Federal Contracting Made Easy

3rd edition

D1111853

Federal Contracting Made Easy

3rd edition

Scott A. Stanberry

MANAGEMENTCONCEPTS

MANAGEMENTCONCEPTS
8230 Leesburg Pike, Suite 800
Vienna, VA 22182
(703) 790-9595
Fax: (703) 790-1371
www.managementconcepts.com

Printed in the United States of America

Library of Congress Cataloging-in-Publication Data

Stanberry, Scott A.
    Federal contracting made easy / Scott A. Stanberry.—3rd ed.
        p. cm.
    ISBN 978-1-56726-231-5
    1. Public contracts—United States. 2. Government purchasing—Law and legislation—United States. I. Title.

KF850.S73 2009
346.7302'3—dc22   2008024552

10   9   8   7   6   5

BERRY'S WORLD cartoons reprinted by permission of Newspaper Enterprise Association, Inc.

Glasbergen cartoons reprinted by permission of Randy Glasbergen.

About the Author

Scott A. Stanberry has been working with government contractors for over 15 years. He specializes in providing auditing and accounting services for commercial clients with federal government contracts and in assisting government agencies in the administration of federal contracts. Scott is a certified public accountant and is highly experienced in the application and interpretation of the Federal Acquisition Regulation.

"Life moves pretty fast. If you don't stop and look around once in a while, you could miss it."

—*Ferris Bueller*

Ten years ago, when this book was first published, the Internet revolution had hardly begun. Remember EC/EDI and the Federal Acquisition Computer Network (FACNET)? Today we live in the very different world of search engines, video streaming, interactive maps, telecommuting, video chat, multiplayer games, online mega-stores, and virtual realities, transforming the way we live, work, and play.

This new third edition has been revised to reflect these changes and expands on the first two editions. So without further ado . . . *Federal Contracting Made Easy* Version 3.0!

Best wishes and happy contracting!

Scott Stanberry

Contents at a Glance

Contents

Preface

© 1999 Randy Glasbergen.
www.glasbergen.com

SUZY'S LEMONADE INC.

GLASBERGEN

"I can offer you a great benefits package:
liberal use of the company bike, paid nap time,
free cootie insurance, and a pension at age 10."

Did you ever run a lemonade stand as a kid? Ever sit by the side of the road for hour after hour in the hot sun, waiting for someone—the mail carrier, the obnoxious neighbor kid, anyone—to walk by? Or maybe, as you got older, you decided to open a bicycle repair shop in your garage, dreaming of owning a bicycle empire, only to find that your business was still essentially sitting by the side of the road, waiting for customers?

That's the story of thousands of businesses that fail each year: a good idea or product, but no knowledge of how to run a business or attract customers.

This book was written to help you attract and make the most of the biggest customer of all: the U.S. government. The federal government spends more than $400 billion on supplies and services each year. Look at it this way: Every 20 seconds of every working day, the federal government awards a contract with an average value of $465,000.

That's a lot of lemonade! What's more, every major federal agency and department is required by law to provide free assistance to businesses interested in bidding on federal work. So whether you're an entrepreneur interested in breaking into the federal market or a mid- to large-sized company seeking to maximize your use of (and financial return on) subcontractors, this book tells you what you need to know.

What's the downside to government business? Marketing to the federal government is like trying to learn the rules to your kid's video games. The characters all have incomprehensible names, some players seem to have secret powers, and any second somebody can throw a bomb that completely knocks you off the screen. How can you win if you're not the 11-year-old king of the arcade with a never-ending roll of quarters and the insider knowledge that comes from devoting yourself to the game 16 hours a day?

That's why I've written this book: to help you decode all the confusing rules, get to know the other players, understand the obstacles thrown in your path, and maybe acquire some secret powers of your own. This book spells out everything you need to know to succeed in the federal marketplace—from the people who oversee the contracting process, to the regulations that govern contracting, to the types of contracts awarded. You'll get the inside scoop on government contracting—all from one source.

All you need to know is inside this book, and you can refer to these pages again and again as your business grows and you go after greater government opportunities. And while much of this book deals with small business programs and services, it also contains a significant amount of information that applies to all types of companies. Even if you or your staff are familiar with some pieces of the federal contracting puzzle, there may be areas where you could use some explanation or insight.

Of particular interest to current contractors, this book offers specific suggestions on how mid- to large-sized companies can take advantage of some of those small business programs through subcontracting—something virtually every government contractor too big to qualify as a small business does on a regular basis. In short, if you're currently working for a business (large or small) or thinking of starting your own, this book is for you!

One word of caution: Government regulations and procedures do not make for keep-you-up-all-night, can't-put-it-down reading. Wading through some of this information may take patience and persistence but, just like that 11-year-old who suffers through hours of frustration to learn the video game, you'll find rewards at the end of the process. You can make good money—even big money—doing business with the federal government. Contracting with the government can make you king of the arcade *and* give you the biggest lemonade stand on the block!

PART 1

What Is Federal Government Contracting?

"You miss 100 percent of the shots you never take."

—*Wayne Gretzky*

How Does Federal Government Contracting Work?

What's in this chapter?

- The big picture
- Top buyers
- Future of federal contracting
- Can you sell to the federal government?
- Should you sell to the federal government?

Our federal government (a.k.a. Uncle Sam) enters into contracts with American citizens like you to acquire the supplies and services needed to run its operations or fulfill its mission requirements. It uses a specific process designed to give business concerns the maximum practical opportunities to participate in federal contracting. Each year (actually, fiscal year, which begins on October 1 and ends on September 30), the federal government spends billions of dollars buying from nonfederal sources, or "commercial contractors."

Generally we hear only about government purchases for multimillion-dollar aircraft or those famous $1,000 toilet seats and $500 hammers. But are you aware that there are currently over 310,000 government contractors, receiving more than $400 billion worth of contracts each year—$45 billion of which goes to small businesses?

The government initiates or modifies more than 450,000 contracts each year, two-thirds of which it grants to contractors outside the Washington, D.C., area. The key to sharing in these contracting opportunities is to understand how the federal government does business. This chapter describes what federal government contracting is all about.

THE BIG PICTURE

By any measure, the U.S. government is by far the biggest consumer in the world. No other nation, or corporation for that matter, can begin to match its purchasing power. Every 20 seconds of each working day, the federal government awards a contract with an average value of $465,000. And the government must tell us what, from where, and from whom it buys.

The government purchases every type of supply and service, ranging from high-technology items like homeland security programs, missiles, ships, aircraft, and telecommunication systems to more mundane items like office furniture, maintenance services, shoes, computers, food, janitorial services, carpeting, accounting services, and real estate. You name it and the government probably buys it!

Because the government's needs vary from those that individuals and small, singly owned enterprises can meet to those requiring the resources of large corporations, everyone has a potential share. In fact, it is no exaggeration to suggest that a small business can probably provide a service or create a product for nearly every federal agency.

Furthermore, a business can supply the government with its products or services from wherever it customarily operates. In other words, contractors are not restricted to selling to federal agencies in their communities. A contractor in Memphis, Tennessee, can supply the Naval Surface Warfare Center in Dahlgren, Virginia, just as easily as a contractor operating from Dahlgren. Anyone looking for more customers or thinking about starting a new business should consider the federal government as a prospect.

To help small businesses participate in federal contracting, the government offers a variety of programs and services, including credit assistance, procurement opportunities, technical support, management assistance, and grants. (See Chapter 4 for what constitutes a small business in the eyes of the government.) These programs and services have created and sustained thousands of small business firms, generating many millions of jobs in the process. As a result, many of these small businesses have grown into large businesses.

I have personally seen firms go from zero to $50 million or more in federal business in less than five years. No other industry provides more opportunities for small businesses than government contracting. Yet only 1% of the 22 million small businesses in the United States participates in federal contracting.

Why doesn't everyone contract with the government? Contracting with the government can be cumbersome, with its regulations, rules, laws, bureaucracy, and red tape. The primary purpose of these detailed rules and regulations is to ensure that the government spends public funds— our tax dollars—wisely. To be successful as a government contractor, you must understand these rules and regulations (see Chapter 2).

Although federal contractors use many of the same business practices as commercial vendors, a number of characteristics clearly differentiate the two. To begin with, the federal government operates in a market termed "monopsonistic"—one with only one buyer and many sellers. As a result of this sovereignty, the government has certain unusual powers and immunities that differ significantly from those of more typical buyers. Congressional mandate, rather than state laws, controls federal policy.

Significant differences include:

Government Contracting	Commercial Contracting
General:	
Federal policy establishes formal competition criteria for purchases or procurements.	Company determines competition criteria.
Congress appropriates all available funds.	Many sources provide funds.
Laws, directives, policies, and procedural regulations define procurement actions.	Company determines procurement actions within legal boundaries.
Profit Margins:	
The government may negotiate a separate profit/fee.	Contractor builds profit into "total price."
The government may apply profit ceilings to certain contracts. (Profit/fee on federal contracts rarely exceeds 6%.)	Contractors rarely use profit ceilings. (Profit/fee on commercial contracts is often as high as 10%–20% of the total contract price.)
Contract Clauses:	
Federal contracts contain extensive clauses, many of which are "take-it-or-leave-it."	Standard commercial code and those clauses agreed to by the parties regulate performance.
Contract Termination:	
The government may terminate a contract for failure to make progress.	Termination is normally not available to commercial contractors.

The government may terminate a contract for its convenience.

Commercial regulations (such as the Uniform Commercial Code) ensure adequate performance.

Social and Economic Policies (such as a policy requiring contractors to maintain a drug-free workplace):

Federal contracts must incorporate these policies.

Social pressures typically dictate company policies; however, some policies are required by law.

The government may use incentive contracts.

Commercial contractors rarely use incentive contracts.

Federal law prohibits gratuities.

Company policy determines gratuities.

The government may penalize contractors for noncompliance.

Penalties are illegal in commercial contracts.

Government business varies vastly, depending on the products or services being sold. Selling copiers has little in common with selling jet engines. Also, contracting with the Department of Defense (DOD) differs from contracting with civilian federal agencies.

You need to determine which federal agencies purchase your goods and services and what solicitation procedures those agencies use to acquire them. Part 3 of this book touches on a number of methods for soliciting and marketing to the various federal agencies.

It's not so much that doing business with the federal government is difficult; it's just different. Instead of selling directly to decision makers, as in the commercial world, government contractors must patiently wade through the government procurement process, which makes the sale more complex and longer to complete. If you learn the system and are patient and persistent, the federal government can be a great source of business revenue for both new and established businesses.

This page intentionally left blank

This page intentionally left blank

TOP BUYERS

During FY2005, the federal government purchased over $390 billion worth of supplies and services. The following table shows the major federal agencies and categories in federal procurement.

Federal Agency	FY2005 Expenditures ($ billion)
Department of Defense (DOD):	
Army	$ 94.7
Navy	$ 64.1
Air Force	$ 55.6
Defense Logistics Agency (DLA)	$ 27.9
Other DOD	$ 25.9
Non-Defense (Civilian):	
Department of Energy (DOE)	$ 22.8
General Services Administration (GSA)	$ 13.6
National Aeronautics and Space Admin (NASA)	$ 12.5
Other Civilian	$ 18.7
Department of Homeland Security (DHS)	$ 10.3

Department of Veterans Affairs (VA)	$	8.8
Department of Health and Human Services (HHS)	$	7.9
Department of the Interior (DOI)	$	4.7
Department of Treasury (USTREAS)	$	3.5
Department of Agriculture (DOA)	$	3.4
Department of Transportation (DOT)	$	1.3

Top Product or Service Categories:

Other services	$	162.4
Supplies and equipment	$	129.0
Research and development (R&D)	$	47.7
ADP equipment and services	$	22.8
Construction	$	17.3
Real property purchase/lease	$	5.0
Architect-engineering	$	4.7

The value of federal contracts awarded, by state (top ten) during FY2005, in billions of dollars, is as follows:

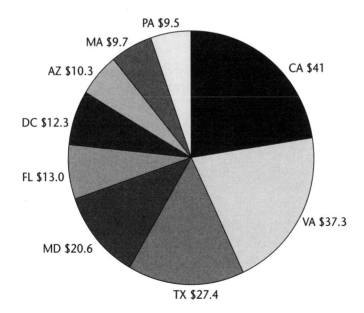

FUTURE OF FEDERAL CONTRACTING

You hear it more and more every day: The federal government is too big and bureaucratic. Both Republicans and Democrats are pushing for a smaller bureaucracy, with all but the most essential government functions (such as national security) being contracted out to private industry. Congress is constantly introducing legislation that eliminates government functions that compete with the private sector.

Current projections estimate that the number of nonpostal government employees will shrink from 1.8 million to 500,000 within the next dozen years. These jobs will not go away; they'll be contracted out to private industry. The belief is that the competitive forces of the commercial marketplace will produce better products and services at cheaper prices. There has never been a better time to look for contracting opportunities with the federal government.

CAN YOU SELL TO THE FEDERAL GOVERNMENT?

To be eligible for federal contracts, contractors must furnish proof that they are both "responsive" and "responsible," that they comply with many of the government's socioeconomic goals, and that they offer prices that are fair and reasonable. In general, the government wants to know the following about a potential contractor:

- Is the contractor eligible, under existing laws, to do business with the government?

- Does the contractor have adequate financial resources to do the job?

- Does the contractor have a good performance record?

- Does the contractor's record demonstrate ethics and integrity?

- Does the contractor have the necessary skills to perform the job, or can it acquire them?

■ Does the contractor have the necessary facilities and production capacity to deliver its products?

■ Can the contractor meet the performance schedule (or delivery schedule), given other commitments?

The government then uses the information to determine whether a potential contractor is eligible for federal contracts.

SHOULD YOU SELL TO THE FEDERAL GOVERNMENT?

Once you understand the contracting process, the next step is to decide whether you should sell to the federal government.

Advantages

Working with the federal government offers tremendous advantages:

■ The government purchases practically every type of supply and service.

■ The government has more than 2,500 buying offices (or "contracting activities") throughout the United States.

■ Each major federal agency must provide free assistance to contractors.

■ In some cases, the government provides financial assistance, such as progress payments (payments made to a contractor based on a percentage of costs incurred as work progresses under the contract) and guaranteed loans.

■ The government has "preference programs" to encourage small business participation.

■ During FY2007 the government had an annual budget of more than $2.6 trillion.

■ The government mandates "full and open competition." In other words, a contractor can compete for federal contracts without having to belong to an exclusive country club.

■ The government spends approximately 25 cents of every dollar spent in the United States.

■ Generally, contractors do not need a massive product distribution system or a substantial advertising budget.

■ Numerous regulations governing federal contracting ensure fair play by both the government and the contractor. (These regulations do, however, create a certain amount of red tape.)

■ If you perform the work required by the contract, you will get paid. Checks cut by the federal government never bounce!

■ Federal business programs often lead to business with other federal agencies, as well as with state and local governments.

■ Many government contracts run for a base year with up to seven option years. So if you live up to expectations, you can expect to get your contract renewed.

■ Average government orders/contracts tend to be larger than commercial orders—$10 million to $100 million is not uncommon.

■ Government business might complement your commercial business. It's common for contractors to sell a product to the government and then sell additional versions of the product to government vendors that are required (or choose) to be compatible with the government's requirements.

■ In spite of legal changes in recent years, the government awards about 45% to 50% of its contracts to sole-source providers. A sole-source award is a contract that a federal agency awards after soliciting and negotiating with only one source. Therefore, contractors may be able to locate and bid on federal contracts that have limited competition.

■ Contracting with the government is patriotic.

With all these advantages, what businessperson wouldn't want to contract with the government? But as with any type of business, there are disadvantages to working with the federal government.

Disadvantages

The disadvantages of contracting with the government include:

■ Government red tape can produce volumes of paperwork. Contractors must fill out numerous federal forms, and even not knowing which one to do next, or to whom to send it, can be a major obstacle to your success. The best way to keep current with these forms is to use the General Services Administration's website at:

www.gsa.gov/forms

This book will also help you untangle the red tape.

■ To be successful in government contracting, you must learn how the government operates. This includes learning the clauses, terms, conditions, proper terminology, and methodology.

■ Once you sign a federal contract, you are locked into performing according to the terms of that contract. (The only exception is for a contract under $25,000, which may be canceled by a contractor at any time before performance begins.)

■ The requirements and specifications for government contracts tend to be much more stringent than those for commercial contracts.

■ For many contracts, the government requires a company to establish a detailed quality control program.

■ Government contracting can be very competitive—and seemingly unfair if competitors have established a personal relationship with a particular buying office.

■ Certain common practices in commercial business, such as entertaining personnel, are illegal in government contracting. (See Allowable Costs in Chapter 15.)

■ Your company personnel may be unfamiliar with federal contracting regulations.

These disadvantages are not intended to discourage you from seeking to do business with the government. On the contrary, if prospective contractors can become aware of and obtain the necessary information before embarking on government business, the chances of success—in terms of both profit and efficiency—are greatly enhanced. If you can avoid learning through trial and error, everyone comes out ahead!

■   ■   ■

Dr. Martin Luther King, Jr., said it best: "Give me an opportunity, not a handout." This book will help you learn how to do business with the federal government and take advantage of the many contracting opportunities the government offers.

■   ■   ■

2

The Rules
of the Game

Berry's World

Bureaucrat studying
a foreign language

6-11-98

What's in this chapter?

- Constitutional authority
- Congressional responsibilities
- Central Contractor Registration
- Federal Acquisition Regulation
- Federal Acquisition Streamlining Act
- Cost Accounting Standards
- Defense Contract Audit Agency
- Government Accountability Office
- Federal Acquisition Reform Act
- Competition in Contracting Act
- Buy American Act
- Truth in Negotiations Act
- Service Contract Act
- Freedom of Information Act

Understanding the opportunities the federal government has to offer is one thing. It is quite another to understand the federal contracting rules and regulations. They are probably the biggest barrier for businesses looking to participate in the federal marketplace. In fact, a contractor would find navigation through the government's market almost impossible without a reasonable level of knowledge about its requirements.

Although the government doesn't intend to put anyone out of business, it nevertheless expects a contractor to know and understand the technical and administrative requirements of a signed contract. In other words, the government will not rescue a company from the consequences of a bad business decision. Far too many contractors watch their profits on a government contract drastically shrink or totally disappear because they overlooked, misunderstood, or just plain ignored the applicable regulations.

The bottom-line philosophy is the more you know the rules of the game or the more you know about government contracting, the greater the likelihood you'll succeed. This chapter will help guide you through the maze!

CONSTITUTIONAL AUTHORITY

The U.S. Constitution gives the federal government the legal authority to enter into contracts with private citizens and commercial organizations. This is the case even though the Constitution does not contain any language that specifically authorizes such actions. The authority derives from a statement in the Preamble that says that the federal government shall "provide for the common defense, promote the general welfare, and secure the blessings of liberty."

For a contract to become the legal obligation of the federal government, it must be based on statutory authority. The federal government may actually avoid liability for a contract that is unsupported by a legally enacted provision.

CONGRESSIONAL RESPONSIBILITIES

The U.S. Congress is responsible for passing the laws that regulate federal contracting. More than 4,000 of those laws are in effect. In addition, numerous bills pending in Congress could affect how the government exercises its contracting functions.

Congress is also responsible for drafting and passing the laws and statutes that establish the various federal agencies and the specific programs proposed by those federal agencies. These laws and statutes are called "authorization acts."

Congress derives its powers from article I, section 8, of the Constitution—General Powers of Congress—which states that Congress will:

1. . . . lay and collect taxes, duties, imports and excises, to pay the debts and provide for the common defense and general welfare of the United States;

12. . . . raise and support Armies;

13. . . . provide and maintain a Navy;

14. . . . make rules for the government and regulation of the land and naval forces;

18. . . . make all laws which shall be necessary and proper for carrying into execution the foregoing powers, and all other powers vested by the Constitution in the Government of the United States, or in any Department or Officer thereof.

Why are these regulations so confusing? Is the government trying to hide something from us? I keep thinking about a political advertisement I saw a while back that said "there's got to be something in the water" in Washington, D.C. The government is notorious for binding its affairs with red tape, and federal contracting regulations certainly entail their fair share.

Well, believe it or not, these regulations are convoluted for a good reason, so to speak, and no, it's not because the government is hiding something. Although the Constitution gives the federal government the power to contract for supplies and services, it also mandates that "no money shall be drawn from the Treasury, but in Consequence of Appropriations made by law. . . ." This basically means the government may purchase only those items that Congress votes to fund. Sounds simple enough.

In approving funds, Congress often places restrictions and conditions on the money for various programs and socioeconomic goals. It's those restrictions that create many of the contradictions, exceptions, and loopholes in the contracting regulations.

Suppose a senator includes a new code of contractor ethics in an appropriations bill. If Congress approves the bill and the President signs it, the regulation becomes applicable to all future agency pronouncements. Regulation writers, therefore, must prepare a new regulation that accurately reflects this change.

Congress also passes laws that affect government contracts. If Congress passes a law that restricts the purchase of products from Iraq, regulation writers must write a regulation to reflect this law. The gradual pileup of these laws and restrictions over the years has created a contracting process that is convoluted, confusing, and inefficient.

Funding Requirements

Congress supports each federal agency and its programs by putting into law an appropriations act. This act provides the funds with which that federal agency functions. Congress derives the authority to enact appropriations acts from article I, section 9, of the Constitution.

Each appropriations act specifies the period for which the funds are available for use by the agency. The appropriation can be for a single year, for multiple years, or unrestricted. Most appropriations are awarded for a single year. This approach requires federal agencies to return annually to Congress to justify the budgets for their operations and programs.

Multiyear appropriations usually apply to major multiple-year programs and projects, such as research and development. Federal agencies prefer multiyear appropriations because they tend to provide significant savings to both the government and contractors. For the savings to be realistic, however, the multiyear program requirements must remain stable and predictable, and the requesting agency must ask for enough money to carry out the contract. Once Congress approves the funds, they are available for use.

Budget Process

The budget process is long and tedious. Each fiscal year (October 1 to September 30), federal agencies are required to submit budgets to Congress detailing their operation costs for the upcoming year. Preparing these proposed budgets usually takes federal agencies several years.

Once a federal agency completes its budget, it submits that budget to the President through the Office of Management and Budget (OMB). OMB holds hearings on the proposed budget and makes recommendations to the federal agency. Upon agreement between the parties, OMB passes the budget on to Congress.

Once Congress receives the proposed budget, the budget is forwarded to the Congressional Budget Office (CBO) and the individual budget committees for in-depth review. During this review process, the CBO and the committees within Congress set targets and ceilings for the various federal functions or programs. The budget is then dissected by the CBO and sent to various House and Senate authorization and appropriation committees. These committees and their subcommittees hold hearings on the proposed programs and draft legislation.

This draft legislation then moves on to the House and Senate for debate and approval. Only after both legislative bodies approve the final budget is it returned to the President for signature. If this process is not completed by the start of the government's fiscal year (October 1), the agency is in jeopardy of being shut down because of inadequate funding.

CENTRAL CONTRACTOR REGISTRATION

Central Contractor Registration (CCR) is the primary registrant database for the federal government. It collects, validates, stores, and distributes specific data about government and commercial contractors (or trading partners). All prospective contractors must be registered in the CCR prior to the award of any federal contract.

Once registered, contractors must update or renew their information at least once a year to maintain an active status. The CCR:

■ Provides contractors worldwide with visibility to government buyers

■ Increases efficiency and lowers costs by simplifying and streamlining the procurement process

■ Allows contractors (or trading partners) to avoid registering with multiple buying offices

■ Reduces errors and saves time by creating an accurate record of data for each business

■ Provides banking information to the Defense Finance and Accounting Service (DFAS), which enables contractors to be paid by means of electronic funds transfer.

To register in the CCR, you must first contact Dun & Bradstreet to obtain a DUNS (Data Universal Numbering System) number, which is a unique, nine-character company identification number. For assistance, contact:

Dun & Bradstreet
Phone (800) 234-3867
www.dnb.com

After getting your DUNS number, you'll need the following information to register:

■ Taxpayer identification number or Social Security number

■ Legal business name

■ Business address

■ Corporate status

■ North American Industry Classification System (NAICS) codes (see Chapter 4)

■ Banking and electronic funds transfer information.

To register in the CCR, go to:

www.ccr.gov

Contractors must ensure the accuracy of their data.

Once your information has been successfully entered into the CCR, you will be assigned a Commercial and Government Entity (CAGE) code. The CAGE code is a five-character (alphanumeric) identifier generated by the Defense Logistics Information Service (DLIS). If you already have a CAGE code, DLIS will validate it during this process.

To find your current CAGE code, call (877) 352-2255. The CAGE code supports a variety of mechanized systems throughout the government, such as those for a facility clearance or a pre-award survey.

FEDERAL ACQUISITION REGULATION

If you plan to contract with the federal government, the Federal Acquisition Regulation (FAR) will serve as your "bible." The FAR is the body of regulations governing federal acquisitions. It contains uniform policies and procedures for all procurements, whether obtained through purchase or lease and regardless of whether the products already exist or must be developed. In laymen's terms, the FAR contains "the rules of the game."

Each federal agency is required to adhere to rules of the FAR when making purchases with congressionally appropriated funds. The FAR is jointly issued and maintained by the General Services Administration (GSA), the Department of Defense (DOD), and the National Aeronautics and Space Administration (NASA). Currently, the FAR includes more than 1,600 pages divided into 53 parts, each dealing with a separate aspect of the procurement process.

FAR Numbering System

Each of the 53 parts of the FAR addresses a separate aspect of procurement. The first six parts address general contracting matters, and the next six cover acquisition planning. Part 13 describes simplified acquisition procedures (see Chapter 10), and Parts 14 through 17 address solicitation procedures for contracts over $100,000. (See Part 4 of this book.)

Parts 19 through 26 include procedures and regulations affecting small and small disadvantaged businesses (see Chapter 5). The remaining sections address such matters as labor laws, contract administration, and standard clauses. The FAR also contains sample forms.

Each part is further subdivided into sections and paragraphs according to the numbering system shown below.

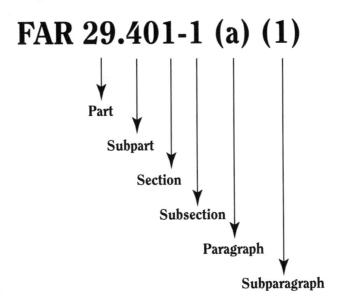

As an example, here's the current outline for Part 29:

PART 29   **TAXES**

SUBPART 29.4   **CONTRACT CLAUSES**

29.401   **DOMESTIC CONTRACTS**

29.401-1   **Indefinite-delivery contracts for leased equipment.**

29.401-2   **Construction contracts performed in North**
Carolina.

29.401-3   **Federal, state, and local taxes.**

29.401-4   **New Mexico gross receipts and compensating tax.**

1.000 Scope of part.

This part sets forth basic policies and general information about the Federal Acquisition Regulations System including purpose, authority, applicability, issuance, arrangement, numbering, dissemination, implementation, supplementation, maintenance, administration, and deviation. Subparts 1.2, 1.3, and 1.4 prescribe administrative procedures for maintaining the FAR System.

Subpart 1.1—Purpose, Authority, Issuance

1.101 Purpose.

The Federal Acquisition Regulations System is established for the codification and publication of uniform policies and procedures for acquisition by all executive agencies. The Federal Acquisition Regulations System consists of the Federal Acquisition Regulation (FAR), which is the primary document, and agency acquisition regulations that implement or supplement the FAR. The FAR System does not include internal agency guidance of the type described in 1.301(a)(2).

1.102 Statement of guiding principles for the Federal Acquisition System.

(a) The vision for the Federal Acquisition System is to deliver on a timely basis the best value product or service to the customer, while maintaining the public's trust and fulfilling public policy objectives. Participants in the acquisition process should work together as a team and should be empowered to make decisions within their area of responsibility.

(b) The Federal Acquisition System will—

(1) Satisfy the customer in terms of cost, quality, and timeliness of the delivered product or service by, for example—

(i) Maximizing the use of commercial products and services;

(ii) Using contractors who have a track record of successful past performance or who demonstrate a current superior ability to perform; and

(iii) Promoting competition;

(2) Minimize administrative operating costs;

(3) Conduct business with integrity, fairness, and openness; and

(4) Fulfill public policy objectives.

(c) The Acquisition Team consists of all participants in Government acquisition including not only representatives of the technical, supply, and procurement communities but also the customers they serve, and the contractors who provide the products and services.

(d) The role of each member of the Acquisition Team is to exercise personal initiative and sound business judgment in providing the best value product or service to meet the customer's needs. In exercising initiative, Government members of the Acquisition Team may assume if a specific strategy,

practice, policy or procedure is in the best interests of the Government and is not addressed in the FAR, nor prohibited by law (statute or case law), Executive order or other regulation, that the strategy, practice, policy or procedure is a permissible exercise of authority.

1.102-1 Discussion.

(a) *Introduction.* The statement of Guiding Principles for the Federal Acquisition System (System) represents a concise statement designed to be user-friendly for all participants in Government acquisition. The following discussion of the principles is provided in order to illuminate the meaning of the terms and phrases used. The framework for the System includes the Guiding Principles for the System and the supporting policies and procedures in the FAR.

(b) *Vision.* All participants in the System are responsible for making acquisition decisions that deliver the best value product or service to the customer. Best value must be viewed from a broad perspective and is achieved by balancing the many competing interests in the System. The result is a system which works better and costs less.

1.102-2 Performance standards.

(a) *Satisfy the customer in terms of cost, quality, and timeliness of the delivered product or service.* (1) The principal customers for the product or service provided by the System are the users and line managers, acting on behalf of the American taxpayer.

(2) The System must be responsive and adaptive to customer needs, concerns, and feedback. Implementation of acquisition policies and procedures, as well as consideration of timeliness, quality, and cost throughout the process, must take into account the perspective of the user of the product or service.

(3) When selecting contractors to provide products or perform services, the Government will use contractors who have a track record of successful past performance or who demonstrate a current superior ability to perform.

(4) The Government must not hesitate to communicate with the commercial sector as early as possible in the acquisition cycle to help the Government determine the capabilities available in the commercial marketplace. The Government will maximize its use of commercial products and services in meeting Government requirements.

(5) It is the policy of the System to promote competition in the acquisition process.

(6) The System must perform in a timely, high quality, and cost-effective manner.

(7) All members of the Team are required to employ planning as an integral part of the overall process of acquiring products or services. Although advance planning is required, each member of the Team must be flexible in order to accommodate changing or unforeseen mission needs. Planning is a

Sample Page of Federal Acquisition Regulation

Suppose you wanted to locate information on time-and-materials (T&M) contracts. The first step is to determine which part of the FAR would likely contain this information.

Federal Acquisition Regulation by Part

Part 1 Federal Acquisition Regulation System	Part 27 Patents, Data, and Copyrights
Part 2 Definitions of Words and Terms	Part 28 Bonds and Insurance
Part 3 Improper Business Practices	Part 29 Taxes
Part 4 Administrative Matters	Part 30 Cost Accounting Standards
Part 5 Publicizing Contract Actions	Part 31 Contract Cost Principles
Part 6 Competition Requirements	Part 32 Contract Financing
Part 7 Acquisition Planning	Part 33 Protests, Disputes, and Appeals
Part 8 Required Sources of Supplies/ Services	Part 34 Major System Acquisition
Part 9 Contractor Qualifications	Part 35 R&D Contracting
Part 10 Market Research	Part 36 Construction Contracts
Part 11 Describing Agency Needs	Part 37 Service Contracting
Part 12 Acquisition of Commercial Items	Part 38 Federal Supply Schedules
Part 13 Simplified Acquisition Procedures	Part 39 Acquisition Resources
Part 14 Sealed Bidding	Part 40 [Reserved]
Part 15 Contracting by Negotiation	Part 41 Acquisition of Utility Services
Part 16 Types of Contracts	Part 42 Contract Administration
Part 17 Special Contracting Methods	Part 43 Contract Modifications
Part 18 Emergency Acquisitions	Part 44 Subcontracting Policies
Part 19 Small Business Programs	Part 45 Government Property
Part 20 [Reserved]	Part 46 Quality Assurance
Part 21 [Reserved]	Part 47 Transportation
Part 22 Labor Laws to Acquisitions	Part 48 Value Engineering
Part 23 Occupational Safety	Part 49 Termination of Contracts
Part 24 Privacy Protection	Part 50 Extraordinary Contractual Actions
Part 25 Foreign Acquisition	Part 51 Use of Government Sources
Part 26 Other Socioeconomic Programs	Part 52 Solicitation Provisions/Contract Clauses
	Part 53 Forms

After examining this list, the best place to start would be Part 16—Types of Contracts. The next step would be to examine the subparts within this part. Part 16 currently consists of the following subparts:

Subpart 16.1 Selecting Contract Types
Subpart 16.2 Fixed-Price Contracts
Subpart 16.3 Cost-Reimbursement Contracts
Subpart 16.4 Incentive Contracts
Subpart 16.5 Indefinite-Delivery Contracts
Subpart 16.6 Time-and-Materials, Labor-Hour, and Letter Contracts
Subpart 16.7 Agreements

In this example, the most obvious choice would be Subpart 16.6.

Finally, go to section 16.601 to find the required information. Once you get the hang of this numbering system, you will be able locate information in the FAR with ease.

Federal Acquisition Circulars

Amendments or changes to the FAR are issued in Federal Acquisition Circulars (FACs). Simply stated, FACs are updates to the FAR. Changes to the FAR are typically the result of congressional actions or presidential orders. GSA, DOD, and NASA are responsible for issuing these circulars.

FACs are published daily in the *Federal Register*. (The *Federal Register* is the official publication used by the government to inform the public of congressional and federal enactments.)

Each FAC is issued sequentially, using the following numbering system:

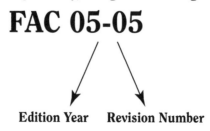

FAC 05-05

Edition Year   Revision Number

The first two digits in the FAC number identify the FAR edition. This particular FAC amends the 2005 edition of the FAR. The final two digits represent the revision number. This is the fifth revision to the 2005 FAR edition. (FAC 05-05 revises the definition of *information technology*.) The best way to keep current with FACs is to access the FAR using the Internet.

Agency Supplements

Each federal agency is authorized by Congress to issue its own supplement to the FAR. These supplements contain policies and procedures that apply only to that particular agency. The Department of Defense FAR Supplement (DFARS) provides contracting personnel detailed procedures for acquiring military-specific items.

The rules and regulations included in these supplements should not contradict the FAR; they just provide additional guidance for dealing with a particular agency. Only by congressional order may a federal agency deviate from the FAR. For instance, the FAA was permitted to deviate from the FAR for the purpose of creating a simplified Acquisition Management System (AMS).

Currently more than 20 federal agencies issue supplements to the FAR, including:

■ DFARS—Department of Defense

■ HHSAR—Department of Health and Human Services

■ AGAR—Department of Agriculture

■ GSAR—General Services Administration

■ AIDAR—Agency for International Development.

You can find a complete list of these supplements in Title 48 of the *Code of Federal Regulations* (CFR). The CFR is available at:

www.gpoaccess.gov/cfr/index.html

Potential contractors must follow the rules of the FAR or risk being eliminated from consideration. Although some contractors feel that the FAR does not allow enough latitude, government officials must adhere to the regulations protecting the expenditure of public funds.

Contractors should always have access to a current copy of the FAR. Because the FAR is updated throughout the year, however, you need to ensure that your copy remains current. Subscriptions with updates (including each agency's FAR supplements) are available from:

Commerce Clearing House
www.cch.com
Phone (800) 248-3248

The latest version of the FAR is also available at:

www.arnet.gov/far

FEDERAL ACQUISITION STREAMLINING ACT

Congress enacted the Federal Acquisition Streamlining Act (FASA) of 1994 to help simplify and streamline the federal acquisition process. FASA was passed in response to calls for government downsizing and the recognition that red tape had caused the acquisition process to become convoluted and inefficient.

FASA directs federal agencies to maximize the use of commercial buying practices, thus avoiding federal specifications and standards, which prolong the procurement process and create red tape. For example, if a contracting activity in DOD wants to purchase an all-terrain boot, it must first seek commercial sources before issuing a solicitation for a military-specific boot.

Also, FASA requires the government to accept the terms and conditions offered by the private sector unless it can negotiate better terms and conditions through commitment guarantees or volume purchases. Other significant provisions of FASA include:

■ A requirement that contracts between $3,000 and $100,000 must be reserved for small businesses unless the government cannot obtain at least two offers with competitive market prices. (More than 90% of annual federal purchase transactions are under $100,000.)

■ A micropurchase threshold of $3,000 (see Chapter 10). Purchases valued at less than the threshold are not subject to small business set-aside requirements or to the Buy American Act. The government can therefore makes purchases without obtaining competitive quotes, assuming the prices are reasonable.

■ A requirement for prompt notice of award. When a federal agency issues a solicitation, it must notify losing offerors in writing within three days of award (see Part 4).

COST ACCOUNTING STANDARDS

Cost accounting standards (CAS) typically apply to large-dollar-value contracts (those in the millions). They provide uniformity and consistency in estimating, accumulating, and reporting costs in connection with the pricing and administration of negotiated procurements (see Part 5). Refer to the Appendix of the FAR for a complete listing of the cost accounting standards.

By following CAS, contractors are able to track costs that apply to each contract or major task they undertake. This is not the same as financial accounting, which is the accumulation of information that enables contractors to know how much total cost they incur and profit they make during a particular period. Financial accounting alone does not tell a contractor what each individual job costs and the profit or loss on that particular job.

DEFENSE CONTRACT AUDIT AGENCY

The Defense Contract Audit Agency (DCAA) performs contract audit functions required by DOD and many civilian agencies. These audits typically include the examination of records, documents, and other financial data relating to contract pricing; performance costs; and any cost, funding, or performance reports required under the specific contract.

Virtually all federal contracts are subject to audit. However, because audits require significant time and expense to perform, they are typically not used for purchases under $100,000. DCAA has more than 300 field offices worldwide.

In addition to performing contract audits, DCAA assists federal agencies in reviewing and evaluating contractor:

■ Efficiency

■ Internal control systems

■ Accounting system suitability

■ Performance.

DCAA is probably the best known and most influential (or feared) of the government audit agencies because of its reputation for being an aggressive defender of the taxpayers' money. DCAA's website is:

www.dcaa.mil

GOVERNMENT ACCOUNTABILITY OFFICE

The Government Accountability Office (GAO) is the investigative arm of Congress. GAO has broad authority to oversee federal programs and operations and to review government contracts to ensure that appropriated funds are spent in accordance with the laws enacted by Congress. GAO also gets involved with:

■ Contract award disputes or protests

■ Defective cost and pricing data

■ Investigations requested by a member of Congress

■ Fraud allegations.

GAO's findings and recommendations are published as reports to congressional members or delivered as testimony to congressional committees. GAO's website is:

www.gao.gov

FEDERAL ACQUISITION REFORM ACT

The Federal Acquisition Reform Act (FARA) of 1996, also called the Clinger-Cohen Act, expands on the Federal Acquisition Streamlining Act of 1994. FARA reinforces the commercial buying preference and limits the number of regulatory FAR clauses that apply to simplified acquisitions. Also, this act significantly changed protest and claim procedures by expanding the use of alternative dispute resolution for disagreements between the government and private industry. (Protests are written objections by interested parties to a solicitation, proposed award, or award of a contract; see Chapter 12.)

COMPETITION IN CONTRACTING ACT

The Competition in Contracting Act (CICA) of 1984 is the basic law governing contract formation. It explicitly requires the government to use "full and open competition" in purchasing supplies and services. This means that all responsible sources must be allowed an opportunity to compete for government contracts. Government officials do not have the luxury of buying from sources based on past good business relations.

Also, procurement officials may not restrict their sources to suppliers known for quality products and on-time delivery. This regulation is in marked contrast to the selection criteria of commercial and private sector businesses, which return to favorite vendors repeatedly rather than risk disappointment by using a vendor with which they have no business experience.

CICA specifies seven exceptions to the "full and open competition" requirement. These exceptions come into play if:

■ Only one responsible source (or vendor) is available, and no other supplies or services will satisfy the agency's requirements.

■ An unusual and compelling urgency (such as a war) exists.

■ Vital supplies or facilities are needed for national emergencies.

■ An international agreement between the United States and a foreign government regulates the conditions of a contract.

■ A statutory requirement (such as the Small Business Act) calls for an exception.

■ Disclosure of the government's needs would threaten national security.

■ "Full and open competition" contradicts the public's best interest.

Note: This act does not apply to simplified acquisition procedures or purchases under $100,000 (see Chapter 10). Different rules on competition also apply for small businesses eligible to participate in the 8(a) program (see Chapter 5).

BUY AMERICAN ACT

The Buy American Act requires the federal government to buy domestic articles, materials, and supplies for public use. An article, material, or supply is considered domestic if:

■ It is an unmanufactured end product mined or produced in the United States.

■ It is an end product that is manufactured in the United States (i.e., if the costs of its components mined, produced, or manufactured in the United States exceed 50% of the cost of its components).

The primary purpose of this act is to discourage the government from buying foreign products. There are six exceptions to the Buy American Act:

■ Items to be used outside the United States.

■ Domestic items that are unreasonably priced. (Unless an agency determines otherwise, the offered price of a domestic item is considered unreasonable when the lowest acceptable domestic offer exceeds the lowest acceptable foreign offer by more than 6% if the domestic offer is from a large business, or more than 12% if the domestic offer is from a small business.)

■ Information technology that is a commercial item.

■ Situations in which compliance with the Buy American Act would not be in the government's best interest.

■ Items that are not mined, produced, or manufactured in the United States in sufficient and reasonably available commercial quantities.

■ Items purchased specifically for commissary resale.

The Buy American Act does not apply to purchases under the micropurchase threshold.

DOD and NASA have determined that it is inconsistent with the public interest to apply the restrictions of the Buy American Act to certain acquisitions. (See their respective FAR supplements for a detailed listing.)

TRUTH IN NEGOTIATIONS ACT

Congress enacted the Truth in Negotiations Act (TINA) to protect the government from unscrupulous contractors that falsify their cost proposals with erroneous information or defective pricing. Contractors are required to submit cost and pricing data in support of their proposals.

Cost and pricing data include more than just historical accounting data. They are facts and information that reasonably can be expected to contribute to the soundness of estimates of future costs and to the validity of costs already incurred. Examples of cost and pricing data include:

■ Vendor quotations

■ Cost trends

■ Information on management decisions that could have a bearing on costs (such as changes in production methods)

■ Lease or buy decisions

■ Data supporting projections of business costs.

The requirements of TINA generally apply to contracts greater than $650,000. However, the government may require cost and pricing data for negotiated contracts over $100,000. A contractor is exempt from providing cost and pricing data if:

■ The cost or pricing data are at or below the simplified acquisition threshold of $100,000.

■ The government determines that the agreed-upon prices are based on adequate price competition.

■ The prices are set by law or regulation.

■ Commercial items are being acquired.

■ A waiver has been granted.

The head of a contracting activity may also waive the cost and pricing submission requirement in exceptional cases. The rationale for the waiver must be in writing. For example, if a contractor furnished cost or pricing data on previous production buys and the contracting head determines that such data are sufficient, a waiver may be granted.

If a contract is subject to TINA, the contractor and subcontractor must also certify, to the best of their knowledge and belief, that the data provided are current, accurate, and complete. If the cost and pricing data are not certified, the government may institute a defective pricing claim. Many contracts use the following certification:

Certificate of Current Cost or Pricing Data

This is to certify that, to the best of my knowledge and belief, the cost or pricing data (as defined in section 15.801 of the Federal Acquisition Regulation [FAR] and required under FAR subsection 15.804-2) submitted, either actually or by specific identification in writing, to the contracting officer or to the contracting officer's representative in support of [Identify the proposal, quotation, request for price adjustment, or other submission involved, giving the appropriate identifying number (e.g., Solicitation No._____)] are accurate, complete, and current as of _____. This certification includes the cost or pricing data supporting any advance agreements and forward pricing rate agreements between the offeror and the government that are part of the proposal.

Part 5 of this book details cost and pricing techniques used by many successful government contractors.

SERVICE CONTRACT ACT

The Service Contract Act (SCA) was enacted to ensure that government contractors compensate their employees fairly and properly. It generally applies to federal contracts and subcontracts for services (performed in the United States) that are over $2,500.

Service contracts must contain mandatory provisions regarding minimum wages and fringe benefits, safe and sanitary working conditions, and equivalent employee classifications and wage rates. The following services are generally covered by the SCA:

■ Parking, taxi, and ambulance

■ Packing and storage

■ Janitorial, housekeeping, and guard services

■ Food service and lodging

■ Laundry services

■ Repair and maintenance

■ Data collection, processing, and analysis.

The SCA does not apply to:

■ Contracts for construction or repair of public buildings

■ Contracts for transporting freight or personnel

■ Contracts subject to the Communications Act of 1934 (radio, phone, cable, etc.)

■ Contracts for public utility services

■ Any employment contract providing for direct services to a federal agency

■ Contracts for operating postal contract stations for the U.S. Postal Service.

The Department of Labor defines the prevailing wage rates and fringe benefits by locality. The minimum wage requirement is specified in the Fair Labor Standards Act. All federal contracts are subject to this minimum wage. For more information on the Service Contract Act, see FAR 22.10.

FREEDOM OF INFORMATION ACT

The Freedom of Information Act (FOIA) is less a regulation to follow than it is an opportunity for contractors to get valuable information. Contractors are encouraged to use FOIA when they conduct market research. FOIA is particularly useful in obtaining information on federal agency buying trends and past contractual data. Even competitors' proposals can be obtained under FOIA.

FOIA was enacted into law on July 4, 1967, to give the public access to information that the federal government assembles, creates, and maintains. This act significantly changed the government's information disclosure policy. Before the enactment of FOIA, the individual bore the burden to establish the right to examine government records or documents. No statutory guidelines or procedures existed to help individuals seeking federal information. In addition, no remedies (judicial or otherwise) were available for those denied access.

With the passage of FOIA, the burden of proof shifted from the individual to the government. The "right to know" doctrine replaced the "need to know" standard. Therefore, individuals who seek federal information no longer must show a need for the requested information.

The government must now justify the need for secrecy. FOIA further requires federal agencies to provide the fullest possible disclosure of information to the public, and it provides administrative and judicial remedies for individuals who are unjustly denied access to federal records.

FOIA applies to documents or records held by federal agencies in the government's executive branch. The executive branch includes cabinet departments, military departments, government corporations, government-controlled corporations, and independent regulatory agencies. FOIA does not apply to federally elected officials, including the President, Vice President, senators, and members of Congress.

Each federal agency must have FOIA request and response procedures. Citizens may request any record in the possession of a federal agency that is not exempt under the provisions of FOIA. Exemptions include:

■ Matters specifically required by executive order to be kept secret in the interest of national defense or foreign policy

■ Matters related solely to the internal personnel rules and practices of a federal agency

■ Matters specifically exempt from disclosure by statute

■ Trade secrets and commercial or financial information received by the government in confidence

■ Internal memoranda related to the decision-making process of the federal agency

■ Personnel or medical files

■ Investigative records compiled for law enforcement purposes

■ Geological data (such as maps).

In addition to these exemptions, there are other, common sense reasons for which the government would reject a FOIA request. Perhaps, for example, the agency does not hold the requested record or the requested record does not exist. In general, if you request information that does not fall under one of the exemptions listed above, you are entitled to it.

Potential contractors should not have reservations about referencing FOIA for fear of being blackballed. Negotiation with FOIA is an accepted part of the procurement process. Actually, exhibiting an understanding of FOIA indicates a contractor's knowledge of the contracting process.

The first step in making a request under FOIA is to identify the federal agency that has the information. If you are unsure which agency has the information you seek, consult a government directory, such as the *United States Government Manual*. This manual (available from the Government Printing Office at (202) 512-1800) lists all federal agencies, a description of their functions, and their addresses.

Each federal agency must institute FOIA implementation procedures or instructions, which are contained in the agency's FAR supplement. Also, each agency has a FOIA officer, whose function is to ensure that vendors (or contractors) obtain the legitimate information they seek.

The best way to get in touch with an agency FOIA center or officer is to contact USA Services:

www.info.gov

If you prefer, you can call the USA Services at:

(800) FED-INFO

Your FOIA request should be in writing and addressed to the agency's FOIA officer. If you plan to mail your FOIA request, be sure to mark the envelope "Freedom of Information Act Request" on the bottom left corner to expedite the process. In your letter, identify the documents or records you need and state that your request is being made under the Freedom of Information Act.

When you make a request under FOIA, try to be as precise as possible. If you don't know the document title, describe what you seek as accurately as possible. A prospective contractor might say, "I would like the names of small businesses that were awarded contracts within the past six months for 5 x 12 white envelopes." Put your phone number on your request, so the agency employee can call you with questions.

Sample FOIA Request

Date

FOIA Officer
Name of Agency
Address

RE: Freedom of Information Act Request

Dear [Name of FOIA Officer]:

XYZ Corporation is hereby requesting under the Freedom of Information Act a copy of the winning technical proposal for Solicitation No._____. Please forward the following information:

- Incumbent's name and address;
- Contract number; and
- Subsequent contract amendments.

If you deny all or any part of this request, please cite each specific exemption you think justifies your refusal to release the information and notify me of appeal procedures available under the law. Also, if there are any fees ([optional] greater than $30) for copying or searching for the records, please let me know before you fill my request.

As prescribed under 5 U.S.C. section 552, XYZ Corporation anticipates response within 10 working days upon receipt of this request. Portions of this request may be forwarded as you locate the documents.

If you have any questions, please feel free to call me at (800) 867-5309. Thank you for your cooperation.

Sincerely,

Joe Smith
President

Federal agencies typically charge you for the costs associated with obtaining and reproducing the FOIA information (usually between $10 and $30). If you request a small amount of information that is easy to obtain, the agency might provide it for free.

Federal agencies must respond to a FOIA request within 10 working days of receiving it. If an agency needs more time, it must acknowledge receipt of the request within 10 days and attempt to fulfill the request within 10 additional working days. The total response time of a federal agency should not exceed 20 working days.

Any FOIA request denial may be appealed to the U.S. District Court. Keep in mind that government records are public property and you have the right to this public information. For more detailed information on FOIA, obtain a publication called *Your Right to Federal Records* by calling the Federal Citizen Information Center at (888) 878-3256.

■   ■   ■

The government needs extensive rules and regulations because of its dual role in the marketplace. The government's contracting capacity establishes it as a vast business organization, purchasing a wide variety of supplies and services from every segment of the private sector. At the same time, it is a political entity that must establish policies and procedures that not only represent good business judgment but also are fair to all concerned.

A contractor should not look at these unique requirements as insurmountable barriers to the economically rewarding experience of doing business with the government. Just keep in mind that the government can be a good customer only when a contractor understands the rules and regulations and the specific actions required.

■   ■   ■

The Key Players

3

© 1999 Randy Glasbergen.

"I'm paid $4,000,000 a year. You're paid $40,000. The only difference is a few zeros. Everyone knows that zero equals nothing. So what's the problem?"

What's in this chapter?

- Head of agency
- Contracting officer
- Competition advocates
- Small business specialists
- Requirements personnel

With the federal government having more than 1.8 million (nonpostal) employees and more than 2,500 contracting activities (or buying offices) throughout the United States, it is essential for a contractor to be familiar with its "key players." This chapter details many of the government's key players and describes their main functions.

HEAD OF AGENCY

The head of agency (or agency head) has the responsibility and authority to contract for supplies and services needed to run an agency's mission requirements. The agency head also establishes "contracting activities" and delegates the duties of these activities to authorized representatives. An authorized representative is any person or persons, other than the contracting officer, authorized to manage an agency's contracting functions.

Each agency head must establish a system for selecting, appointing, and terminating contracting officers and must maintain a procurement career management program. (The contracting officer is the only federal employee authorized to bind the government to a contract over $3,000.) These selections and appointments must be consistent with the Office of Federal Procurement Policy's standards for skill-based training in performing contracting and purchasing duties.

In selecting a contracting officer, the appointing official considers the complexity and dollar value of the acquisitions to be assigned and the candidate's experience, training, education, judgment, and character. The appointing official will want to know whether the candidate has:

- Experience in government contracting and administration, commercial purchasing, or related fields

- Education or special training in business administration, law, accounting, engineering, or related fields

- Knowledge of acquisition policies and procedures

■ Specialized knowledge in the particular assigned field of contracting

■ Satisfactory completion of the acquisition training courses.

CONTRACTING OFFICER

A contracting officer enters into, administers, or terminates contracts and makes related determinations and findings. The contracting officer is the only person who can bind the government to a contract that is greater than the micropurchase threshold of $3,000. There are currently more than 28,000 contracting officers in the government (three-quarters of whom work at DOD).

When appointed by the head of agency, a contracting officer is issued a Certificate of Appointment, Standard Form 1402. This certificate is also referred to as a "warrant." Each Certificate of Appointment identifies the contracting officer, the federal agency for which he or she works, and any limitations on his or her authority.

A contracting officer may bind the government only to the extent of the authority delegated. The Certificate of Appointment might, for example, limit a contracting officer's purchasing authority to supplies and services that are less than $200,000. If you have any doubts about a contracting officer's authority, ask to see his or her warrant. Further, the contracting officer's name and agency/department must be typed, stamped, or printed on the contract.

Contracting officers ensure compliance with the terms of the contract and safeguard the interests of the government in its contractual relationships. If the contracting officer is unable to ensure that all requirements of law, executive orders, regulations, and all other applicable procedures, including clearances, have been met, he or she is prohibited from executing the contract. The contracting officer ensures that:

■ Sufficient funds are available for the obligation.

■ The price paid by the government is "fair and reasonable."

Certificate of Appointment

Under authority vested in the undersigned and in conformance with
Subpart 1.6 of the Federal Acquisition Regulation

Scott Stanberry

is appointed

Contracting Officer

for the

United States of America

Subject to the limitations contained in the Federal Acquisition Regulation and to the following:

Unless sooner terminated, this appointment is
effective as long as the appointee is assigned to:

_____
Contracts Division
(Organization)
General Services Administration
(Agency/Department)

_____
(Signature and Title)
Head of Contracting Activity

10/15/08
(Date)

GSA-115
(No.)

STANDARD FORM 1402 (10-83)
Prescribed by GSA
FAR (48 CFR), 53.201-1

NSN7540-01-152-5815
1402-101

Sample Certificate of Appointment

■ The contractor receives impartial, fair, and equitable treatment.

■ The contract meets the requirements of the applicable laws and regulations.

Because the contracting officer is the only government official with this authority, he or she is always under intense scrutiny from both contractors and government personnel. The Federal Acquisition Regulation (FAR) is written specifically for the contracting officer, and it offers hundreds of options to consider. The contracting officer often requests the help of specialists in audit, law, engineering, and other fields when making determinations.

In many cases, the contracting officer delegates some of his or her authority and duties to other persons. These authorized representatives include the following.

Procuring Contracting Officer

The procuring contracting officer (PCO) is responsible for issuing solicitations, accepting bids, and making the original award of the contract. If you have a problem with a solicitation before award, the PCO is the person to call. By law, the PCO's name and phone number must be on the cover of the solicitation and in the FedBizOpps synopsis. FedBizOpps is where government buyers publicize their business opportunities on the Internet (see Chapter 8).

Administrative Contracting Officer

The contracting officer may delegate administrative responsibility for your contract to the administrative contracting officer (ACO). These functions typically include monitoring the contractor's performance, inspecting and accepting the contractor's supplies and services, and ensuring that the contractor is properly paid.

Administrative contracting officers are stationed around the country to keep a close eye on contractor performance. This practice allows the contracting officer to concentrate on awarding new contracts. The contracting officer still has the final authority on issues that have a significant impact on the contract.

Termination Contracting Officer

For companies contracting with the government, the possibility that the contract may be terminated is a fact of life. In cases where a contract is terminated for the government's convenience or because of a contractor's default, a termination contracting officer (TCO) is typically used. FAR Part 49 contains the uniform policies and procedures on contract terminations.

When a contracting officer terminates a contract, the settlement process is turned over to the TCO. A settlement proposal details the charges (or expenses) a contractor is seeking as reimbursement for work done to date.

Once the contractor completes the settlement proposal, the TCO (with the help of government auditors) examines the proposal to verify its accuracy. When the TCO is satisfied with the settlement proposal, he or she signs the agreement and binds the government. The TCO may approve the settlement proposal without the contracting officer's approval.

Contracting Officer's Representative

Most federal agencies allow the contracting officer to appoint a contracting officer's representative (COR) or a contracting officer's technical representative (COTR). They assist the contracting officer in ensuring that the contractor's performance proceeds in accordance with the terms and conditions of the contract. Typically, the COR will provide technical advice and guidance regarding the contract's specifications and statements of work.

The COR also keeps the contracting officer updated on the contract's status or progress by performing inspections and quality assurance functions. These functions include updating the contracting officer on any unusual circumstances, such as security violations or whether the contractor has assigned adequate personnel to perform the contract's requirements.

The contracting officer appoints a COR to a contract in writing. This appointment letter must state the COR's duties and authority, along with any limitations placed on that authority. Only the contracting officer handles any changes involving unit cost, total price, quantity, or delivery schedules. The contracting officer may appoint as many CORs as necessary to adequately perform the requirements of the contract or program.

COMPETITION ADVOCATES

The Competition in Contracting Act of 1984 requires each federal agency to appoint a competition advocate, who is responsible for promoting full and open competition. Competition advocates do this by challenging barriers to competition, such as restrictive statements of work, unnecessarily detailed specifications, and burdensome contract clauses.

Competition advocates also review the agency's contracting operations to ensure that appropriate actions are being taken to encourage competition and the acquisition of commercial items. For example, a competition advocate might examine solicitations expected to exceed $100,000 that are being conducted without full and open competition. The agency's senior procurement executive then reviews the findings.

The competition advocate is a member of the agency's executive staff. However, the competition advocate may hold no duties or responsibilities that would conflict with his or her primary responsibilities.

Competition advocates are always looking for ways to increase competition. If you find that a solicitation contains unnecessary restrictions, contact the contracting officer listed on the cover page. If you are not satisfied with the contracting officer's response, contact the competition advocate.

SMALL BUSINESS SPECIALISTS

Each major federal agency and department has an Office of Small and Disadvantaged Business Utilization, with at least one small business specialist. These specialists, also referred to as Small and Disadvantaged Business Utilization Specialists (SADBUS), assist and counsel small businesses on acquisition regulations and practices, finding buying offices for their supplies or services, and acquiring data on current or future procurements.

Small business specialists ensure that their departments or contracting activities award a fair portion of their contracts to small businesses. The Small Business Act of 1953 requires each federal agency to establish goals for contract awards to small businesses. The Department of Defense currently has an agency goal of awarding 5% of its contracts to women-owned small businesses (see Chapter 4).

Small business specialists review all purchase transactions over the simplified acquisition threshold of $100,000 to determine whether they can be performed by a small business. If such purchase transactions are identified, the specialist may recommend to the contracting officer that the purchase be *set aside* for small businesses. Finally, a small business specialist can introduce you to the actual customer (or contracting personnel) who will purchase your supplies and services.

Small business specialists are an invaluable resource. For a current list of small and disadvantaged business utilization offices, visit:

www.acq.osd.mil/osbp

The Government Printing Office also has a publication called *Small Business Specialists*, which lists DOD small and disadvantaged businesses by state, including their addresses, phone numbers, and contacts. For information about this publication, contact:

**Superintendent of Documents
Government Printing Office
Washington, DC 20402-9371
Phone (202) 512-1800**

REQUIREMENTS PERSONNEL

The government personnel responsible for determining which supplies and services a federal agency needs to run its operations are usually referred to as "requirements personnel" or "users." There is no universal title for these persons. The following illustration should help clarify which government personnel would be considered requirements personnel.

Each contracting activity in the Defense Advanced Research Projects Agency (DARPA) must submit an annual budget for the items it will need to run its research projects. DARPA is the central research and development organization for DOD.

DARPA requires two separate groups to prepare budget requests. The first group consists of the agency's program managers (or head scientists), who prepare budgets for the supplies and services they will need to run their research projects during the upcoming fiscal year. The second group consists of the agency's logistics managers, who prepare budgets and make purchases for commonly used items like pens, computers, and office furniture.

Completed budgets are then submitted to the Comptroller or equivalent person, for approval. Once approved, they are sent to DARPA's budget office, where they are grouped together with the budgets of other buying offices to establish the total budget of the contracting activity.

In this example, there are two types of requirements personnel: program managers (or head scientists) and logistics managers. If you want to market your products or services to DARPA, you need to find out which program and logistics managers typically purchase your products. The best way to get in touch with a contracting activity's requirements personnel is to have the small business specialist set up an appointment for you.

The government encourages prospective contractors to contact requirements personnel directly because it enables the parties to gain valuable information about each other. The requirements personnel find out which supplies and services are available to fulfill their needs. The contractor discovers the types of items the contracting activity typically purchases.

Meeting with an agency's requirements personnel is a great way to learn about a contracting activity's current and future needs. I can't think of a better way to get a head start on your competition.

■   ■   ■

These key players are not the only government personnel you will run into—just the ones that seem to pop up most frequently. The trick to being a successful contractor is to know who the key players are and to focus your attention and efforts on them.

■   ■   ■

PART 2

How Your Business Size Offers Opportunity

Chapter 4: Opportunities for Small Businesses/ Independent Contractors

Chapter 5: Small Business Preference Programs

Chapter 6: Subcontracting Opportunities

Chapter 7: Federal Supply Schedules/ GSA Schedules

"Ginger Rogers did everything Fred Astaire did, except backwards and in high heels."

—*Bob Thaves*

By now you know that the federal government has an enormous impact on business. But are you aware that the government provides a variety of programs and services to assist small businesses, including technical, management, and financial assistance? In fact, the policy of the U.S. government is to give small businesses the maximum practical opportunity to participate in federal contracting. Congress has enacted numerous laws and regulations that promote the participation of small businesses in the federal contracting process.

What's more, mid- to large-sized companies can benefit from these small business programs by providing subcontracting opportunities to businesses that meet the government's criteria on their contracts.

Opportunities for Small Businesses/ Independent Contractors

4

© 1999 Randy Glasbergen.

"We're the only company in the world that sells organic cookies made with goat urine, but the government isn't trying to break up *our* monopoly."

What's in this chapter?

- Small Business Act
- Government-wide goals
- North American Industry Classification System
- Size certification
- Small business affiliates
- Certificate of competency
- Small business set-asides

Everyone knows that there is a big size difference between a major corporation like Microsoft and the Mom-and-Pop convenience store on your street corner. But how do you determine your actual business size? Is yours a small business? And, if so, what happens when your business grows? When does your business cease to be small? These are very important questions because many of the government's programs and services are targeted toward small businesses specifically.

Did You Know That . . .

According to the Small Business Administration (see www.sba.gov):

- More than 25.8 million small businesses are operating in the United States?

- New business formation reached a record high in 1998?

- Thirty-five percent of federal contracts go to small businesses each year?

- During FY2006, the government issued more than $77 billion worth of federal contracts to small businesses?

Small Businesses . . .

- Create three out of every four new jobs

- Produce 51% of the gross national product

- Represent 99.7% of all employees

- Provide 55% of innovations

- Account for 53% of the private sector output

- Represent 96% of all U.S. exporters

- Account for 38% of jobs in high-technology sectors

■ Provide 47% of all sales in the country

■ Employ 58% of the private workforce

■ Provide 67% of workers with their first jobs.

As you can see, the federal government offers tremendous opportunities for people looking to start new businesses or increase the size of their existing businesses. This chapter will help you determine your business size and discuss some of the advantages of being a small business.

SMALL BUSINESS ACT

In the mid-1900s, the government began to recognize a problem with its procurement process. It seemed that a few large companies dominated some industries almost to the point of monopolization, and smaller companies were unable to compete for federal contracts. As a result, Congress passed the Small Business Act of 1953.

The Small Business Act requires the government to award a "fair proportion" of its federal contracts to small businesses. It also requires the government to provide small and small disadvantaged businesses with the maximum practical opportunity to participate in federal contracting. To help ensure these requirements are met, the act established the Small Business Administration (SBA).

GOVERNMENT-WIDE GOALS

Congress establishes government-wide goals for awards of federal contracts and subcontracts to small businesses. These goals are typically stated as percentages of the procurement dollars spent by the government each year. (See www.sba.gov for more details.)

Congress established the following government-wide goals for FY2007: 23% of all federal contracts should go to small businesses, 5% to small "disadvantaged" businesses (SDBs), 5% to small women-owned businesses (WOBs), 3% to small HUBZone businesses, and 3% to small disabled veteran-owned businesses.

Note: Contract awards to small disadvantaged, women-owned, HUBZone, and disabled veteran-owned businesses each count toward the 23% goal for all small businesses.

SBA negotiates with each federal agency to determine an estimate for contract awards to small businesses. These estimates might be higher or lower than the government-wide goals, depending on the types of supplies and services being purchased. For example, a federal agency with a $40 million annual budget might have the following agency goals:

Awards to SDBs: 6% x $40,000,000 = $2,400,000

Awards to small WOBs: 4% x $40,000,000 = $1,600,000

                                              $4,000,000

Awards to small businesses: 15% x $40,000,000 = $6,000,000

Total small business awards   25% $10,000,000

SBA then compares each agency's estimates against its actual results to determine its success in meeting its goals. Federal agencies pay close attention to these results because they are given to Congress for review.

Agency goals provide two primary advantages for small businesses. First, they ensure that each federal agency has plans for awarding federal contracts to small businesses. Second, the goals give federal agencies a baseline against which to measure their progress yearly. If, six months into the year, a federal agency notices that it has awarded only 2% of its contracts to small disadvantaged businesses, government policy mandates that it concentrate in this area over the next six months.

NORTH AMERICAN INDUSTRY CLASSIFICATION SYSTEM

SBA has taken the lead in defining what constitutes a small business in the eyes of the federal government. It issues a body of definitions called "size standards" classified on an industry-by-industry basis. Size standards are defined by number of employees, average annual sales, assets (for financial organizations), or total electric output (for utility firms).

SBA uses the North American Industry Classification System (NAICS, pronounced "nakes") to identify the various types of industries and establishments. On April 9, 1997, NAICS officially replaced the U.S. Standard Industrial Classification (SIC) system.

Why Switch from SIC to NAICS?

For more than 60 years, the SIC system served as the structure for collecting, aggregating, presenting, and analyzing data on the U.S. economy. It was developed in the 1930s, at a time when manufacturing dominated the U.S. economic scene. However, today's services-centered economy has rendered the SIC system obsolete because the system often fails to adequately account for new and emerging service industries.

Enter NAICS! NAICS focuses on how products and services are created as opposed to the SIC system, which focuses on what is produced. This "process"-oriented classification methodology yields industrial groupings that are more homogenous and thus better suited for economic analysis.

Under the SIC system the category of food services was classified as retail trade, where it accounted for over one-third of that sector's employment. Consequently, retail trade represents a smaller share of the economy under NAICS than under the SIC system.

Retail Trade

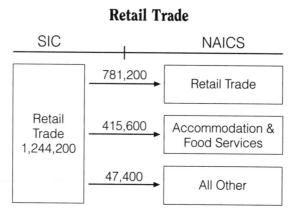

NAICS groups the economy into 20 broad sectors, up from the 10 divisions of the SIC system.

Code	NAICS Sectors	Previous SIC Divisions
11	Agriculture, Forestry, and Fishing	Agriculture, Forestry, and Fishing
21	Mining	Mining
23	Construction	Construction
31-33	Manufacturing	Manufacturing
22	Utilities	Transportation, Communications, and Public Utilities
48-49	Transportation and Warehousing	
42	Wholesale Trade	Wholesale Trade
44-45	Retail Trade	Retail Trade
72	Accommodation and Food Services	
52	Finance and Insurance	Finance, Insurance, and Real Estate
53	Real Estate and Rental and Leasing	

51	Information	
54	Professional, Scientific, and Technical Services	
56	Administrative Support/Waste Mgmt Services	Services
61	Educational Services	
62	Health Care and Social Assistance	
71	Arts, Entertainment, and Recreation	
81	Other Services	
92	Public Administration	Public Administration
55	Management of Companies	(Parts of all divisions)

The shift to NAICS means a break in historical time series. SIC and NAICS industry groupings are not directly comparable because the code changes for NAICS have split some SIC groups.

NAICS industries are identified by a six-digit code, in contrast to the four-digit SIC code. This six-digit hierarchical structure allows for greater coding flexibility.

XX	Industry Sector (31–33 = Manufacturing)
XXX	Industry Subsector (321 = Wood Product Manufacturing)
XXXX	Industry Group (3219 = Other Wood Product Manufacturing)
XXXXX	Industry (32191 = Millwork)
XXXXXX	Country–U.S., Canadian, Mexican (321911 = Wood Window/ Door Manufacturing)

The NAICS coding system was developed to focus on the identification of high technology and new and emerging industries. Currently, NAICS has identified more than 350 new industries, including pet supply stores, casinos, interior design services, convenience stores, and HMO medical centers.

In developing NAICS, the United States, Canada, and Mexico agreed that the five-digit codes would represent the level at which the system is comparable among the three countries. The sixth digit allows for country-specific detail. In cases where the United States did not choose to create additional detail, the five- and six-digit categories within U.S. NAICS are the same and the six-digit U.S. NAICS code ends in zero.

Comparison of SIC and NAICS Codes	
NAICS	**SIC**
Six-digit industry code	Four-digit industry code
1,170 industry codes	1,005 industry codes
21 sectors	Ten major divisions
Industry's classifications based on production processes it uses	Industry's classifications based on its primary type of activity

SBA Size Standards

Suppose SBA is issuing a small business solicitation for construction services and you want to determine whether your firm is eligible to bid. As a general construction contractor, your NAICS code is "236210."

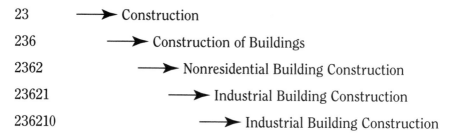

23	→ Construction
236	→ Construction of Buildings
2362	→ Nonresidential Building Construction
23621	→ Industrial Building Construction
236210	→ Industrial Building Construction

The following website allows you to search SBA's size standard by NAICS:

www.census.gov/naics

In this case, any company independently owned and operated with $28.5 million or less in average revenues over the past three years could submit a bid. SBA makes these size determinations annually.

The amount of average gross revenue over a three-year period usually determines size. An accounting firm, for instance, is considered a small business if it has less than $7 million in average gross revenue. On the other hand, engineering services on military equipment (NAICS code 541330) has a small business size standard of $23 million.

Occasionally, number of employees is used as a size standard. A regular dealer or wholesale trader is considered a small business if it has fewer than 100 employees (500 for government contractors) averaged over a 12-month period. Manufacturers in certain industries may have up to 1,500 employees and still be considered small businesses. An aircraft manufacturer, NAICS code 336411, has a small business size standard of 1,500 employees. Companies with multiple business lines may, in certain circumstances, qualify as small businesses when proposing for a particular requirement.

You probably think that these classifications are too high for most small businesses—and you're probably right. The government's aim is to let small businesses grow into thriving medium-sized businesses before taking away the small business benefits or perks. The government wants to make sure that a small business is self-sufficient before it graduates from the small business program.

SBA also establishes small business size standards for federal programs and services, such as financial assistance loans, 8(a) program participation, and participation in the Small Business Innovative Research (SBIR) program. For more information about these size standards, contact:

Small Business Administration
Size Standard Division
(202) 205-6618

www.sba.gov/size/indexsize.html

SIZE CERTIFICATION

Each contractor must self-certify that it is a small business. It is the responsibility of the contracting officer to accept this certification or request that SBA formally determine the company's size. Competitors to a particular solicitation may also compel the contracting officer to make a formal size determination by submitting a timely protest. (A protest is a written objection by an interested party to a solicitation, proposed award, or award of a contract.)

A competitor may protest the winning small business on several grounds, including:

■ The winning small business is affiliated with or controlled by a large business.

■ It has an agreement with a large business to be purchased.

■ It is really a large business when the time period and methodology for measuring annual receipts are properly considered.

If a company's owners intentionally misrepresent the company's size on a federal procurement, they might be subject to fines.

Protests must be submitted to the contracting officer within five working days of notification of the winner or ten working days of being notified of the competitive range. If the protest is not made in that period, SBA's findings will apply only to future purchases.

SMALL BUSINESS AFFILIATES

The most significant stumbling block for determining whether you qualify as a small business is the concept of affiliates. Business concerns, organizations, or individuals are considered affiliates of each other, directly or indirectly, if either one has the power to control the other, or if a third party controls or has the power to control both.

Affiliates must combine their respective incomes and employees when determining their status as a small or large business. SBA's rule for affiliation is that "size determinations shall include the applicant concern and all its domestic and foreign affiliates."

Most business owners think of affiliates as divisions or subsidiaries, but SBA looks at an affiliation in terms of substance rather than mere form. SBA looks at who has the control. If a company can directly or indirectly control (or has the power to control) another company, the two are considered affiliates and SBA treats them as one company. Whether the controlling company exercises its power is of no consequence as long as the ability to control is present.

CERTIFICATE OF COMPETENCY

SBA also manages the Certificate of Competency (COC) program. This program's primary purpose is to assist small businesses in obtaining federal contracts for which they were determined to be the lowest responsive and responsible bidder. If your business is the low bidder on a federal contract and the contracting officer questions your ability to perform the contract, you may apply to SBA for a COC.

The COC applies to all federal acquisitions. It does not, however, extend to questions concerning regulatory requirements that federal agencies impose and enforce. Here's how the program works:

1. Upon determining and documenting that an apparently successful small business lacks certain elements of responsibility, the contracting officer withholds the contract award for a period of 15 business days. Elements of responsibility include, but are not limited to, capability, competency, credit, and integrity. The documented areas of nonresponsibility are then referred to the appropriate SBA regional office.

2. SBA informs the small business that it has been determined nonresponsible and offers the business an opportunity to apply for a COC.

3. Once SBA receives an acceptable COC application, an authorized SBA representative visits the small business and reviews the areas of non-responsibility cited. SBA also performs an on-site survey of the firm's facilities, management, performance record, and production capacity in relationship to the contract in question. The SBA representative then sends his or her findings to the SBA regional director.

4. The regional director decides whether to issue a COC.

5. If the regional director decides to issue a COC, the contracting officer usually awards the contract to the small business. (The regional director's decision may not be appealed if the award is valued at $100,000 or less.) If the contracting officer disagrees with the determination, he or she appeals the case to SBA headquarters in Washington, D.C.

SMALL BUSINESS SET-ASIDES

All procurements between $3,000 and $100,000 are, by law, set aside for small business and may only be awarded to large business if a small business cannot provide the supply or service at a reasonable price. Set-asides ensure that a fair proportion of the government's procurements go to small and small disadvantaged business concerns. All solicitations involving set-asides must specify the applicable small business size standard and product classification.

The contracting officer is responsible for reviewing acquisitions to determine whether they can be set aside for small business. Small business set-asides may be conducted using simplified acquisition procedures, sealed bidding, or negotiated procurement procedures (see Part 4).

Rule of Two

The "rule of two" states that purchases (other than federal supply schedules purchases—see Chapter 7) with an anticipated dollar value exceeding $3,000 must be set aside exclusively for small business participation if there is a reasonable expectation that:

■ Offers will be received from at least two responsible small business concerns.

■ Awards will be made at fair market prices.

If the contracting officer receives no acceptable offers, the set-aside requirement may be withdrawn and the procurement resolicited on an unrestricted basis.

The "rule of two" should be looked at seriously. When applied literally, it can be a strait-jacket to someone who wants to consider large businesses in the procurement process. When you see a FedBizOpps synopsis that is being done for market research purposes, it is most often being done to either establish a basis for determining if the acquisition is legitimately a sole-source procurement or if the acquisition should be set aside for small businesses.

Don't confuse small business set-asides with simplified acquisition procedures (see Chapter 10). The main difference between them is that set-asides typically are used for purchases greater than $100,000. The following example should clarify this difference.

Suppose a major computer manufacturer and a regular dealer work together to sell computers to the government. The manufacturer is considered a large business and the regular dealer, a small business. A firm qualifies as a regular dealer if:

■ It regularly maintains a stock of products (computers, in this case) for which it claims to be a dealer.

■ The stock maintained is true inventory from which sales are made.

■ Sales to the public are made regularly in the usual course of business.

- Sales are made regularly from stock on a recurring basis.

- The business is established and ongoing.

Now, let's assume the contracting officer plans to make two separate purchases using small business set-aside procedures. The first purchase is for 20 computers with an anticipated value of $80,000. This purchase would fall under simplified acquisition procedures because it's less than $100,000. Under these procedures, a small business regular dealer may furnish any domestically manufactured products, regardless of the manufacturing company's size. In this example, then, the regular dealer would be eligible for this solicitation.

The second purchase is for 40 laser printers with an anticipated value of $200,000. When a small business set-aside is greater than the simplified acquisition threshold, the regular dealer and the manufacturer must both qualify as small businesses. The regular dealer, therefore, would not be eligible for the solicitation because the manufacturer is a large business.

Partial Set-asides

Partial set-asides enable the contracting officer to set aside a portion of a contract for small businesses. They may be used when:

- A total set-aside is not appropriate. (Suppose the Defense Advanced Research Projects Agency has issued an R&D contract to study the atmosphere on Mars. Because this contract requires sophisticated equipment, it cannot be performed exclusively by a small business. Therefore, the contracting officer decides to set aside the reporting requirements of the study for a small business.)

- The procurement can be split into two or more economic production runs.

- One or more small business concerns are expected to have the technical competence and production capacity to satisfy the set-aside portion of the requirement at a fair market price.

■ More than one large and one small business are expected to submit bids.

To set aside a portion of an acquisition, the contracting officer divides the requirement into a set-aside portion and a non-set-aside portion. The non-set-aside portion is awarded using normal contracting procedures.

To be eligible for the set-aside portion of the procurement, a small business must submit its bid and proposal at the time the non-set-aside portion is due. Once all the awards have been made on the non-set-aside portion, the contracting officer negotiates the set-aside portion with the eligible small business concerns. The small business that submits the lowest responsive bid is awarded the contract. Partial set-asides may be conducted using sealed bidding or negotiated procedures.

Class Set-asides

Class set-asides are particular classes of products and services reserved for small businesses. A buying office might decide to create a class set-aside for stationery supplies. Accordingly, only small businesses may bid on pencil sharpener procurements for that particular office.

■ ■ ■

The Small Business Act requires the government to award a fair share of its contracts to small businesses. To be successful in federal contracting, you must ensure that your business size standard accurately reflects your company's business size. For more detailed information on small business size standards, size status, and size protests, visit:

www.sba.gov/size

or consult a size determination specialist in one of SBA's six Offices of Government Contracting.

■ ■ ■

5 Small Business Preference Programs

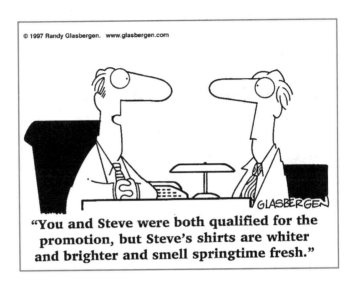

© 1997 Randy Glasbergen. www.glasbergen.com

GLASBERGEN

"You and Steve were both qualified for the promotion, but Steve's shirts are whiter and brighter and smell springtime fresh."

What's in this chapter?

- Definition of small disadvantaged businesses
- Evaluation preference for SDBs
- 8(a) business development program
- Status of preference programs
- Women-owned small businesses
- Veterans business outreach program
- Labor surplus area set-asides
- SBA HUBZone empowerment contracting program
- Small business competitiveness demonstration program
- Small business innovative research program

The federal government gives preference to certain kinds of businesses in awarding federal contracts. These preference programs ensure that every U.S. citizen has an opportunity to participate in government contracting. Because they are preference programs, however, they are always under intense scrutiny. This chapter describes some common preference programs and offers insight into what the future holds for these programs.

DEFINITION OF SMALL DISADVANTAGED BUSINESSES

To qualify as a small disadvantaged business (SDB), a firm must be a small business that is at least 51% owned by persons belonging to a socially and economically disadvantaged group. Socially disadvantaged persons are those who have been subjected to racial or ethnic prejudice or cultural bias based on their identity as a member of a particular group. Disadvantaged groups include:

■ Asian Americans

■ Black Americans

■ Hispanic Americans

■ Native Americans.

Economically disadvantaged persons are those whose ability to compete in the free market system has been impaired as a result of diminished capital and credit opportunities, compared to others in the same or a similar line of business. In determining the degree of economic disadvantage, the government considers:

■ Personal financial condition of the disadvantaged individual (Program participants must have a net worth of less than $750,000—some of us are more disadvantaged than others!)

■ Business financial condition

■ Access to credit and capital

■ Comparisons with other businesses in the same or a similar line of business.

Handicapped persons and women are not presumed to be socially and economically disadvantaged. See FAR 19.001 for a more detailed definition of small disadvantaged business concerns.

EVALUATION PREFERENCE FOR SDBs

The Federal Acquisition Streamlining Act of 1994 allows federal agencies to use an "evaluation preference" when evaluating offers received from SDBs on unrestricted solicitations. This preference allows an SDB to receive a contract even if its bid is higher than that of its competitors, up to a limit of 10% of the proposed contract price, thus helping federal agencies attain the government's goal of awarding 5% of its contract dollars to SDBs. These set-asides are still subject to the rule of two, however.

To be eligible for an evaluation preference, a contractor must submit a certification, obtained within the past three years, that one or more socially disadvantaged persons own and control the business. Businesses owned by persons who are not members of the statutorily presumed groups can qualify as SDBs by submitting evidence demonstrating their social and economic disadvantage.

An evaluation preference may not be used if the acquisition is:

■ 100% set aside for SDBs.

■ Partially or totally set aside for small businesses.

■ Made pursuant to the 8(a) program or the labor surplus area program (which are discussed later in this chapter).

■ Under the simplified acquisition threshold of $100,000.

■ Under the U.S. Trade Agreement Act and other agreements with foreign governments.

■ Made in a designated industry group. The four designated industry groups are construction, architect and engineering services, non-nuclear ship repair, and refuse system and related services (see Small Business Competitiveness Demonstration Program later in this chapter).

This example should help clarify how the evaluation preference works. Let's assume DOD plans to award a contract that has an evaluation preference of 10% for SDBs. Two businesses, one of which is an SDB, are competing for the contract. The firms make the following bids:

> Regular business bid $ 475,000
> SDB bid $ 500,000

Assuming the contract will be awarded on price-related factors alone, which contractor do you think would win? Let's do the math.

> SDB bid $500,000
>   × 10%   SDB evaluation preference
> Evaluation preference
> adjustment $50,000

The evaluation preference gives the regular business the following bid price:

> Regular business bid $ 475,000
> Evaluation preference $50,000
> Regular business bid (after preference) $525,000
> SDB bid $500,000

In this example, the SDB would win the contract because its bid is $25,000 lower than that of the regular business.

8(a) BUSINESS DEVELOPMENT PROGRAM

The 8(a) Business Development Program fosters business ownership by persons who are socially and economically disadvantaged. This is a major preference program and permits agencies to award (sole-source) contracts directly to eligible small businesses, especially if the total value is to be less than $3,000,000 for services or $5,000,000 for supplies. It is named for the section of the Small Business Act from which it derives its authority.

SBA is responsible for awarding these noncompetitive contracts to eligible program participants. More than 4,000 companies are currently in this program.

8(a) Qualifications

A small business qualifies for the 8(a) program if it is at least 51% owned by one or more socially and economically disadvantaged persons. Persons who are not black, Hispanic, Native American, or members of any other group presumed to be socially disadvantaged may qualify for the 8(a) program by establishing social disadvantage based on a "preponderance of evidence."

Applicants to the 8(a) program must have been in operation for at least two full years, as evidenced by business tax returns that show operating revenues in their primary industry. Applicants can obtain a waiver from this two-year requirement if they meet the following five conditions:

■ The person or persons upon whom eligibility is based have substantial business management experience.

■ The applicant firm can demonstrate the technical expertise to carry out its business plan.

■ The applicant firm has adequate capital to sustain its business operations.

■ The applicant firm has a record of successful performance on contracts from governmental or nongovernmental sources in its primary industry.

■ The applicant firm can demonstrate that it has the ability to obtain the personnel, facilities, and equipment needed to perform on the contracts, in a timely manner, if admitted to the 8(a) program.

Eligibility Constraints

The conditions governing the definition of socially and economically disadvantaged persons impose constraints on the way in which an 8(a) business organization is structured and operated. Transactions that are routinely permissible for non-8(a) companies could jeopardize an 8(a) contractor's continued program participation. If your enterprise is to maintain its program eligibility, you must be aware of these constraints.

If a business is organized as a corporation, it must comply with the unconditional ownership requirement, as evidenced by at least 51% ownership of each class of voting stock by socially and economically disadvantaged persons. The business must maintain this level of ownership throughout its participation in the program.

The 8(a) program can be a powerful tool for assisting disadvantaged persons and their companies in the federal marketplace. A thorough understanding of the program's qualifications and requirements can help 8(a) contractors avoid situations that could jeopardize their continued program eligibility.

Program Participation and Duration

Program participation is divided into two stages: the developmental stage and the transitional stage. The developmental stage lasts for four years and helps 8(a) firms overcome their economic disadvantage through business development assistance. During this stage, SBA wants participants to achieve the following objectives:

■ Maintain an existing business base

■ Develop and implement a business plan and marketing strategy to facilitate the achievement of non-8(a) revenues.

During the transitional stage, which lasts five years, participants prepare to leave the 8(a) program. SBA encourages contractors to increase their non-8(a) support levels during the transitional stage. For example, targeted non-8(a) total revenue should be:

Transitional Stage Year	Non-8(a) Revenue/ Total Revenue
1	15%–25%
2	25%–35%
3	35%–45%
4	45%–55%
5	55%–75%

If your company is to survive or prosper, you need to develop an "exit strategy" from the 8(a) program as soon as possible. That strategy might include developing a mix of government and commercial contracts and establishing long-term business partnerships with major prime contractors.

On an interesting note, an 8(a) firm in its, say, final (ninth) year of eligibility for preference, can be awarded a contract lasting up to five years under this program. For contracts lasting longer than five years, an agency cannot claim credit toward its small business goals if, after the fifth year, the firm no longer qualifies for that status even though the contract may still remain in effect.

Here's an example of how the 8(a) Business Development Program works. Typically, three parties are involved in the process:

- The federal agency that awards the contract

- SBA, which receives the contract (the party that receives the contract is referred to as the prime contractor)

- The 8(a) firm that performs the contract (in this scenario, the 8(a) firm would be considered the subcontractor).

The General Services Administration (GSA) plans to award a contract for security services. The contract is for two years at an estimated contract value of $200,000 per year. After reviewing the plans for the job, the contracting officer decides it would be perfect for an 8(a) firm and contacts SBA. To help meet their agencies' goals, contracting officers are always on the lookout for 8(a) opportunities.

SBA then looks for qualified 8(a) firms to perform the contract. Several 8(a) firms are selected and told to submit competitive bids for the work. The contract is then awarded to the 8(a) firm with the lowest bid (without any negotiations).

Once SBA selects a qualified 8(a) firm to perform the contract, it negotiates a price for the contract with the contracting officer. When the parties agree, the contracting officer mails the solicitation to the 8(a) firm and awards the contract to SBA. SBA then awards a subcontract to the 8(a) firm, and the 8(a) firm begins the work.

During contract performance, the 8(a) firm deals directly with the federal agency that awarded the contract. Payments are also made directly from the federal agency to the 8(a) firm.

Nowadays, many federal agencies, under an agreement with SBA, award contracts directly to 8(a) firms. Also, in the matter of 8(a) firms securing business, they can, and very often do, get agencies to go directly to the SBA and request authorization to make an award to the identified 8(a) firm. Why might they do this? Because, if they're comfortable with the 8(a) firm, they avoid going through a lengthy competitive process and can negotiate a contract directly with them.

Other Assistance

Financial assistance in the form of loans and advance payments is available to 8(a) program participants. SBA also offers a wide range of management assistance, including counseling and seminars.

Reporting Requirements

SBA annually reviews 8(a) firms for compliance with eligibility requirements. As part of the annual review, each participant firm submits the following items:

■ Certification that the company meets the 8(a) program eligibility requirements

■ Certification that no changes that could adversely affect the participant's program eligibility have been made

■ Personal financial information for each disadvantaged owner

■ Record of all payments, compensation, and distributions (including loans, advances, salaries, and dividends) made by the company to each of its owners, officers, and directors, or to any person or entity affiliated with such individuals

■ IRS Form 4506, Request for Copy or Transcript of Tax Form

■ Other information SBA deems necessary.

If a participant fails to provide this information for the annual review, SBA may initiate termination proceedings.

How to Apply for 8(a) Status

Any individual or business has the right to apply for section 8(a) assistance, regardless of whether it appears to be eligible. To get an application, contact:

SBA Answer Desk
800-U-ASK-SBA (800-827-5722)

www.sba.gov

Once you complete your application, you will need to file it at the SBA field office that serves your company's principal place of business. (SBA has more than 100 field offices.) Your principal place of business is the location of your books and records and the office at which the persons who manage the company's day-to-day operations work.

Once your application is submitted, the regional Division of Program Certification and Eligibility (DPCE) has 15 days to review it for completeness. If the application is incomplete, you will have 15 days to provide the additional information and resubmit it. If DPCE determines the application is complete, SBA will make a final decision regarding 8(a) program eligibility within 90 days.

If your application is rejected, you may request that SBA reconsider it. During the reconsideration process, you may submit additional or revised information. If your application is declined after reconsideration, you must wait a year from the date of reconsideration to submit a new application.

SDB Program/8(a) Program Comparison

The purpose of the SDB program is to encourage minority-owned businesses, including contractors that were 8(a)-certified, to seek federal contracts. The SDB program, therefore, provides an alternative to SBA's 8(a) program for small minority-owned businesses seeking to participate in the economic mainstream. Here are a few characteristics that differentiate the two programs:

> ■ The eligibility requirements for the SDB program are less stringent than those for the 8(a) program.
>
> ■ SDBs may compete directly for any federal contracts for which they are qualified, whereas 8(a) firms rely on SBA to identify and approve sole-source contracts.
>
> ■ An SDB may self-certify that it meets the definition of an SDB, whereas an 8(a) firm must be certified by SBA to receive an 8(a) contract.

STATUS OF PREFERENCE PROGRAMS

Preference (or affirmative action) programs are always under intense scrutiny and change with the nation's moods or political views. Are they fair? Do they do enough to help disadvantaged U.S. citizens? Are they constitutional? Is there a way to make everyone happy? What does the future hold for these preference programs?

These are some questions that affirmative action programs evoke, and unfortunately there really isn't a definitive answer to any of them. However, if there is an indication of what the future holds for these preference programs, it would have to be the Supreme Court case of *Adarand Constructors, Inc. v. Pena.*

On June 12, 1995, the Supreme Court made a decision that had a profound impact on affirmative action programs. The case of *Adarand Constructors, Inc. v. Pena* involved a Department of Transportation (DOT) contract clause that rewarded the prime contractor on the job for exceeding an SDB subcontracting goal. The contract clause stated the following:

> Monetary compensation is offered for awarding subcontracts to small business concerns owned and controlled by socially and economically disadvantaged individuals. . . . Compensation is provided to the Contractor to locate, train, utilize, assist, and develop SDBs to become fully qualified contractors in the transportation facilities construction field. The contractor shall also

provide direct assistance to disadvantaged subcontractors in acquiring the necessary bonding, obtaining price quotations, analyzing plans and specifications, and planning and management of the work. . . . The Contractor will become eligible to receive payment under this provision when the dollar amount . . . of the DBE subcontract(s) awarded exceeds [10% for Colorado] of the original [prime] contract award.

In other words, the government would pay a prime contractor a 1.5% bonus if it awarded more than 10% of its subcontracts to SDBs.

Adarand Constructors, Inc. (owned by a white male), submitted the low bid for a guardrail subcontract. The prime contractor (Mountain Gravel) awarded the guardrail subcontract to the second lowest bidder, a certified SDB, to collect the contract bonus. Adarand filed suit against the government, claiming that it had violated the 14th Amendment of the Constitution, which guarantees "every citizen equal protection under the law."

Adarand claimed that, because the contract was awarded on class-based, noncompetitive grounds, the company did not receive equal protection under the law. All the lower courts ruled against Adarand's lawsuit, and the case was sent to the Supreme Court. The Supreme Court found DOT's subcontractor clause to be neither constitutional nor unconstitutional. Rather, it used the case to set a standard of review that courts must follow when evaluating such preferences.

The Supreme Court altered the playing field in some important respects, holding that "all racial classifications, imposed by whatever federal, state, or local governmental actor, must be analyzed by a reviewing court under strict scrutiny." In other words, preferences or programs based on racial classifications are constitutional only if they are narrowly tailored measures that further compelling governmental interests.

Although the Supreme Court raised the bar that affirmative action programs must clear, the strict scrutiny standard does not necessarily spell the end of preference programs. Seven justices expressed continued support for affirmative action, and the Supreme Court emphasized that the government is not disqualified from acting in response to the lingering effects of racial discrimination. The SBA interprets these guidelines by limiting the credits offered to SDBs bidding in industries that show the ongoing effects of discrimination.

WOMEN-OWNED SMALL BUSINESSES

Women-owned small businesses (WOSBs) are businesses that are at least 51% owned and controlled by one or more women who are U.S. citizens. The government offers WOSBs many outreach programs and services that provide counseling and assistance.

Women as a group, however, are not considered socially or economically disadvantaged, and their businesses are therefore treated like any other small business—although the government has established a goal of awarding WOSBs 5% of the total value of contracts each year.

If the WOSB owner happens to be socially or economically disadvantaged, the business qualifies for all three business categories: small business, small disadvantaged business, and small women-owned business. Federal agencies look for firms with this particular combination because con-tracts awarded to such firms can be applied to all of their small business goals.

Here are a few incredible statistics SBA has gathered on women business owners:

■ Women create new businesses and new jobs at twice the national rate.

■ Seventy-five percent of new businesses started by women succeed, com-pared to only 25% of those started by men.

■ More than one-third of all businesses are now owned by women.

■ Over the past 20 years, the number of women-owned businesses has nearly doubled.

www.womenbiz.gov

VETERANS BUSINESS OUTREACH PROGRAM

The Veterans Business Outreach Program (VBOP) provides entrepreneurial development services such as business training, counseling, and mentoring to eligible veterans who own or are considering starting a small business. A veteran is a person who served in the active military, naval, or air service and who was honorably discharged. Like women, veterans as a group are not depicted as socially or economically disadvantaged, and therefore veteran-owned small businesses are treated like any other small businesses.

Federal agencies are, however, responsible for ensuring that veterans receive fair consideration in agency purchases. Congress has established a government-wide goal of awarding 3% of all federal contracts to disabled veteran-owned small businesses.

www.vetbiz.gov

LABOR SURPLUS AREA SET-ASIDES

The Labor Surplus Area Program restricts competition to businesses that agree to perform most (at least half) of the contract work in areas that have higher-than-average unemployment, even if their headquarters are not located in the designated areas. This program directs government contract dollars into areas of severe economic need. Labor surplus area set-asides are applied only when enough qualified businesses are expected to bid, so that SBA can award contracts at fair and reasonable prices. The government also encourages contractors to place subcontracts with businesses located in labor surplus areas.

The U.S. Department of Labor defines and classifies labor surplus areas. It puts out this information in a monthly publication called *Area Trends in Employment and Unemployment,* which is available from the Government Printing Office.

SBA HUBZONE EMPOWERMENT CONTRACTING PROGRAM

This program encourages economic development in historically underutilized business zones (HUBZones) by establishing preferences for awarding federal contracts to small business concerns located in such areas. A HUBZone is an area with an unemployment rate that is at least 140% of the state's average or an average household income of no more than 80% of the nonmetropolitan state median. The HUBZone Empowerment Contracting Program was enacted into law as part of the Small Business Reauthorization Act of 1997.

Under this statute, SBA:

■ Determines whether small business concerns are eligible to receive HUBZone contracts

■ Maintains a list of qualified HUBZone small business concerns for use by acquisition agencies in awarding contracts under the program

■ Adjudicates protests of eligibility to receive HUBZone contracts

■ Reports to Congress the degree to which the HUBZone Empowerment Contracting Program has yielded increased employment opportunities and investment in HUBZones.

All federal agencies participate in the HUBZone program. Currently, Congress has established a government-wide goal of awarding 3% of all federal contracts to small HUBZone businesses.

Qualifications

For a small business to qualify for this program, at least 35% of its employees must reside in a designated HUBZone area. Small business concerns must be certified by SBA as meeting the HUBZone requirements. Metropolitan areas qualify as HUBZones based on census tract criteria. Nonmetropolitan counties must meet a specific income or unemployment test. Lands within the external boundaries of an Indian reservation also qualify.

The Bureau of the Census estimates that approximately 9,000 census tracts (out of 61,000) and 900 nonmetropolitan counties (out of 3,000) are HUBZones. SBA estimates that approximately 30,000 firms will apply to become certified HUBZone small business concerns. For more details on the HUBZone Empowerment Contracting Program, visit:

www.sba.gov/hubzone

Program Benefits

HUBZone awards take precedence over small business set-asides. Contracting officers must set aside acquisitions over $100,000 for HUBZone small business concerns if two or more HUBZone small businesses make fair market offers. If a sole-source HUBZone contract is made, it must be greater than $100,000 but less than $3 million ($5 million for manufacturing contracts), and the award must be at a fair market price.

Small business concerns located in HUBZone areas receive a 10% price evaluation preference in full and open procurements. This evaluation preference works just like the SDB evaluation preference. The price offered by a HUBZone small business is considered lower than the price offered by a non-HUBZone firm, as long as the HUBZone business's price is not more than 10% of the price offered by the otherwise lowest responsive bidder.

The HUBZone preference may not be used when price is not a selection factor (as in certain architectural-engineering contracts) or the successful bidder is a non-HUBZone small business. Another significant provision of this program is that a firm that is both a HUBZone small business concern and an SDB can receive the evaluation preference for each qualification.

Suppose Sandy's Script Services is located in a HUBZone area and is owned by a socially and economically disadvantaged person. Sandy Spellman, the owner, wants to bid on a Department of Agriculture (USDA) contract for editing services. USDA receives the following bids for this contract:

Sandy's Script Services	**$300,000**
Edit, Inc.	**$250,000**

This solicitation is subject to full and open competition, and Edit, Inc., is not eligible for any preferences. The final bids are calculated as follows:

Sandy's original bid price	**$300,000**
SDB evaluation preference (300,000 x 10%)	**(30,000)**
HUBZone preference (300,000 x 10%)	**(30,000)**
Sandy's bid price (after preferences)	**$240,000**
Edit, Inc., bid price	**$250,000**

Assuming the contract is awarded on price-related factors alone, Sandy's Script Services would win because its recalculated bid is $10,000 lower than that of Edit, Inc.

SMALL BUSINESS COMPETITIVENESS DEMONSTRATION PROGRAM

For years now, certain industry groups have complained that a disproportionately large number of contracts were being set aside for small businesses. The Small Business Competitiveness Demonstration Program Act of 1988 was established to assess whether small businesses in certain industry groups can compete successfully with larger businesses for federal contracts on an unrestricted basis.

The program consists of two major components:

1. Unrestricted competition in four designated industry groups

2. Enhanced small business participation in ten agency-targeted industry categories.

The four designated industry groups are:

- Construction (under NAICS codes, Major Groups 236, 237, and 238)

- Refuse systems and related services

- Architectural and engineering services

- Non-nuclear ship repair (NAICS code 336611).

The following federal agencies participate in the program:

- Department of Agriculture

- Department of Defense (except Defense Mapping Agency)

- Department of Energy

- Department of Health and Human Services

- Department of the Interior

- Department of Transportation

- Department of Veterans Affairs

- Environmental Protection Agency

- General Services Administration

- National Aeronautics and Space Administration.

Under the program, small business set-asides are eliminated for federal procurements with an anticipated value of more than $25,000 in the four designated industry groups. (Purchases made under section 8(a) of the Small Business Act are exempt from this program.) If any designated industry group falls below a 40% small business award goal, the set-asides are reinstituted. Participating agencies conduct quarterly reviews to provide a floor of protection for small businesses.

SBA also monitors the individual NAICS codes in the designated industry groups. If the small business participation rate for a particular code falls below 35% during a four-quarter period, SBA reinstitutes set-asides under that code.

Let's assume DOT had the following participation rates during each quarter of FY2010 for construction groups 236, 237, and 238.

Construction—Major Groups

	236	237	238
Participation Rates:			
1st Qtr	39%	20%	31%
2nd Qtr	42%	29%	39%
3rd Qtr	40%	28%	43%
4th Qtr	41%	30%	45%
Total for FY2010	41%	28%	42%

In this example, major groups 236 and 238 exceeded the participation goal of 40%. Set-asides were therefore not reinstituted. Major group 237, however, was far below the 40% goal, and set-asides were therefore reinstituted under that group.

Emerging Small Business Concerns

The Small Business Competitiveness Demonstration Program also measures the extent to which contract awards are being made to a new category of small businesses called emerging small businesses (ESBs). An ESB must be no greater than 50% of the applicable small business size standard. For example, a manufacturer of office furniture, NAICS code 337214, has a small business size standard of 500 employees. Therefore, a firm with 250 or fewer employees is eligible to be an ESB.

The four designated industry groups reserve acquisitions that have an estimated value of $25,000 or less for ESBs, assuming there is a reasonable expectation of obtaining offers from two or more responsible businesses. SBA requires that ESBs receive 15% of the dollar value of contracts awarded in each designated industry group.

Targeted Industry Categories

Finally, the Small Business Competitiveness Demonstration Program requires federal agencies, in consultation with SBA, to designate 10 targeted industry categories for enhanced small business participation. Targeted industry categories represent products and services that are purchased by a federal agency that has a small business participation rate below the government-wide goal. Small business participation is expanded through the continued use of set-aside procedures, increased management attention, and specifically tailored acquisition procedures.

For example, NASA selected the following targeted industry categories during FY2008:

NAICS Code	Industry Category
334111	Electronic Computer Manufacturing
334418	Printed Circuit Assembly Manufacturing
334613	Magnetic and Optical Recording Media Manufacturing
334119	Other Computer Peripheral Equipment Manufacturing

334220   Radio and Television Broadcasting and Wireless
          Communication Equipment Manufacturing

336415   Guided Missile and Space Vehicle Propulsion Unit and
          Propulsion Unit Parts Manufacturing

336419   Other Guided Missile and Space Vehicle Parts and Auxiliary
          Equipment Manufacturing

334511   Search, Detection, Navigation, Guidance, Aeronautical, and
          Nautical Systems Manufacturing

333314   Optical Instrument and Lens Manufacturing

541511   Custom Computer Programming Services

541512   Computer Systems Design Services

514210   Data Processing Services

541519   Other Computer-Related Services

Each participating agency's targeted industry categories are listed in its FAR supplement.

SMALL BUSINESS INNOVATIVE RESEARCH PROGRAM (SBIR)

The SBIR program is an extremely active and valuable program for the development of new ideas and innovative approaches. Federal agencies, especially the Department of Defense, award SBIR contracts for various R&D projects.

Since the enactment of SBIR in 1982, as part of the Small Business Innovation Development Act, it has helped thousands of small businesses to compete for federal contracts. The Internet was developed with funding from a government program similar to SBIR.

An individual or firm can become involved with federal research and development (R&D) projects in two ways:

■ By responding to Small Business Innovation Research (SBIR) solicitations

■ By initiating an unsolicited proposal (see Chapter 13).

Note: The government also has a R&D program called the Small Business Technology Transfer Research (STTR) program, which works almost exactly like the SBIR program. For our purposes, these programs are treated as if they were the same.

Qualified small businesses are encouraged to propose innovative ideas through this program to meet the government's R&D needs. SBIR is designed to:

■ Encourage small business participation in government research programs

■ Foster and encourage participation by minority and disadvantaged persons in technological innovations

■ Stimulate technological innovations

■ Provide incentives for converting research results into commercial applications.

During FY2007, the government spent more than $2 billion on R&D projects under this program. This program is a major channel for obtaining research funding!

Participating Agencies

Federal agencies that fund more than $100 million in external R&D projects must participate in the SBIR program. These agencies currently include:

■ Department of Agriculture

■ Department of Commerce

■ Department of Defense

■ Department of Education

■ Department of Energy

■ Department of Health and Human Services

■ Department of Transportation

■ Environmental Protection Agency

■ National Aeronautics and Space Administration

■ National Science Foundation

Every year the participating agencies assemble solicitations that briefly describe the topics they are interested in. Most agencies allow potential contractors to propose subjects not included in their announcements as well. Proposals submitted in direct response to an SBIR solicitation are competitively evaluated on their scientific and technical merit.

SBIR Qualifications

A small business must meet certain eligibility criteria to participate in the SBIR program:

■ The business must be American-owned and independently operated.

■ The business must be a for-profit business.

■ The principal researcher must be employed by the business.

■ The company size is limited to 500 employees.

■ The principal place of business must be located in the United States.

For most contractors, eligibility isn't a problem. Your primary challenge will be to communicate your idea and why it should be funded in 25 pages or less.

Obviously, a well-written proposal is critical for success in this program. Because only a small fraction of R&D funding actually results in a commercial product, the evaluators look for convincing arguments that describe the innovation, its use to the federal agency, and the contractor's qualifications. Only after the prospective contractor establishes its technical competence and the value of its idea do the evaluators consider the cost proposal.

R&D Brochure

If your firm is interested in obtaining R&D contracts, you should consider preparing a brochure describing your organization and its capabilities. Obtaining R&D contracts requires marketing to the technical personnel of the appropriate contracting (or purchasing) activity. Experienced firms report that a well-thought-out brochure quickly establishes their basic qualifications and fields of endeavor.

At a minimum, an R&D brochure should identify work you have done or are doing, the type of work for which you are qualified, and the names and qualifications of technical personnel on your staff. When you contact a contracting activity, you should present your brochure to both the contracting and technical personnel.

The Three-Phase Program

SBIR uses a highly competitive, three-phase award system.

Phase I is the start-up phase. Phase I awards are typically in the neighborhood of $100,000 for approximately six months. This phase is intended to determine the scientific or technical merit and feasibility of the ideas submitted.

Phase II is the performance phase. During this time, the R&D work is performed and the developer evaluates commercialization potential. Only Phase I award winners are considered for Phase II. Roughly 50% of the Phase I award winners go on to Phase II. Awards of up to $750,000, for as long as two years, allow contractors to expand their Phase I results. Phase II R&D projects result in a well-defined deliverable product or process. Phase I and II contracts may include a profit/fee.

Phase III is the period during which Phase II innovation moves from the laboratory into the marketplace. No SBIR funds support this phase. The small business must find funding in the private sector, or federal agencies may award non-SBIR-funded follow-on contracts for products or processes that meet the mission needs of those agencies.

Work for all phases of this program must be performed in the United States.

More than 35,000 SBIR awards have been made to date, and the Government Accountability Office (GAO) estimates that more than one-quarter of the awards have produced commercial products.

SBA's Role

SBA plays an important role as the coordinating agency for the SBIR program. It directs each participating agency's implementation of the SBIR program, reviews agency progress, and reports annually to Congress on the program's operation. Use it as your point of contact and information source.

SBA also collects solicitation information from participating agencies and publishes it in a presolicitation announcement. Presolicitation announcements provide contractors with the topics and anticipated release dates of potential acquisitions. These announcements are published periodically throughout the year and include the requesting agency's address and phone number. Presolicitation announcements are available only on the Internet at:

www.sba.gov/sbir

SBA also publishes the *SBIR Proposal Preparation Handbook,* available on the above website.

For more information on the SBIR program, contact:

U.S. Small Business Administration Office of Technology
409 Third Street, SW
Washington, DC 20416
Phone (202) 205-6450

■   ■   ■

Preference programs give small businesses a chance to compete with large firms for government contracts. The qualifications and restrictions of some of these programs require a little work to understand, but the effort certainly pays off in government assistance and procurement preferences.

■   ■   ■

6 Subcontracting Opportunities

© Randy Glasbergen, 1996

GLASBERGEN

"It is important to learn from your mistakes, Bob...but let's try not to learn quite so much."

What's in this chapter?

- Selecting a subcontractor
- Awarding the subcontract
- DOD Mentor-Protégé Program

When a company enters into a contract to perform work for a customer (or the government) and another firm provides a portion of the goods or services necessary to fulfill the contract, the company is said to be "subcontracting" part of its contractual requirements. For many small businesses, subcontracting to a prime contractor is the most effective way to share in the federal marketplace.

A company's contract with the government is usually referred to as the prime contract, and the company's contracts with its suppliers are referred to as subcontracts. The subcontractor does not have a direct contractual relationship with the government. Some examples of major prime contractors are Lockheed Martin, Northrop Grumman, Cisco, General Dynamics, and Westinghouse.

The Small Business Administration (SBA) develops and promotes subcontracting opportunities for small businesses by referring small contractors to prime contractors. The market for subcontract work is nearly as large as the basic government market for contracting. During FY2006, DOD prime contractors awarded more than $85 billion in subcontracts—$32 billion (or over 37%) of which went to small businesses.

Another good reason to look for subcontracting opportunities is to take advantage of contracts that are available only through prime contractors. Most construction projects, for example, are awarded as "turnkey" contracts. A turnkey contract is a contract that places the responsibility for completion completely on the winning contractor or prime contractor.

Suppose Weitz Construction was awarded a contract to build an office building. Weitz (the prime contractor) is unable to perform the air-conditioning portion of the building project. If an air-conditioning firm wanted to be part of this building project, it would need to get a subcontract for the work with Weitz.

Besides the obvious reason that few companies are able to offer a full spectrum of supplies and services, why would a prime contractor want to subcontract? SBA requires large businesses receiving contracts valued at over $550,000 ($1 million for construction) to develop plans and goals for awarding subcontracts to qualified small business concerns, thus forcing federal contracting dollars to flow down.

The subcontracting plan must include a statement of total dollars planned to be subcontracted, as well as percentage goals for awarding subcontracts to small, small disadvantaged, and women-owned small businesses. Descriptions of the needed supplies and services, along with the methods used to identify potential sources, are also included in the plan.

If a prime contractor fails to submit a small business subcontracting plan or fails to negotiate an acceptable plan with SBA, it becomes ineligible for the contract. The government can also assess "liquidated damages" to a prime contractor that fails to make a good faith effort to meet its subcontracting goals.

A contracting officer may also encourage increased subcontracting opportunities in negotiated acquisitions by providing monetary incentives to prime contractors, such as award fees. The amount of the incentive is negotiated and depends on the prime contractor's achieving its small business goals and the technical assistance and outreach programs it intends to provide.

When significant subcontracting opportunities exist, a contracting officer may publish in FedBizOpps the names and addresses of prospective prime contractors (see Chapter 8). In addition, the contracting officer synopsizes in FedBizOpps contract awards exceeding $25,000 that are likely to result in the award of subcontracts. Prime contractors and subcontractors are also encouraged to publicize subcontracting opportunities in FedBizOpps.

SELECTING A SUBCONTRACTOR

Subcontracting is also an excellent way to "learn the ropes" in dealing with the federal government. Prime contractors consider a number of factors when selecting a subcontractor, including the:

■ Degree to which the company's products or services fit the requirements of the contract

■ Degree to which a mutually agreeable deal can be struck between the parties

■ Size and socioeconomic status of the firm

■ Company's asking price for its goods or services

■ Technical superiority of the company's goods or services.

Perhaps the most important consideration in a subcontracting relationship is that the terms and conditions in the prime contractor's agreement with the government generally flow down to the subcontractor. In other words, the subcontractor is equally bound to comply with the applicable acquisition rules and regulations. The solicitation enumerates the terms and conditions, and the potential subcontractor should understand their significance before entering into any agreement.

Note: There is no "privity of contract" between the government and any subcontractor. That is, to say, the government's contractual relationship is with the prime contractor only. The subcontractor has no right to seek redress from the government but must do it with the prime contractor, even if it means filing a civil lawsuit to settle a disagreement.

AWARDING THE SUBCONTRACT

Companies may negotiate and sign a subcontract agreement at any point during the solicitation process. Generally, it is advantageous to the prime contractor if the agreement is signed prior to award because it locks in the subcontractor's terms and pricing. It also allows the prime contractor to calculate the total amount of risk it is taking on. Conversely, the subcontractor must devote resources to negotiating a subcontract that might, in fact, never be executed.

Subcontracting is a great way for small businesses to build up their resumes and make new industry contacts. But in many cases the subcontracting arrangement leads to misunderstandings and disputes between the parties. Having a rock-solid subcontracting agreement in place is the best way to protect against disagreements.

Once you receive the subcontracting agreement, be sure to look it over and go back to the prime contractor with any areas of concern. It is better to err on the side of caution beforehand than to sort out contracting disputes once the work has begun.

Most federal agencies publish a list of businesses that received contracts over $550,000 ($1 million for construction) and are subject to subcontracting goals. For example, DOD maintains a subcontracting directory at:

www.acq.osd.mil/osbp/doing_business

The directory lists DOD prime contractors alphabetically, including their addresses, phone numbers, and contacts, and the products or services purchased.

SUB-*Net*

Although there is no single point of entry for subcontracting opportunities in the federal marketplace, SBA's SUB-*Net* encourages prime contractors, federal agencies, state and local governments, and educational entities to post solicitations and notices there.

http://web.sba.gov/subnet

DOD MENTOR-PROTÉGÉ PROGRAM

The Mentor-Protégé Program provides incentives to major contractors to assist small disadvantaged businesses (SDBs) and qualified organizations that employ disabled persons in enhancing their capabilities for performing DOD contracts. The mentor assists the protégé by sharing its management expertise and technical skills to enhance the protégé's competitiveness.

Through such assistance, the program attempts to increase the participation of SDBs in DOD contracting. Many federal agencies (e.g., DOE, EPA, NASA) have their own mentor-protégé programs. Any prime contractor with an active subcontracting plan negotiated with DOD may participate as a mentor.

Contracting officers encourage mentors (prime contractors) to take a small business under their wing by providing such incentives as cost reimbursement, credit toward SDB subcontracting goals, or a combination of both. Mentors are also encouraged to strengthen and expand their own capabilities throughout their program participation.

Protégé Qualifications

To qualify as a protégé, a firm must be a small disadvantaged business, as defined by section 8(d)(3)(C) of the Small Business Act. Any firm (excluding 8(a)-certified firms) that seeks eligibility as a small disadvantaged business for participation as a protégé must be certified by SBA. Self-certifications are insufficient.

To qualify, contact your local SBA District Office for an application package.

www.sba.gov

Submit the completed application to SBA's Assistant Administrator for Small Disadvantaged Business Certification and Eligibility.

Finding a Mentor

You can identify a mentor in *Subcontracting Opportunities with Department of Defense (DOD) Major Prime Contractors*. This publication lists most major DOD prime contractors that have negotiated subcontracting plans, including the names and phone numbers of their small business liaison officers and the firms' primary products or service lines. You can download this publication at the following website:

www.acq.osd.mil/osbp/doing_business

As a prospective protégé, you need to select a firm with the technical capabilities you seek and a similar business focus. Look for one that might afford you the best future partner for teaming relationships. Keep in mind that a mentor might want to establish a subcontracting relationship before negotiating a mentor-protégé agreement. Be prepared to market your firm's capabilities and address what you will bring to the table.

To participate in the program, the mentor and the protégé must formalize their relationship through a letter of intent and a mentor-protégé agreement. These documents set forth the duration of the mentor-protégé relationship and detail the developmental assistance to be provided. Although DOD must approve these documents, it will have a limited oversight role during the program.

Mentor Responsibilities

The mentor can provide a broad array of assistance to the protégé, but the protégé must perform its own contracts and subcontracts. DOD will not, however, give credit for or reimburse the mentor for any costs related to direct work the mentor performs on the protégé's contracts. The program aims to produce viable SDBs capable of performing contracts that require high-technology skills.

Visit the following website for more information about this program:

www.acq.osd.mil/osbp/mentor_protege

■   ■   ■

Both large and small companies can benefit from establishing subcontracting agreements. Mid- to large-sized companies can strengthen and expand their own capabilities while meeting their goals for providing opportunities for small, small disadvantaged, and women-owned small business concerns. As a result, federal contracting dollars flow down to small business concerns.

■   ■   ■

7 Federal Supply Schedules/GSA Schedules

What's in this chapter?

- Federal Acquisition Service
- Multiple Award Schedule
- Schedules e-Library
- GSA Advantage
- *MarkeTips* magazine
- Problems with federal supply schedules

If you're in the business of selling commercial products and services, the Federal Supply Schedule program might be a good option for you. Federal supply schedules are the government's fastest-growing procurement method, especially for services. Historically, this program accounts for over 10% of all federal purchases, which adds up to over $40 billion each year. Only commercial items are solicited.

Federal supply schedules are designed to provide contracting activities (or buying offices) with a simplified process for acquiring commercial items at discounted prices. Both buyers and sellers benefit from the program with its shorter lead times, lower administrative costs, and reduced inventories. The buying power of the government also allows for volume discounts on its purchases.

Although a GSA schedule is an official federal contract, it is not automatically funded. Only when orders are placed by a federal agency does the funding occur. In the simplest terms, schedule contracts make your company's products and services available to federal buyers at pre-approved prices. The disadvantages of federal supply schedules are discussed later in this chapter.

FEDERAL ACQUISITION SERVICE

The Federal Acquisition Service (FAS), a division of the General Services Administration (GSA), manages and operates the Federal Supply Schedule program. Its primary responsibility is to negotiate indefinite-delivery/ indefinite-quantity, no-guarantee-of-sale contracts with commercial firms to provide products and services at stated prices for specific periods (usually three years).

FAS currently negotiates schedule contracts for 62 categories of products and services, ranging from furniture and office supplies, to information technology, to financial services, to travel and transportation services. It awards contracts under negotiated procurement procedures (see Chapter 12). To be eligible for the Federal Supply Schedule program, a contractor must have its schedule contract approved by FAS.

Once approved by FAS, the schedule contract is assigned a classification code and published in a catalog or listing called a federal supply schedule (or GSA schedule). Each schedule covers a particular product or group of products, or a particular type of service. For example, schedule group 76, Publication Media, includes publications, encyclopedias, instructional/ technical books and pamphlets, medical guides, almanacs, and geography maps and atlases.

Each federal supply schedule contains ordering information, including covered products and services, the eligible contractors and their contact information, terms and conditions, prices, maximum and minimum order sizes, and ordering instructions. Federal buying offices place their orders directly with the vendor or contractor. In many cases, federal agencies are required to use federal supply schedules as their primary source of supply.

It is crucial for a contractor to get on a schedule contract that accurately reflects its products or services. Competitive pricing is also vital to your success.

GSA Schedule Sales

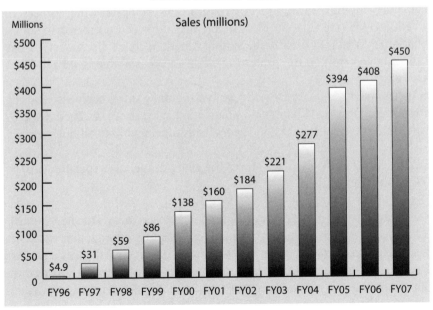

Program Benefits

Federal supply schedules offer the following benefits:

- They expose a contractor's products and services to a vast number of contracting activities or buying offices throughout the government for at least one year and, in some cases, up to five years.

- Schedule holders are preapproved to contract with federal agencies, so your company joins a list of "preferred vendors."

- They enable the government to use its buying power to obtain volume discounts on purchases.

- State and local governments can purchase from Schedule 70—Information Technology. In addition, certain prime contractors are eligible to purchase from federal supply schedules (see Part 51 of the FAR).

- Eighty percent of the contracts under the GSA Schedules Program are small businesses.

- Agency buying offices are not required to synopsize their orders in FedBizOpps (see Chapter 8). Also, buying offices do not perform solicitation procedures on federal supply schedule items because FAS has already determined the prices to be fair and reasonable (see Part 4).

- Agency buying offices are not required to follow small business set-aside requirements (see Chapter 4) when purchasing from a schedule. This permits large contractors, in theory, to compete with small businesses.

- When a schedule is mandatory, the federal agencies specified in the schedule must use it.

FAS may also authorize other federal agencies to award and publish schedule contracts. The Department of Veterans Affairs, for example, awards schedule contracts for certain medical items. DOD uses a similar system for military items that are not part of the FAS program. Approximately 25 states have their own versions of federal supply schedules as well.

MULTIPLE AWARD SCHEDULE

The most common federal supply schedule type is the multiple award schedule (MAS). It is a list of contracts the government establishes with more than one vendor/contractor for the same types of products and services. Each year, federal agencies spend billions of dollars through MASs, buying everything from desks and paperclips to computers and software.

MAS contracts are awarded on a "variable" basis, meaning that contractors can respond to MAS solicitations at any time. There are no government specifications for the items listed in an MAS schedule. Any responsible contractor may submit offers in response to a solicitation for MAS contracts.

Each contractor on the MAS submits a different price list for its products and services and may offer specific options and features. An agency buying office selects the contractor that best meets its particular needs. For the most part, contractors do not participate in head-to-head competition, although agencies may hold competitions among schedule holders.

MAS contract holders must provide the government with prices that are at least as good as the prices they offer commercial clients. This negotiation objective is commonly known as "most favored customer" pricing. Moreover, contractors can offer additional discounts to make their schedule more competitive. Your MAS prices represent a "ceiling" price. Once a schedule price is approved, it can be changed only by GSA approval.

Contracting officers must follow negotiated procurement procedures when issuing MAS contracts. After the MAS contract is issued, the contractor prepares and distributes a catalog and/or price list to the various ordering offices. Agency buying offices then use the catalogs, along with an MAS, to purchase needed products and services. Contractors must accept payment using the government-wide purchase card (see Chapter 10).

Buying offices may not purchase commercial products and services that are available under an MAS. As a result, if a company has a schedule contract, it is likely to have a competitive advantage over contractors that do not participate in the MAS program.

SCHEDULES E-LIBRARY

The Schedules e-Library is GSA's official online source for federal supply schedule information. The site contains basic ordering guidelines, complete schedule listings, and details on schedule program changes. A search engine allows you to search by keyword, schedule number, item number, contractor name, and contract number. It is updated daily to ensure access to the latest award information. For more information on Schedules e-Library, visit:

www.gsaelibrary.gsa.gov

FEDERAL SUPPLY CLASSIFICATION CODES

As a government contractor, it is useful to know the Federal Supply Classification (FSC) codes assigned to each of your products. Buying offices use FSC codes to identify products and services. FSC codes currently consist of 78 groups, which are subdivided into 646 classes.

Although contractors are not required to use FSC codes when registering with the government, they are encouraged to include the codes that apply to their products and services. FSC codes help buying offices identify a contractor's capabilities more accurately.

The FSC code uses a four-digit structure. The first two digits identify the group, such as:

Group	Title
70	Data Processing Equipment
71	Furniture
75	Office Supplies and Devices
81	Containers, Packaging, and Packing Supplies

The last two digits of the code identify the classes within each group. For example, group 71, Furniture, currently has the following classes:

FSC	Title
7125	Cabinets, Lockers, Bins, and Shelving
7105	Household Furniture
7195	Miscellaneous Furniture and Fixtures
7110	Office Furniture

For more information on FSC codes, visit:

www.dlis.dla.mil/h2

Getting Started

Here's a general outline to help you get your products and services listed on a GSA schedule.

1. Review *Getting on a GSA Schedule* at:

www.gsa.gov/gettingonschedule

2. Identify the federal supply schedule that covers your products or services. There are currently more than 40 different federal supply schedules. For example:

FAS Schedule	Schedule I.D.
Financial and Business Solutions (FABS)	520
Office Furniture	711
Leasing of Autos and Light Trucks	751
Professional Engineering Services (PES)	871
Environmental Services	899

Hardware and software schedules generally require the contractor to offer support, such as maintenance or repair service. Visit the following website for a complete listing of federal supply schedules:

www.gsaelibrary.gsa.gov

Note: Each GSA schedule has a point of contact that can provide specific information about individual GSA schedule items.

3. Obtain a copy of a federal supply schedule solicitation for your particular products or services by searching:

www.fedbizopps.gov

4. Obtain a Dun & Bradstreet (D&B) reference check. For more information on reference checks, call Dun & Bradstreet at (800) 234-3867, or apply at:

www.dnb.com

5. Complete all information in the solicitation. Each solicitation has different requirements, so be sure to read it carefully.

6. Be prepared to offer a competitive price.

The GSA Vendor Support Center maintains a library of federal supply schedules and authorized contractor catalog price lists. It is also a receiving point for customer and vendor questions regarding FAS products and services. For more information on the GSA Vendor Support Center, visit:

http://vsc.gsa.gov
or call (877) 495-4849

Now What?

You've just been awarded your first schedule contract. Congratulations! So now you're ready for all those orders to pour in. Unfortunately, having a schedule contract does not guarantee that you will receive government orders. It indicates only that you are an eligible contractor and that your products and services are reasonably priced. Therefore, while the ink is drying on your contract, you should immediately turn your attention to marketing your new award.

The first step in marketing your schedule contract is to develop your contract price list. A contract price list is a "catalog" that lists the items you have been awarded and identifies the terms and conditions of the contract. Your price list is your initial "face" to the customer. When designing your price list, be sure to make it user-friendly. A one-page flyer covering only the required items specified in your contract usually is best.

Once your price list is completed, you'll need to distribute it to potential customers. For many schedules, GSA provides a mailing list of customers who have expressed an interest in the products and services on a particular GSA schedule. Be sure to ask your Procuring Contracting Officer (PCO) if your schedule has a customer mailing list.

Although the government is moving toward a paperless environment, it's not there yet. Contractors should still take the time to mail a hard copy of their price list to prospective customers. Also, in your mailing be sure to include your company brochure and other literature about your products or services.

Sample Price List		
GSA Schedule Price List Contract # GS-35F-0213M		
Products:		
Part #	**Product Description**	**GSA Price**
DS01	GEMS	$80,607.00
PS01	mCAT!	$6,525.36
CA01	LaserCat 2003	$4,310.00
Software Maintenance:		
Part #	**SW Maintenance Description**	**GSA Price**
DS01-2	GEMS Year 2	$9,521.24
DS01-3	GEMS Year 3	$17,258.47

Labor Rates:

Cat #	Labor Category	Year-1	Year-2	Year-3	Year-4	Year-5
L001	Program Manager	$116.03	$120.56	$126.33	$133.08	$138.63
L002	Senior Network Engineer	$85.68	$93.04	$95.57	$100.35	$106.37
L003	Software Engineer	$59.38	$62.27	$65.43	$68.65	$73.09
L004	Database Administrator	$54.38	$57.48	$62.45	$63.37	$66.54
L005	Financial Analyst	$54.38	$57.48	$62.45	$63.37	$66.54
L006	Network Engineer	$54.74	$587.48	$62.45	$63.37	$66.54
L007	Technical Writer	$51.06	$53.78	$55.21	$57.97	$61.35
L008	Administrative Support	$23.43	$25.55	$26.82	$28.13	$29.61

Buy Now Using GSA Advantage!
For more information, contact: 800-555-3000 ext. 101
or email: GSA@baystate.com

GSA ADVANTAGE

Your price list also needs to be posted to GSA Advantage, an online shopping service or ordering system for government buyers. GSA Advantage provides access to several thousand contractors and millions of products and services. During FY2007 GSA Advantage did more than $120 million in sales.

Government buyers use GSA Advantage to:

■ Search for items using keywords, part numbers, national stock numbers, supplier names, contract numbers, etc.

■ Compare features, prices, and delivery options

■ Configure products and add accessories

■ Place orders directly online

■ Review and choose delivery options

■ Select a convenient payment method

■ View order history.

Contractors use GSA Advantage to:

■ Research the competition

■ Check out the market

■ Sell to the federal marketplace.

To post a company catalog/profile/price list to GSA Advantage, go to:

http://vsc.gsa.gov

Click on the Schedule Input Program (SIP) Web Training user link to begin.

The SIP also allows contractors to post product photos to GSA Advantage. It is the contractor's responsibility to keep its GSA Advantage catalog/ profile information current, accurate, and complete.

GSA Advantage gives contractors an opportunity to put a controlled marketing spin on their products and services by linking their company website to their catalog/profile. Be sure to make your website "GSA-friendly." Put GSA's logo and your contract number on an easy-to-spot location on your website. Also, set up a separate e-mail account for GSA schedule inquiries only.

For more information on GSA Advantage, visit:

www.gsaadvantage.gov

MARKETIPS MAGAZINE

Another way to market your products and services to potential customers is to supply advertisements to *MarkeTips*, a bimonthly publication for GSA customers. Advertising space in *MarkeTips* is free and is offered on a first-come, first-served basis. Because of limited ad space, vendors are restricted to two ads per year, per GSA contract. *MarkeTips* is sent to over 110,000 federal and military subscribers worldwide and is available at:

http://apps.fas.gsa.gov/pub/marketips.cfm

Getting a GSA schedule is just the tip of the iceberg when it comes to generating sales through your schedule contract. You must still aggressively market to agency buying offices that could potentially purchase your products and services. Call them. Send brochures. Be sure to use GSA logos on all of your marketing materials. Remember, most federal supply schedules will have many suppliers, so you must find a way to get your products or services noticed!

PROBLEMS WITH FEDERAL SUPPLY SCHEDULES

You would think federal supply schedules would be a gold mine for small- and medium-sized companies—and in many ways they are. However, selling or wholesaling common-use commercial products and services to the federal government is extremely competitive. Markups of 8% to 12% are the norm for many products. In the face of this competition, small businesses are at a disadvantage because they are unable to maintain a large enough sales volume to be profitable.

Suppose that your small business is a regular dealer of Dell equipment and your agreement allows you to purchase computers for $1,000 each (which would be considered the unit price of the computer). After reading this book, you decide to apply to FAS to get your computer products on a federal supply schedule. You review the GSA Schedules e-Library on the Internet and determine that federal supply schedule 70, Information Technology Equipment, is appropriate for your computers.

Next, you obtain your Dun & Bradstreet (D&B) reference check and use FedBizOpps to obtain the solicitation for federal supply schedule 70. Finally, you complete the solicitation.

Let's assume the Department of Commerce plans to purchase 200 Dell computers and has selected your federal supply schedule. The contracting officer making this purchase does not need to be concerned about the price of the computers because FAS has already determined your schedule prices to be fair and reasonable. Assuming you have a 10% markup, your total sales price for this order will be:

> 200 Dell computers x $ 1,000 = $ 200,000
> Markup   x 10%
> **Total sales price**   **$ 220,000**

You will earn a total gross profit (or margin) of $20,000 on this transaction. The next step is to apply your indirect costs against this sales transaction.

Indirect costs are expenses incurred by a contractor that cannot be attributed to any one particular contract. Lighting in a manufacturing area that houses the work of several contracts would be an example of an indirect cost.

Indirect costs are classified further as either overhead (O/H) expenses or general and administrative (G&A) expenses.

O/H expenses are general costs like indirect labor, rent, supplies, insurance, and depreciation.

G&A expenses are any management, financial, or other expenses incurred for the general management and administration of the company as a whole.

The following breakdown shows the indirect costs and profit of this sales transaction.

Total gross profit (or margin)	**$ 20,000**
LESS:	
O/H expenses:	
Salaries	$ 3,500
Supplies	$ 750
Equipment rental	$ 500
Depreciation	$ 2,250
G&A expenses:	
Executive salaries	$ 4,000
Personnel costs	$ 1,500
Professional services	$ 1,750
Training costs	$ 1,250
Total (net) profit	**$ 4,500**

When you consider these indirect costs, you barely break even on this transaction. That's the main problem with serving as a small business regular dealer or wholesaler to the government. How can a small business survive with such a low markup on its sales? In addition, what happens to the small business if the government doesn't consistently buy its products or services?

The key to being a successful regular government dealer or wholesaler is to have a large sales volume. Because many indirect costs remain consistent, regardless of sales volume, a large sales volume allows a contractor to cover more indirect expenses, increasing total profit. These indirect costs are referred to as fixed costs.

Suppose Joe's Janitorial Services provides your office cleaning services for $1,000 per month. This expense would be considered a fixed cost because it remains the same regardless of sales volume. If you increase product sales, you earn a greater total profit because your fixed costs remain at $1,000, even though you take in more sales. Large businesses enjoy a tremendous advantage because they can maintain lower markups with larger sales volumes.

Another problem for small business regular dealers is that there is not much incentive for a large business or manufacturer to use a regular dealer to sell products to the government. Why would a large manufacturer need to use the services of a regular dealer if the government ordering activities can contact the manufacturer directly? Think about it: If your company were a large manufacturer like Dell, wouldn't you want to sell your products directly to the government so you could charge a more competitive price?

■ ■ ■

GSA schedules are like fishing licenses to go after government contracts. They give commercial contractors an excellent opportunity to increase market share while taking on only some of the red tape that usually accompanies government purchases. Schedule holders must have adequate cash flow, an effective delivery system, and an aggressive marketing plan to be successful.

The Federal Supply Schedule program is designed to closely mirror commercial buying practices. All government buying offices—large or small, and even those in remote locations—receive the same services, convenience, and pricing.

■ ■ ■

How to Find Government Contracting Opportunities (Marketing)

"Opportunity does not knock; it presents itself when you beat down the door."

—*Kyle Chandler*

How to Market to the Federal Government

8

© 1999 Randy Glasbergen.

GLASBERGEN

"The number one rule in sales is:
'Find Out What The Customer Wants'.
The customer wanted me to go away."

What's in this chapter?

- Finding markets for your supplies and services
- Using the Internet
- FedBizOpps
- Federal Supply Schedules/GSA Schedules
- Federal Register
- Federal agency acquisition forecasts
- Bidders' lists
- TECH-*Net*
- Federal Procurement Data System
- Year-end procurements

You would think that marketing to the federal government would be an easy subject to write about. The government has more than 310,000 contractors, which receive more than $400 billion worth of contracts each year. But as I began asking successful contractors and government officials about marketing to the government, I was amazed at how little they actually knew about the subject. Don't get me wrong—they all had some good ideas, but in the end they all seemed to conclude that *who you know* is the deciding factor in getting government contracts.

Now that's great, and I'm sure that to be successful in any business, who you know is very important. But my question is: Who is it that I should get to know, and how do I get to know them? And that question has gotten me a lot of blank stares and answers like "You've just got to find a way." So that's what Part 3 of this book is all about: learning how to market to the federal government.

Marketing to the government differs from marketing to other types of industries because the government makes purchases with funds that are financed by the public (that is, tax dollars). This means that the government has a higher degree of accountability for the ways in which those funds are spent. Federal buying offices, for example, must allow full and open competition for their purchases. This mandate helps ensure that contractors can compete for federal contracts without having to belong to an exclusive country club.

The bottom line is there really is no one way to market your supplies or services to the government because each federal agency makes acquisitions in a different way. But understanding the government's procurement methods (or sources) and the support services it offers to contractors can surely help.

This chapter touches on a number of marketing methods. Hopefully, you will be able to incorporate some of them into your business marketing plans.

FINDING MARKETS FOR YOUR SUPPLIES AND SERVICES

One important thing to remember about government contracting is that you do not have to be located near a federal agency to compete for contracts. The government currently has more than 2,500 buying offices (or contracting activities) throughout the United States. SBA has grouped them into 10 regions.

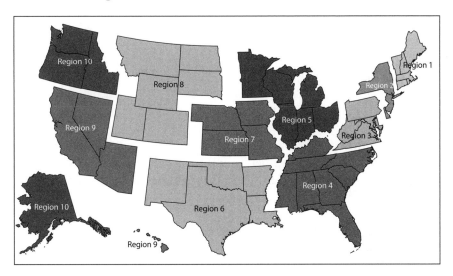

To market successfully in the large and diverse federal marketplace, a contractor must focus on a specific area that offers the greatest opportunity for success based on available resources. The following questions might help you decide which markets to concentrate on:

■ *Where is your business located?* Is it in a densely populated area like New York City or a rural area like Greenville, North Carolina? In a densely populated area, you can concentrate on using a business center that is close to your location because heavily populated areas tend to have larger government markets. On the other hand, in a rural area, you will probably use a business center that is farther away because these areas have fewer buying offices.

■ *What is your business type?* If you are in a business that requires you to work at the job site, you should consider a smaller geographical area. For example, if you operate a construction company, most of your work will take place at the job site. It is therefore beneficial to work close to your home office.

■ *How much experience do you have?* If yours is a relatively new business and you are still learning the ropes, you should probably look for opportunities near home. If you have been in business for many years and have a good share of the local market, you might consider expanding your market base.

At the outset, you should have a pretty good feel for how far your company can venture and still successfully perform the contract's requirements. Reaching out too far to perform government contracts could be a mistake that endangers your company's future business opportunities. Carefully identify the government market that you want to go after and stick to that plan. Once you determine your target markets, your next step is to locate opportunities within those markets. The following website lists SBA offices by state:

www.sba.gov/localresources/index.html

USING THE INTERNET

If the first two editions of my book haven't convinced you, I'll say it one more time: The Internet provides unlimited marketing potential, so please take advantage of this amazing resource. Each federal agency has its own website, and one of the best ways to familiarize yourself with a particular agency is to browse its site. You'll quickly notice that most federal government websites end in .gov, an abbreviation for "government."

Agencies typically use their acronym names as their web addresses. To find the Department of Energy's website, you would type:

www.doe.gov

If you wanted the Department of Health and Human Services, you would type:

www.hhs.gov

If an agency's web address doesn't agree with its acronym name, you can try to locate it using another agency's site (each agency's website allows you to transfer—or link—to other agencies' sites). You can use DOE's website to link to the Department of Commerce's website and vice versa.

FEDBIZOPPS

FedBizOpps is the single government point of entry on the Internet for federal procurement opportunities over $25,000. It was designed to broaden the federal marketplace and minimize the effort and cost associated with finding government business opportunities. FedBizOpps helps level the playing field for small businesses.

> Note: In the "olden days" solicitations were printed in a newspaper called the *Commerce Business Daily* (CBD). On January 4, 2002, FedBizOpps replaced the CBD as the official source for procurement opportunities and information.

Government buyers publicize their business opportunities by posting information directly to FedBizOpps through the Internet. Contractors looking to do business with the government are able to search, monitor, and retrieve opportunities solicited by the entire federal contracting community.

FedBizOpps lists synopses and notices of proposed contract actions, contract solicitations, amendments/modifications, subcontracting leads, contract awards, and other business opportunities. Although the General Services Administration (GSA) is responsible for the operation and maintenance of the website, the content of a notice is the sole responsibility of the buying office that issues/posts the notice.

Approximately 500–1,000 new notices are posted each business day. FedBizOpps currently supports more than 22,000 federal buyers in 96 federal agencies and hosts more than 380,000 solicitation documents. Over 95% of all federal opportunities are listed on FedBizOpps.

Getting Started

Let's assume you want to identify opportunities for Facilities Support Services (NAICS code 561210).

1. Go to www.fedbizopps.gov

   Note: If you're new to FedBizOpps, be sure to read the "User Guide" located at the far right of this screen. Click the "Vendor" link.

2. Locate the "Finding Opportunities" section of the web page (near the center) and click the double-arrows icon. This will take you to the FBO Synopsis/Awards Search page. FBO search options include:

   ■ Full Text/Keyword Search

   ■ Documents to Search (Active or Archived)

   ■ Opportunity/Procurement Type

   ■ Dates to Search (e.g., Last 3 Days, One Week)

   ■ Place of Performance (Zip Code)

   ■ Set-Aside Code

   ■ Classification Code

   ■ NAICS Code (select from dropdown menu)

   ■ Search by Agency (select from list).

   Note: The full text/keyword search can be used in a number of ways, including searches for NAICS codes, keywords, and opportunities in your state.

In this case, we are going to search by NAICS code 561210, using the full text search and a search by agency, Department of Agriculture (USDA). Once you have filled in the appropriate criteria, click the "search" button.

3. Search results:

Search Results Business Opportunities **Synopsis and Solicitation Grouped by Organization and Posted Date**
Active Postings: 27/89099
July 21, 2010 **Agency:** Department of Agriculture **Office:** Forest Service **Location:** R-5 Northern Province Acquisitions, Yreka Office ➡ **Posted:** July 21, 2010 **Type: <u>Synopsis</u>**
Title: Z — USDA Forest Service, Region 5, Pacific Southwest, Grounds and Facilities Maintenance Services
SOL: Reference-Number-R5NP072103-GFM-TB
August 12, 2010 **Agency:** Department of Agriculture **Office:** Forest Service **Location:** R-5 Northern Province Acquisitions, Yreka Office ➡ **Posted:** August 12, 2010 **Type: <u>Solicitation</u>**
Title: Z — USDA Forest Service, Region 5, Pacific Southwest, Grounds and Facilities Maintenance Services
SOL: Reference-Number-R5NP072103-GFM-TB

In this case, a "synopsis" and "solicitation" have been posted. A good idea might be to review the synopsis first, since it gives a basic description of the opportunity, along with point-of-contact information. To view the synopsis listing, click on the highlighted link (i.e., Synopsis).

**Z—USDA Forest Service, Region 5, Pacific Southwest, Grounds
and Facilities Maintenance Services**

General Information
Document Type: Presolicitation Notice
Solicitation Number: Reference-Number-R5NP072103-GFM-TB
Posted Date: Jul 21, 2010
Original Response Date: Sep 05, 2010
Current Response Date: Sep 16, 2010
Original Archive Date: Sep 27, 2010
Classification Code: Z — Maintenance, repair, and alteration of real
property

Contracting Office Address
Department of Agriculture, Forest Service, R-5 Northern Province
Acquisitions, Yreka Office, 1312 Fairlane Road, Yreka, CA, 96097

Description
Region 5, USDA Forest Service intends to issue a solicitation for Grounds
and Facilities Maintenance Services, pursuant to and in accordance with
an Office of Manpower and Budget (OMB) Circular No. A-76, 'Performance
of Commercial Activities'. The agency anticipates up to three (3) subsequent awards - one each for the Northern, Central and Southern California
areas. The solicitation will be available on or around August 6, 2010 for
electronic download only. The NAICS code for this acquisition is 561210.
The small business size standard is $6.0 million.

Point of Contact
Doris Broussard, Contracting Officer, Phone 530-242-2219,
e-mail tbroussard@fs.fed.us

| Add to Watchlist | Add Me To Interested Vendors |

Note: Many solicitations are reserved, or "set aside," for small businesses, minority-owned businesses, women-owned firms, and veteran-
owned businesses and they are listed as such.

Be sure to click on the "Add To Watchlist" box at the bottom of the synopsis and provide your e-mail address. This is a subscription to a mailing
list for all future announcements on this particular solicitation.

Vendor Notification Service

By registering for the Vendor Notification Service (under "Vendors— Search, Monitor, and Retrieve Opportunities" on the FedBizOpps homepage), vendors can register to receive procurement announcements by email. A vendor can specify notices it wishes to receive by solicitation number, selected organizations, and product service classification. To date, more than 150,000 vendors are registered to receive business opportunities from FedBizOpps.

FedBizOpps includes the capability to join and view a published list of vendors interested in a particular solicitation. This is useful for vendors who are interested in teaming on procurement opportunities. The "Register as Interested Vendor" button will be on the listing page of the solicitation, if it is available. Eventually, federal agencies/buying offices will use this site regularly to receive proposals electronically.

Be Realistic!

If you're new to the federal marketplace, it can be tempting to bid on every government contract that comes along, but your time and effort would be better spent targeting the best opportunities for your business. Look objectively at your company's resources. If the project seems too big, if you don't meet all of the solicitation's requirements, or if completing the proposal is going to put an unnecessary strain on your personnel, skip it and find another opportunity more suited to your specialties. Don't burn that midnight oil if you don't have to.

Business Solutions Awards—GSA
Online Business Intelligence

By Shane Harris, Government Executive

In January, the procurement world bid a solemn adieu to the trusted, true and utterly obsolete *Commerce Business Daily,* the government-printed newspaper that for 51 years had been companies' main source of information on what federal agencies were shopping for. In years past, prospective contractors had scoured the CBD, as it was commonly called, like unemployed workers searching the classified ads. Agencies posted their procurement notices in the publication faithfully.

But readership plummeted in recent years, from a high of 55,000 subscriptions in 1986 to 2,600 in 2001, as the government turned to the Web as a vehicle for advertising procurement opportunities. Vendors also used the Internet to hunt for new leads, or simply paid other companies to compile procurement notices for them. The Government Printing Office, which published the CBD, tried to revitalize it in 1996 by launching an online version called CBDNet. But that site didn't aggregate all procurement opportunities.

The time for change had arrived. On Jan. 4, as the CBD and CBDNet were officially terminated, the General Services Administration launched a new website called FedBizOpps.gov. It has quickly become the procurement source of record. Every agency is required to post procurement notices on the site.

FedBizOpps was recognized for acquisition excellence by this year's Business Solutions in the Public Interest Awards because of its simplicity. "One of the major reasons that we all thought it should be a winner," says Allan Burman, the former administrator of the Office of Federal Procurement Policy and one of this year's judges, "is the effort they made at simplifying how people get information from the government—putting it in one place and getting it electronically."

Until the launch of FedBizOpps, vendors had to spend hours looking for agencies' procurement announcements and solicitations. To do so online, they had to visit hundreds of individual agency websites. And many agencies didn't post their procurements online. Michael Sade, procurement chief at the Commerce Department and also one of this year's judges, says FedBizOpps saves time. That's especially helpful, he says, for small vendors, who have fewer resources

to spend hunting in paper documents for new business opportunities.

Burman says judges admired FedBiz Opps for its growth from humble beginnings at a single agency into a massive governmentwide project. NASA officials first came up with the idea of consolidating their own purchasing process online. The agency is one of the biggest single buyers in the government, with $10 billion in spending on prime contracts in fiscal 2001. But NASA officials realized the project was a huge undertaking, even for them. They needed help funding the site, so they joined forces with GSA, says David Drabkin, GSA's deputy associate administrator for acquisition policy. GSA's Office of Governmentwide Policy and the Federal Supply Service took over the project and guided the site into its current form.

In their pitch to judges, Burman says GSA officials predicted that FedBizOpps would have a wide-ranging effect on agencies' business, because it would be a highly reliable system that the whole government could use to simplify the procurement process. Officials said the site had already registered 180,000 vendors and incorporated 23 million documents in its first year of operation. In spring 2000, in preparation for the launch, GSA officials launched a training program and taught 2,000 procurement offices how to use FedBizOpps.

Companies that register at FedBiz Opps receive tailored e-mails about procurements announced in specific agencies or categories. They can search the site for solicitations by selecting from a list of agencies or entering a specific solicitation number. Notices are listed by the contracting agency and the date posted. Each notice presents a link to the full text of the solicitation. Users can search one or all agency solicitations for key words.

Sade says FedBizOpps also is a useful tool for procurement officials. They can search for information about acquisitions similar to theirs conducted at other agencies around the country.

Contracting officers can contact their colleagues, whose names are listed on the notices, to get their advice and discuss challenges in constructing their acquisition efforts.

Most often, Sade says, contracting officers just want to see a document to know how a particular procurement was structured in the past.

FedBizOpps archives past solicitations, so contracting officers can look over the history of a particular kind of procurement and see how its structure might have changed.

The site gives procurement executives control over the quality of solicitations, because executives can go online and see what people at the agency are posting, Sade says. He looks at documents to spot weaknesses and strengths so he can improve training and give people appropriate credit for crafting effective procurements and attracting new vendors. "In a nonobtrusive way, I can see what we're doing out there," he says.

FedBizOpps is widely used, but that doesn't necessarily mean it's easy to use. People with no familiarity with the procurement process and its unique jargon would probably be lost surfing around the site. Of course, FedBizOpps is a professional tool, intended for those who live and breathe the obscure purchasing lexicon, but Burman says the site's managers shouldn't take for granted their users' grasp of minutiae, espe-

cially as use of the site grows. "Too often, people [in government] fall into jargon and use terms that aren't all that understandable by the general public," Burman says.

Paying to keep FedBizOpps in business may be one of GSA's biggest challenges as the site evolves. "Funding is a big issue and hasn't been resolved," Drabkin says. "[The site] doesn't currently pay for itself." Officials have said it takes about $4.3 million a year to operate FedBizOpps. Agencies pay a fee for every solicitation they post. GSA agreed in the first year not to charge agencies more per posting than they paid for CBDNet, Drabkin says. Agencies end up paying about $5 per posting to use FedBizOpps.

However, Drabkin adds, many more agencies use FedBizOpps than ever used CBDNet. The number of postings in February alone exceeded CBDNet's annual rate, Drabkin says. Presumably, higher use might drive fees down. But even with its popularity, FedBizOpps has only collected $650,000 in fees this fiscal year, which is not enough to cover its operating costs, Drabkin says. GSA is considering ways to make the site self-funding. Vendors don't pay to register on the site or to receive e-mail notifications, but Drabkin says GSA might start charging them a small annual fee, which probably would not exceed $30.

GSA officials are looking to enhance FedBizOpps in several ways. One of the most significant would be creating a system to allow vendors to post bids online. Federal officials want agencies to have the capacity to receive online bids, whether through FedBizOpps or some other site. Members of the Executives Council, which includes procurement chiefs from across the government, are discussing how to do this. Sade says procurement officials who are members of the FedBizOpps users group will submit their ideas and suggestions to the council. Those users also want to implement electronic authentication tools for verifying vendors' and purchasers' identities. The Office of Management and Budget has participated in these ongoing discussions. But while a dialogue has started, no firm plans have been made on how to move into the next phase.

Drabkin says he's happy that FedBiz Opps overcame the obstacles that have stalled similar efforts. "All of the agencies that came together to make this happen . . . could have kept it from hap-

pening," he says. Drabkin says the site is a testament to intergovernmental cooperation, something many agencies are trying to emulate these days with a new Homeland Security Department emerging.

Burman says FedBizOpps can serve as a model for the Bush administration's electronic government initiatives, a series of two dozen projects that aim to put government transactions online. FedBizOpps takes information from many sources and puts it in one accessible place, a model that has implications well beyond the scope of procurement.

August 15, 2002

FEDERAL SUPPLY SCHEDULES/ GSA SCHEDULES

Every commercial contractor interested in selling to the federal government should be on a federal supply schedule—just your humble author's opinion! GSA schedules allow you to establish long-term government-wide contracts for your particular products and services. They are a great way to get your foot in the government's door.

Contractors looking for ways to diversify and/or complement their commercial sales base should strongly consider getting on a schedule as well. Government business tends to complement your commercial business. Not only do schedule orders tend to be larger, but government buyers also tend to make purchases at different times of the year, like in September, when the government's fiscal year ends.

Schedule holders are preapproved to contract with federal agencies, so your company joins a list of "preferred vendors." Your approved prices/ rates can also be used to validate your costs on other proposals you submit, thus helping you keep DCAA (the Defense Contract Audit Agency) off your back.

Chapter 7 goes into detail on federal supply schedules.

FEDERAL REGISTER

The *Federal Register* is a daily newspaper that informs the public of congressional and federal enactments and regulatory activities. It is the official publication used by the federal government to announce changes to the FAR. All changes to established agency regulations must be published in the *Federal Register*.

The National Archives and Records Administration is responsible for publishing the *Federal Register*. The publication varies in size from 200 to 600 pages (or more), depending on the number and length of announcements.

Careful attention to the *Federal Register* will help you anticipate the government's priorities and program changes. The *Federal Register* is available at:

www.gpoaccess.gov/fr/index.html

FEDERAL AGENCY ACQUISITION FORECASTS

Among the best sources a contractor can use to anticipate future contract actions or awards are federal agency acquisition forecasts. Each federal agency must compile and make available one-year projections of contracting opportunities that small and small disadvantaged businesses can perform. Most federal agencies announce their acquisition forecasts on the Internet. You can find these at each agency's website, or call the agency to request a copy.

Federal Register / Vol. 68, No. 166 / Wednesday, August 27, 2003 / Notices   51565

Personal Data Record, USAFA Form 146, OMB Number 0701–0064.

Needs and Uses: The information collection requirement is necessary to obtain data on candidate's background and aptitude in determining eligibility and selection to the Air Force Academy.

Affected Public: Individuals or households.

Annual Burden Hours: 3,617.

Number of Respondents: 7,233.

Responses per Respondent: 1.

Average Burden per Response: 30 Minutes.

Frequency: 1.

SUPPLEMENTARY INFORMATION:

Summary of Information Collection

The information collected on this form is required by 10 U.S.C. 9346. The respondents are students who are applying for admission to the United States Air Force Academy. Each student's background and aptitude is reviewed to determine eligibility. If the information on this form is not collected, the individual cannot be considered for admittance to the Air Force Academy.

Pamela Fitzgerald,

Air Force Federal Register Liaison Officer.

[FR Doc. 03–21846 Filed 8–26–03; 8:45 am]

BILLING CODE 5001-05-P

DEPARTMENT OF DEFENSE

Department of the Air Force

Proposed Collection; Comment Request

AGENCY: Department of the Air Force, DoD.

ACTION: Notice.

In compliance with Section 3506(c)(2)(A) of the Paperwork Reduction Act of 1995, Headquarters Air Force Recruiting Service announces the proposed extension of a currently approved public information collection and seeks public comment on the provisions thereof. Comments are invited on: (a) Whether the proposed collection of information is necessary for the proper performance of the functions of the agency, including whether the information shall have practical utility; (b) the accuracy of the agency's estimate of the burden of the proposed information collection; (c) ways to enhance the quality, unity, and clarity of the information to be collected; (d) ways to minimize the burden of the information collection on respondents, including the use of automated collection techniques or other forms of information technology.

DATES: Consideration will be given to all comments received by September 8, 2003.

ADDRESSES: Written comments and recommendations on the proposed information collection should be sent to Department of Defense, HQ AFRS/RSOC, 550 D Street West, Suite 1, Randolph AFB TX 78150–4527.

FOR FURTHER INFORMATION CONTACT: To request more information on this proposed information collection or to obtain a copy of the proposal and associated collection instruments, please write to the above addresses, or call HQ AFRS/RSOC, Officer Accessions Branch at (210) 652–4334.

Title, Associated Form, and OMB Number: Air Force Officer Training School Accession Forms, AETC Forms 1413 and 1422, OMB Number 0701–0080.

Needs and Uses: These forms are used by field recruiters and education counselors in the processing of Officer Training School (OTS) applications.

Affected Public: Civilian and Active Duty OTS Applicants.

Annual Burden Hours: 2,200.

Number of Respondents: 1,700.

Responses per Respondent: 1.

Average Burden per Response: 1 Hour (AETC Form 1413)/2 Hours (AETC Form 1422).

Frequency: On Occasion.

SUPPLEMENTARY INFORMATION:

Summary of Information Collection

Respondents are civilian and active-duty candidates applying for a commission in the United States Air Force. These forms provide pertinent information to facilitate selection of candidates for commission.

Pamela Fitzgerald,

Air Force Federal Register Liaison Officer.

[FR Doc. 03–21848 Filed 8–26–03; 8:45 am]

BILLING CODE 5001-05-P

DEPARTMENT OF DEFENSE

Department of the Air Force

Proposed Collection; Comment Request

AGENCY: Department of the Air Force, DoD.

ACTION: Notice.

In compliance with section 3506(c)(2)(A) of the Paperwork Reduction Act of 1995, Headquarters Air Force Recruiting Service announces the proposed extension of a currently approved public information collection and seeks public comment on the

provisions thereof. Comments are invited on: (a) Whether the proposed collection of information is necessary for the proper performance of the functions of the agency, including whether the information shall have practical utility; (b) the accuracy of the agency's estimate of the burden of the proposed information collection; (c) ways to enhance the quality, unity, and clarity of the information to be collected; (d) ways to minimize the burden of the information collection on respondents, including the use of automated collection techniques or other forms of information technology.

DATES: Consideration will be given to all comments received by September 11, 2003.

ADDRESSES: Written comments and recommendations on the proposed information collection should be sent to Department of Defense, HQ AFRS/RSOC, 550 D Street West, Suite 1, Randolph AFB TX 78150–4527.

FOR FURTHER INFORMATION CONTACT: To request more information on this proposed information collection or to obtain a copy of the proposal and associated collection instruments, please write to the above addresses, or call HQ AFRS/RSOC, Officer Accessions Branch at (210) 652–4334.

Title, Associated Form, and OMB Number: Health Profession Accession Forms, AETC Forms 1402 and 1437, OMB Number 0701–0078.

Needs and Uses: These forms are used by field recruiters in the processing of health professions applicants applying for a commission in the United States Air Force.

Affected Public: Individuals or households.

Annual Burden Hours: 3,600.

Number of Respondents: 3,600.

Responses per Respondent: 1.

Average Burden per Response: 1 Hour.

Frequency: On Occasion.

SUPPLEMENTARY INFORMATION:

Summary of Information Collection

Respondents are civilian candidates applying for a commission in the United States Air Force as healthcare officers. These forms provide pertinent information to facilitate selection of candidates for commission.

Pamela Fitzgerald,

Air Force Federal Register Liaison Officer.

[FR Doc. 03–21849 Filed 8–26–03; 8:45 am]

BILLING CODE 5001-05-P

Sample page of *Federal Register*

BIDDERS' LISTS

Contracting activities (or buying offices) maintain bidders' lists to identify contractors that have expressed an interest in furnishing a particular supply or service. Bidders' lists are also called "solicitation mailing lists" or "bidders' list catalogs."

> Note: Effective October 1, 2003, federal contracting activities are no longer required to establish and maintain manual bidders' lists. This change to the FAR is intended to broaden the use of e-business applications.

Contracting activities typically keep separate bidders' lists for the various types of supplies and services they purchase. For example, a contracting activity might have separate bidders' lists for office supplies, janitorial services, technical support, and computers. The best way to get information about a contracting activity's bidders' list procedures is to contact its small business specialist.

Many contracting activities use Standard Form 129, Solicitation Mailing List Application, as their bidders' list application. Standard Form 129 asks for the following information:

■ Type of organization (corporation or individual)

■ Officers' names

■ Supplies and services offered (use government classification codes, if known)

■ Business size and average number of employees

■ Ownership type (e.g., small disadvantaged business, women-owned business)

Suppose Rick Hanley, of Rick's Hardware, wanted to sell tools his company manufactures to the Defense Logistics Agency. He would submit SF 129 with the information shown in the sample.

SOLICITATION MAILING LIST APPLICATION			1. TYPE OF APPLICATION ■ INITIAL ❑ REVISION	2. DATE 3/30/08	FORM APPROVED OMB NO. 2900-0445	
NOTE: Please complete all items on this form. Insert N/A in items not applicable. See reverse for instructions.						
Public reporting burden for this collection of information is estimated to average .58 hours per response, including the time for reviewing instructions, searching existing data sources, gathering and maintaining the data needed, and completing and reviewing the collection of information. Send comments regarding this burden estimate or any other aspect of this collection of information, including suggestions for reducing this burden, to the FAR Secretariat (MVR), Federal Acquisition Policy Division, GSA, Washington, DC 20405.						

SUBMIT TO	A. FEDERAL AGENCY'S NAME Defense Supply Center Columbus			APPLICANT	A. NAME Rick's Hardware		

	A. FEDERAL AGENCY'S NAME				A. NAME		
	Defense Supply Center Columbus				Rick's Hardware		
	B. STREET ADDRESS				B. STREET ADDRESS		C. COUNTY
	3990 East Broad Street				128 K Street		
	C. CITY	D. STATE	E. ZIPCODE		D. CITY	E. STATE	F. ZIPCODE
	Columbus	OH	43216		Wichita	KS	67201

5. TYPE OF ORGANIZATION (Check one)	6. ADDRESS TO WHICH SOLICITATIONS ARE TO BE MAILED (IF DIFFERENT THAN ITEM 4)	
❑ INDIVIDUAL ❑ NON-PROFIT ORGANIZATION ❑ PARTNERSHIP ■ CORPORATION, INCORPORATED UNDER THE LAWS OF THE STATE OF: KS	A. STREET ADDRESS	B. COUNTY
	C. CITY	D. STATE E. ZIPCODE

6(A). EMAIL ADDRESS

7. NAMES OF OFFICERS, OWNERS, OR PARTNERS

A. PRESIDENT	B. VICE PRESIDENT	C. SECRETARY
Rick Hanley	Susan Snow	Judy Stevens
D. TREASURER	E. OWNERS OR PARTNERS	
Joe Smith	N/A	

8. AFFILIATES OF APPLICANT (Names, locations and nature of affiliation. See definition on reverse)

NAME	LOCATION	NATURE OF AFFILIATION

9. PERSONS AUTHORIZED TO SIGN OFFERS AND CONTRACTS IN YOUR NAME (Indicate if agent)

NAME	OFFICIAL CAPACITY	TELEPHONE NUMBER	
		AREA CODE	NUMBER
Rick Hanley	President		999-888-5616
Susan Snow	Vice President		999-888-5617

10. IDENTIFY EQUIPMENT, SUPPLIES, AND/OR SERVICES ON WHICH YOU DESIRE TO MAKE AN OFFER, AND INCLUDE NORTH AMERICAN INDUSTRY CLASSIFICATION SYSTEM CODE (NAICS)
Stainless Steel Hammers and Stainless Steel Chisels

11A. SIZE OF BUSINESS (See definitions on reverse) ■ SMALL BUSINESS (IF CHECKED, COMPLETE ITEMS 11B AND 11C) ❑ OTHER THAN SMALL BUSINESS	11B. AVERAGE NUMBER OF EMPLOYEES (including affiliates) FOR FOUR PRECEDING CALENDAR QUARTERS 25	11C. AVERAGE ANNUAL SALES OR RECEIPTS FOR PRECEDING THREE FISCAL YEARS $ 250,000

12. TYPE OF OWNERSHIP (See definitions on reverse) (Not applicable for other than small business)		13. TYPE OF BUSINESS (See definitions on reverse)
❑ DISADVANTAGED BUSINESS ❑ HUBZONE SMALL BUSINESS ❑ VERY SMALL BUSINESS ❑ 8(A)	❑ WOMEN-OWNED BUSINESS ■ VETERAN-OWNED BUSINESS ❑ SERVICE DISABLED VETERAN	■ MANUFACTURER OR PRODUCER ❑ SERVICE ESTABLISHMENT ❑ CONSTRUCTION COINCERN ❑ RESEARCH AND DEVELOPMENT ❑ SURPLUS DEALER

14. DUN AND BRADSTREET NUMBER (If applicable) 12-589-1684	15. HOW LONG IN PRESENT BUSINESS 5 years

16. FLOOR SPACE (In square feet)		17. NET WORTH	
A. MANUFACTURING	B. WAREHOUSE	A. DATE	B. AMOUNT
8,000	5,000	12/31/07	$ 50,000

18. SECURITY CLEARANCE (If applicable, check highest clearance authorized)

FOR	TOP SECRET	SECRET	CONFIDENTIAL	C. NAME OF AGENCIES WHICH GRANTED SECURITY CLEARANCES	D. DATES GRANTED
A. KEY PERSONNEL	N/A				
B. PLANT ONLY					

CERTIFICATION – I certify that information supplied herein (including all pages attached) is correct and that neither the applicant nor any person (for concern) in any connection with the applicant as a principal or officer, so far as it known, is now debarred or otherwise declared ineligible by any agency of the Federal Government from making offers for furnishing materials, supplies, or services to the Government or any agency thereof.

19. NAME AND TITLE OF PERSON AUTHORIZED TO SIGN (Type or Print) Rick Hurley, President	20. SIGNATURE	21. DATE SIGNED 3/30/08

AUTHORIZED FOR LOCAL REPRODUCTION	STANDARD FORM 129

Sample SF 129

Registration through an agency's Internet homepage is the best way to submit your bidders' list application.

Placement on a bidders' list does not guarantee that you will receive government orders. Federal regulations require only that a sufficient number of vendors be solicited to ensure competition. If a particular bidders' list includes numerous firms capable of supplying the products or services sought, the contracting activity may select only a portion of those listed to solicit. A rotation system helps ensure each vendor has a fair chance of being selected periodically.

Using a Bidders' List

The following example illustrates how Widget World, a small business, navigates through the Department of Transportation's bidders' list system.

Widget World submits an SF 129 online for widgets to a contracting activity in DOT. On January 5, 2010, the application is received and approved. Currently, the contracting activity has 20 businesses on its widget bidders' list.

Luckily, Mike Mitchell, a contracting officer at this activity, happens to be issuing an order for $2,000 worth of widgets. Although Mike can randomly select businesses from the current bidders' list or send the solicitation to all of them, he decides to rotate the bidders' list and select 10 firms to solicit.

As is typical when a bidders' list is rotated, Mike solicits from the previously successful bidder; firms added since the last order, which include Widget World; and a certain other portion of the list. Firms may also request a copy of the solicitation.

Many times, you will receive a solicitation in which you are not interested. In that case, notify the contracting officer in writing that you
are unable to submit a bid at this time but would like to be retained on
the bidders' list. Be sure to use your company's letterhead so the contracting officer can clearly identify you as the sender. If you are
removed from a bidders' list, you will have to resubmit your SF 129.

Bidders' lists are slowly but surely becoming a thing of the past. In today's
marketplace, they are used primarily by smaller contracting activities to
purchase items that are under the micropurchase threshold.

TECH-*NET*

TECH-*Net*, the Technology Resources *Network*, is a search engine that
features a database of high-tech small businesses. Business profiles are
structured like executive business summaries, with specific data fields
designed to meet the needs of researchers, investors, and other potential
users. Small businesses can use their profiles to market their capabilities
and accomplishments. TECH-*Net* also provides access to SBIR solicitations (see Chapter 5) and other technology procurement opportunities.

Businesses profiled on TECH-*Net* can be searched using NAICS code, keywords, company name, ownership type, technology code, and contract
award year. For more information on TECH-*Net*, visit:

http://tech-net.sba.gov

FEDERAL PROCUREMENT DATA SYSTEM

When pursuing federal contracts, you'll need to identify market changes,
analyze procurement history, and identify spending trends so you can
pinpoint where to concentrate your sales efforts. Congress established the
Federal Procurement Data System (FPDS) as a system for collecting,
developing, and disseminating data on the $400 billion a year the govern-

ment spends on supplies and services. It serves as a government-wide acquisition management information system.

FPDS provides unprecedented visibility into procurement and acquisition activities within federal agencies. Among its many features, FPDS:

■ Provides the public with Internet access to federal data in real time

■ Provides users with extensive online reporting capabilities, including reports with charts and graphs

■ Collects data on over 13 million procurements valued at more than $3,000, including who bought what, from whom, the dollar amounts of each transaction, when the contract was signed, and where the work was performed

■ Maintains a historical trail of all transactions, including interagency transactions conducted through government-wide acquisition contracts (GWACs) and Federal Supply Schedule contracts

■ Enables government acquisition officials worldwide to input and access purchase data via the Internet.

For more information on FPDS, visit:

www.fpds.gov

YEAR-END PROCUREMENTS

The federal government operates on the basis of a fiscal year that begins October 1 and ends September 30. As mentioned in Chapter 2, Congress appropriates funds to federal agencies to run their operations or meet their mission requirements. The appropriations can be for a single year, for multiple years, or on an unrestricted basis. Most appropriations are for a single year.

When Congress appropriates funds to a federal agency on a single-year basis, the agency must spend those funds during that particular fiscal year or lose the funding. Use it or lose it! This situation gives federal agencies no incentive to save money. In fact, it encourages agencies to spend all available funds.

Which quarter during the government's fiscal year historically has the highest level of procurement activity or acquisitions? If you guessed the fourth quarter, you're right. Why do you think this is? Maybe federal personnel go crazy from the heat. (Hey, it happens!)

But more than likely it's because the majority of government funds expire on September 30. If you receive a solicitation during May or June, the agency might have to award the contract before midnight on September 30 or lose its funding.

It is a fact of life that year-end procurements tend to be a little frantic. Mostly this is the result of poor planning by the agencies, internal bickering, and politics. Procurements are often poorly thought out, poorly designed, and fraught with errors that must be corrected after the contract has been awarded. Knowing the government's situation at this time of the year gives you an advantage during the solicitation process.

There are, of course, exceptions to this requirement. Funds appropriated on an unrestricted basis (also referred to as no-year money) or funds appropriated for multiple years do not necessarily expire on September 30. Ask the contracting officer about the status of a contract's appropriated funds.

■   ■   ■

In spite of—or because of—the federal government's size, no one way exists to market your supplies and services. Each federal agency uses different acquisition methods; therefore, the best way to market your items is to contact specific federal agencies to determine exactly how their procurement processes work.

To be successful in marketing to the federal government, you must be persistent. Visit each federal agency's website. Go to the agencies' programs and workshops. Register your supplies and services with the agencies. Talk to each agency's Small Business Specialist. Sign up for a federal supply schedule. Provide buying offices with brochures describing your company. Do whatever it takes to get your products and services noticed!

■   ■   ■

Support Programs and Services for Contractors

9

© 1997 Randy Glasbergen
www.glasbergen.com

HAIR BALLS
50¢

GLASBERGEN

"Business is lousy. Maybe I should have done more market research first."

What's in this chapter?

- Small Business Administration
- Defense Logistics Agency
- General Services Administration
- A-76 Program
- USA Services
- USA.gov
- National Contract Management Association

To help small businesses participate in federal contracting, the government has established numerous programs and services. Each federal agency provides small businesses with information on procurements, guidance on solicitation procedures, and identification of subcontracting opportunities. Many nonfederal sources also offer services. This chapter discusses many of the support programs available to small business contractors.

SMALL BUSINESS ADMINISTRATION

The Small Business Administration (SBA) is in business solely to help the small business owner. It provides small businesses with a wide variety of programs and services covering various business areas, including financial, technical, and management assistance. Specifically, SBA offers five major programs:

■ Business development assistance

■ Procurement assistance

■ Minority small business assistance

■ Advocacy

■ Financial assistance.

SBA also offers counseling services to business owners or potential business owners on all facets of small business matters.

Did You Know That SBA . . .

■ Partners with more than 8,000 private sector lenders to provide capital to small businesses?

■ Guaranteed more than 78,000 loans totaling $16 billion to small businesses during FY2006?

■ Maintains a portfolio guaranteeing more than $40 billion in loans to 220,000 small businesses that otherwise would not have such access to capital?

■ Extended management and technical assistance to nearly one million small businesses through its 1,100 Small Business Development Centers and 10,500 Service Corps of Retired Executives volunteers?

■ Provides loan guarantees and technical assistance to small business exporters through U.S. Export Assistance Centers?

The best place to locate up-to-the-minute information about SBA programs and services is:

www.sba.gov

SBA Answer Desk

The SBA answer desk is a toll-free information center that answers questions about starting or running a business and getting assistance. The toll-free number is:

(800) 8-ASK-SBA

The answer desk can give you a list of SBA offices and their phone numbers.

Service Corps of Retired Executives

SBA developed the Service Corps of Retired Executives (SCORE) to provide one-on-one management counseling to aspiring entrepreneurs and business owners. SCORE's experienced business experts offer general advice on everything from marketing and writing a business plan, to managing cash flow/capital needs, to investigating the market potential for a product or service.

Counselors also give insight into how to start, operate, buy or franchise, and sell a business. SCORE services are free. Currently more than 10,500 volunteer business counselors are located at SBA field offices throughout the United States.

For a current list of SCORE locations, visit:

www.score.org

or call (800) 634-0245.

SBA Small Business Development Centers

Numerous studies have shown that most small businesses fail as a result of poor management. SBA established the Small Business Development Center (SBDC) program to provide management assistance to small business owners. This program coordinates efforts among universities across the country; local, state, and federal governments; and private sector businesses to provide assistance with management techniques and technology to the small business community.

SBDC's services include assisting small businesses with financial, marketing, production, organization, engineering, and technical problems. In addition, SBDC offers specialized programs on international trade, business law, venture capital formation, and rural development.

Currently, there are 57 SBDCs—one in each state (Texas has four), the District of Columbia, Puerto Rico, Guam, and the U.S. Virgin Islands. In each state a lead organization sponsors and manages the SBDC program. The lead organization coordinates program services through a network of subcenters and satellite locations in each state, providing more than 1,100 service locations. Subcenters are located at colleges, vocational schools, local government offices, and economic development centers.

The best way to locate an SBDC is to visit:

www.sba.gov/aboutsba/sbaprograms/sbdc

SBA Women Business Centers

Women Business Centers (WBCs) provide women with long-term training and counseling in all aspects of owning and managing a business. SBA has a network of more than 60 WBCs, with at least one representative in each state. For the phone number of the WBC in your state or district, contact the SBA answer desk at (800) 8-ASK-SBA.

The Office of Women's Business Ownership (OWBO) also provides comprehensive training, counseling, and information.

www.sba.gov/aboutsba/sbaprograms/onlinewbc

SBA Office of Advocacy

SBA's Office of Advocacy encourages policies that support small business development and growth. It works to reduce the burdens that federal policies impose on small businesses and to maximize the benefits small businesses receive. To accomplish these objectives, Congress has specified five statutory duties:

■ Serve as a focal point for receiving complaints, criticisms, and suggestions concerning federal policies that affect small businesses

■ Counsel small businesses on ways to resolve problems in dealing with the federal government

■ Represent small businesses before federal agencies whose actions affect them

■ Recommend changes to better comply with the Small Business Act (see Chapter 4) and communicate such proposals to appropriate agencies

■ Work with federal agencies and private groups to examine ways in which small businesses can make better use of the government's programs and services.

The Office of Advocacy also provides statistics and research studies on small businesses. For more information, visit:

www.sba.gov/advo

SBA Financial Assistance Programs

No matter how carefully you manage your company's cash flow, at some point you will have to borrow money. The two primary reasons a company borrows money are (1) to cover temporary cash-flow shortages and (2) to provide working capital for business growth. One of the best places for a small business to look for financial assistance is SBA.

SBA provides financial assistance in the form of loan guarantees to qualified small businesses that are unable to obtain credit elsewhere. These loans are available for many business purposes, such as acquiring real estate, equipment, working capital, or inventory, or for expanding. To be eligible for an SBA loan, a business must meet the size standards established by industry type (see Chapter 4).

SBA makes loans in conjunction with a bank or other lending institution, which provides the funds. It guarantees up to 90% of the loan. The major benefit to borrowers who obtain loans through SBA is the terms, which are typically longer than those available from commercial lenders. SBA does not provide grants to start or expand a business.

SBA offers many different types of loans, including:

■ Minority prequalification loans

■ Women's prequalification loans

■ Physical disaster business loans

■ Contract loans

■ Surety bond guarantees

▪ Small business energy loans

▪ Microloans

▪ General contractor loans.

To be eligible for an SBA loan, you must first apply—and be rejected—for a loan from at least one qualified commercial lender. The reasons for rejection might include the following: the repayment period was too long, the business had not been in operation long enough, or the loan request was too large. If the lender rejects your loan request for any reason other than your ability to repay, ask if the lender would be willing to make the loan if SBA guaranteed it.

If the lender agrees to the SBA loan arrangement, it contacts SBA to determine whether the agency will guarantee the loan. Assuming that the loan meets SBA's criteria, it's up to the lender whether to make the loan. If the lender agrees, it makes the necessary arrangements to secure the guarantee with SBA. If the lender refuses to make the loan, the borrower must look for another lender.

Borrowers should be prepared to pay closing costs on SBA-guaranteed loans. Closing costs vary, but most tend to be 3% to 5% of the total loan amount.

DEFENSE LOGISTICS AGENCY

The Defense Logistics Agency (DLA), though not exactly a support program, is the organization that contractors interested in selling to the military should be aware of. DLA provides supply support, contract administration, and technical services to all branches of the military and to several civilian agencies. It manages a distribution system of approximately 4 million general supply items, including food and clothing, textiles, medical equipment, auto parts, and construction equipment.

DLA buys and manages these supplies at the following Lead Centers:

■ Defense Supply Center Columbus

■ Defense Supply Center Richmond

■ Defense Supply Center Philadelphia

■ Defense Distribution Center

■ Defense Energy Support Center

■ Defense Reutilization and Marketing Service

www.dla.mil/dla_orgs.aspx

Note: DOD websites typically end in .mil, which is an abbreviation for "military."

Each of these centers manages very specific commodity groupings, so don't be misled by the center names. If you are interested in selling to the military, contact the Small Business Specialist at the supply center that purchases your particular products.

MILITARY OPPORTUNITIES

DOD has published a handbook called *Doing Business with the DoD*, which furnishes general information about DOD contracting. If you plan to contract with DOD, this handbook will be very useful. For more information, visit:

www.acq.osd.mil/osbp/doing_business

GENERAL SERVICES ADMINISTRATION

The General Services Administration (GSA) is the government's landlord. It provides federal agencies with the tools necessary to perform their day-to-day operations. GSA spends several billion dollars annually, providing federal agencies across the country with:

■ Workspace and security

■ Furniture

■ Phones and computers

■ Travel services

■ Motor vehicle fleet management

■ Federal child care

■ Historic building preservation

■ Fine art management.

GSA's website has all kinds of useful information and downloadable forms, probably the best of the federal agencies.

www.gsa.gov

GSA also distributes a handbook called *Doing Business with GSA*.

www.gsa.gov/doingbusinesswithgsa

GSA Regional Centers/Small Business Utilization Centers

GSA Regional Centers serve as a front door for small businesses seeking to market their products and services to GSA. These centers advise and counsel persons interested in contracting with GSA. Each center distributes federal directories, publication lists, references, and a variety of technical publications.

Currently 11 Regional Centers are located throughout the country. GSA's website provides the address and phone number of the Regional Center that serves your area or region.

www.gsa.gov/sbu

Each Regional Center is staffed by specialists who can provide information on how to:

■ Get onto GSA's bidders' lists

■ Introduce items for government purchase

■ Learn about current bidding opportunities with GSA

■ Obtain copies of federal standards and specifications

■ Review bid abstracts to learn the bidding history of various contract awards (abstracts identify the names of successful bidders and the prices they bid)

■ Obtain publications and other documents about government procurements

■ Receive business counseling.

GSA Regional Centers play a central role in GSA's small business set-aside programs by challenging decisions not to set aside procurements for small business. They also review prime contracts to identify subcontracting opportunities for small and small disadvantaged businesses.

Offices of Small and Disadvantaged Business Utilization

Each major federal agency and department must have an Office of Small and Disadvantaged Business Utilization (OSDBU). The OSDBU provides small businesses with information on procurement opportunities, guidance on procurement procedures, and identification of both prime and subcontracting opportunities. For a current list of OSDBU locations and addresses, visit:

www.osdbu.gov

A-76 PROGRAM

The question of whether federal functions should be performed under contract with commercial sources or in-house using government personnel goes as far back as the Constitution itself. In fact, it is the federal government's policy not to compete with its citizens and to rely on commercial sources to fulfill its operational needs.

Certain functions are inherently governmental in nature, being so intimately related to the public interest as to mandate performance only by federal employees. Monetary transactions, such as tax collection and revenue disbursements, typically meet that definition. Those functions do not compete with the commercial sector and therefore should be performed by federal employees.

On the other hand, government should not start or carry on any activity that can be procured more economically from a commercial source. Activities suitable for outsourcing include:

■ Equipment installation, operation, and maintenance

■ Machine, carpentry, electrical, plumbing, painting, etc.

■ Custodial and janitorial services

■ Office furniture

■ Guard and protective services

■ Scientific data studies.

The Office of Management and Budget (OMB) Circular A-76, *Performance of Commercial Activities Program,* was established to study this issue. The terms *downsizing, privatization,* and *outsourcing* are generally synonymous with the A-76 program. OMB Circular A-76 requires each federal agency to maintain a detailed inventory or record of its in-house activities that could be obtained from commercial sources.

These inventories of commercial activities are submitted to OMB yearly. After review and consultation by OMB, the agencies submit a copy of the inventory to Congress and make its contents available to the public. Unless otherwise provided by law, Circular A-76 applies to all federal agencies.

When an inventory activity is identified as a candidate for outsourcing, the contracting officer places a synopsis in FedBizOpps. If sufficient commercial sources are available, a solicitation stating the method of procurement is issued. All competitive methods of procurement are appropriate for cost comparison under the circular (see Part 4).

The federal agency then prepares a cost estimate of its own according to the solicitation's statement of work (or performance work statement). The cost estimate represents the agency's total cost to continue performing the identified activity. Circular A-76, Attachment C—Calculating Public-Private Competition Costs, is used to prepare the cost estimate.

This attachment provides detailed procedures for developing the cost estimate and specifically identifies such factors as tax rates, depreciation rates, fringe benefit rates, insurance costs, repair and maintenance costs, and similar costs. The competed cost estimate is sealed and stored with the other bids or proposals. The contract is then awarded to the offeror that provides the best value to the government.

Each federal agency is responsible for establishing one or more offices as central points of contact to carry out the provisions of the OMB Circular

A-76. Documents and data pertinent to actions taken under the circular are maintained at those locations. Contractors are encouraged to examine various inventories, schedules, reviews, and cost comparison data for outsourcing candidates.

The A-76 program is not designed to simply outsource federal functions. Rather, it tries to balance the interests of both parties by encouraging competition. OMB Circular A-76 and its supplement are available at:

www.whitehouse.gov/omb/circulars

Federal Procurement Conferences

Federal procurement conferences give small businesses the opportunity to meet with acquisition specialists from military and civilian agencies, as well as prime contractors. Conferences are held at various locations throughout the country. For conference times and locations, visit:

www.acq.osd.mil/sadbu/conferences

USA SERVICES

USA Services is a single point of contact for questions about federal programs, benefits, and services. You can access this information center at:

www.info.gov
or
(800) FED-INFO

Information specialists will answer your questions directly, refer you to the correct office, or research your inquiry.

USA.GOV

USA.gov is the federal government's one-stop shopping mall for government information. By linking nearly all government resources, USA.gov allows users to search popular topics; reference sources, such as news releases, forms, and laws and regulations; and services for citizens, businesses, and federal, state, tribal, and local governments.

Federal Yellow Book

The *Federal Yellow Book* is an organizational directory of the departments and agencies of the federal government's executive branch. It lists positions, addresses, and phone numbers of more than 40,000 federal officials. For more information about this publication, contact:

Leadership Directories, Inc.
(212) 627-4140
info@leadershipdirectories.com

www.leadershipdirectories.com

NATIONAL CONTRACT MANAGEMENT ASSOCIATION

The National Contract Management Association (NCMA) is a professional association in the field of contract management with more than 19,000 members. NCMA offers:

■ Training programs

■ *Contract Management* magazine

■ *Journal of Contract Management*

■ National and regional conferences

■ Credential programs.

For more information about NCMA, contact:

**National Contract Management Association (NCMA)
21740 Beaumeade Circle, Suite 125
Ashburn, VA 20147
Phone (800) 344-8096**

www.ncmahq.org

■ ■ ■

In addition to the huge buyers like DOD and GSA, hundreds of lesser-known federal agencies buy from both large and small businesses. An excellent source of names and addresses for federal agencies is:

www.lib.lsu.edu/gov/fedgov.html

■ ■ ■

PART 4

How the Government Issues Procurement Opportunities

Chapter 10: Simplified Acquisition or Small
Purchase Procedures

Chapter 11: Sealed Bidding

Chapter 12: Negotiated Procurements

Chapter 13: The Uniform Contract Format

"Luck is when preparation meets opportunity."

—Neil Peart

The government procures most of its products and services through "full and open competition." But how does the government determine who receives its awards? Is it the contractor that submits the lowest bid or the contractor with the best overall product or service? The answer is: It depends on the solicitation type. The government primarily uses three methods to solicit contractors' offers:

■ Simplified acquisition or small purchase procedures (see Chapter 10)

■ Sealed bidding procedures (see Chapter 11)

■ Negotiated procurement procedures (see Chapter 12).

Each of these solicitation methods specifies the basis on which the award decision will be made. You will need to examine each solicitation carefully to determine exactly which factors the government will use to make its award decisions.

The Uniform Contract Format (UCF) is a blank solicitation package that prospective contractors can use to submit their bids. Chapter 13 walks you through the four parts and 13 sections of the UCF.

10 Simplified Acquisition or Small Purchase Procedures

GLASBERGEN

"Unless we receive the outstanding balance within ten days, we will have no choice but to destroy your credit rating, ruin your reputation, and make you wish you were never born. If you have already sent the ninety-seven cents, please disregard this notice."

What's in this chapter?

- Micropurchases
- Simplified acquisition methods

When the government makes major purchases (greater than $100,000), it follows an extensive set of procedures to ensure that the funds are spent fairly and wisely. However, the federal government cannot afford to spend same amount of time and money on small purchases or commercial items. That's where simplified acquisition procedures come into play; they emphasize simplicity and reduced administrative costs.

Simplified acquisition procedures apply to purchases that are $100,000 or less. This $100,000 limit is referred to as the simplified acquisition threshold (SAT). If an agency estimates that an acquisition will exceed the SAT, the acquisition must be handled using formal acquisition procedures (see Chapters 11 and 12). Simplified acquisition procedures represent 90% of the government's purchase transactions, although they account for less than 20% of the total procurement dollars.

By using simplified acquisition procedures, contracting officers avoid much of the red tape that slows down the purchase of supplies and services. These procedures also reduce the time and resources that a contractor spends in meeting peculiar government standards. The procedures, however, do not apply to orders from Federal Supply Schedules (Chapter 7) or to delivery orders placed against existing contracts.

Federal agencies are required to use simplified acquisition procedures to the maximum extent practicable. In fact, acquisitions with an anticipated dollar value exceeding $3,000 but not over $100,000 are reserved exclusively for small businesses, provided there is a reasonable expectation of obtaining offers from two or more responsible small business concerns. If that doesn't convince you that government contracting offers exceptional opportunities for small businesses, nothing will.

Commercial Item Test Program

As part of the Federal Acquisition Streamlining Act (FASA) of 1994, the Commercial Item Test Program defined in FAR 13.5 authorizes the use of simplified acquisition procedures to acquire commercial items that cost $5.5 million or less. The goal of this commercial item preference is to simplify the procurement process to encourage private sector companies to sell to the government. It applies to commercial items only!

MICROPURCHASES

Purchases that are $3,000 or less are referred to as *micropurchases*. (The micropurchase limit is $2,000 in the case of construction.) These purchases typically cover routine supplies and services. Micropurchases allow the government to keep less documentation, pay bills more quickly, and handle discrepancies less formally. They account for 70% of the government's purchasing actions.

Micropurchases use the following guidelines:

■ Purchases must be distributed equitably among qualified suppliers to the maximum extent practical.

■ Micropurchases may be awarded without soliciting competitive quotes if the price is deemed reasonable.

The requirements of the Buy American Act do not apply to micropurchases (see Chapter 2). Federal agencies may authorize employees who are not designated acquisition officials to make micropurchases, thus allowing the contracting officer to concentrate on major purchases. Micropurchases may be made from any type of seller, not just small businesses.

Acquisition Methods	
$3,000 or less	Micropurchase procedures
$3,001 to $100,000	Simplified acquisition procedures
Over $100,000	Formal solicitation procedures

SIMPLIFIED ACQUISITION METHODS

Simplified acquisition procedures allow the government to use several authorized methods for entering into contracts.

Request for Quotation

A request for quotation (RFQ) is a document (Standard Form 18) that the government uses to solicit prices for purchases that are under the simplified acquisition threshold (less than $100,000). The government typically uses RFQs when it does not intend to award a contract on the basis of the solicitation but wishes to obtain price, delivery, or other market information as the basis for preparing a purchase order. Your response to this type of announcement is called a *quote.*

Suppose James Statton, president of Answer Me, Inc., receives an RFQ for a phone answering machine and decides to submit a quote. James enters the price of the answering machine on Block 12 of SF 18, signs Block 15, and returns the form to Becky Harper, the contracting officer, by the date specified on Block 10. James' response to the RFQ is not considered an offer, and it cannot be used to form a binding contract. Becky also has the option of obtaining oral quotes from vendors.

Becky Harper then issues a purchase order to the contractor that submits the lowest quote.

Purchase Order

A purchase order (PO) is a contract document that the government uses to buy supplies and services at a price quoted by a seller or vendor. Contracting officers typically use POs to make over-the-counter purchases. All POs are issued on a firm-fixed-price basis (see Chapter 14).

POs detail what the parties must know to complete the sales transactions, such as:

■ The quantity of supplies or scope of services ordered

■ When and where the supplies are to be delivered or the services performed

■ Inspection requirements (if applicable)

REQUEST FOR QUOTATION *(This is not an order)*	THIS RFQ ☐ IS ☒ IS NOT A SMALL BUSINESS SET-ASIDE		PAGE OF PAGES 1 / 6

1. REQUEST NO. RFQ-DC-03-00228	2. DATE ISSUED 05/29/08	3. REQUISITION/PURCHASE REQUEST NO. PR-DC-03-01902	4. CERT. FOR NAT. DEF. UNDER BOSA REG. 2 AND/OR DMS REG. 1	RATING

5a. ISSUED BY US EPA   Mail Drop: 3805R
EMERGENCY RESPONSE SERVICE CENTER
1200 PENNSYLVANIA AVE., NW
WASHINGTON, DC 20460

6. DELIVER BY (Date) 07/30/08

7. DELIVERY ☒ FOB DESTINATION ☐ OTHER (See Schedule)

5b. FOR INFORMATION CALL: (No collect calls)
Name CHRISTINE EDWARDS
TELEPHONE NUMBER (202) 564-2182   Fax: (202) 565-2558

8. TO:
a. Name
b. Company
c. Street Address
d. City   e. State   f. Zip Code

9. DESTINATION
a. Name of Consignee US EPA   Mail Drop: MS101
U.S. EPA - ERT-EAST
b. Street Address 2890 WOODBRIDGE AVE., BLDG 18
c. City EDISON
d. State NJ   e. Zip Code 08837-3679

10. PLEASE FURNISH QUOTATIONS TO THE ISSUING OFFICE IN BLOCK 5A ON OR BEFORE CLOSE OF BUSINESS (Date) 07/10/2003

11. IMPORTANT: This is a request for information, and quotations furnished are not offers. If you are unable to quote, please so indicate on this form and return it to the address in Block 5A. This request does not commit the Government to pay any costs incurred in the preparation of the submission of this quotation or to contract for supplies or services. Supplies are of domestic origin unless otherwise indicated by quoter. Any representations and/or certifications attached to this request for Quotations must be completed by the quoter.

12. SCHEDULE (Include applicable Federal, State and Local taxes)

ITEM NO. (a)	SUPPLIES/SERVICES (b)	QUANTITY (c)	UNIT (d)	UNIT PRICE (e)	AMOUNT (f)
1	Centech Chemical Agent Centech UC AP2Ce (or equivalent) Accessories to be included in the quote: Battery Charger Carrying Case Straps for carrying equipment (quote on any available) RS 232 cables and software for laptop computer Minimum Specifications: 1. Detects phosphoreus and sulphur compounds, nerve and blister agents 2. Detects vapors and liquids. 3. Flame photometric detector for HD, G, V agents. 4. Operational temperature range: -10 C to 55 C, not effected by relative humidity. Operational to 3000m altitude. 5. Storage temperature range: -39 C to	36	EACH		

12. DISCOUNT FOR PROMPT PAYMENT ▶

a.10 Calendar Days (%)	b.20 Calendar Days (%)	c.30 Calendar Days (%)	d. Calendar Days Number / Percent

NOTE: Additional provisions and representations ☒ are ☐ are not attached.

13. NAME AND ADDRESS OF QUOTER	14. SIGNATURE OF PERSON AUTHORIZED TO SIGN QUOTATION	15. Date Of Quotation
a. NAME OF QUOTER		
b. STREET ADDRESS		
	16. SIGNER	
c. COUNTY	a. NAME (Type or Print)	b. TELEPHONE Area Code
d. CITY e. STATE f. ZIP CODE	c. TITLE (Type or Print)	Number

AUTHORIZED FOR LOCAL REPRODUCTION / Previous edition not usable   STANDARD FORM 18 (REV. 6-95) / Prescribed by GSA - FAR (48 CFR) 53.215-1(a)

Sample SF 18

- Contract and acquisition numbers

- Any trade and prompt payment discounts.

Several contractual clauses may appear on the reverse of the PO or be attached to it. For the most part, these clauses apply during the performance of the work.

The PO process typically works as follows:

- The contracting officer lists the items he or she plans to purchase on Standard Form 44, Purchase Order–Invoice–Voucher.

- If the contracting officer pays cash, he or she signs the SF 44 and gives a copy of this PO to the seller as a record/receipt of the transaction. If the contracting officer doesn't pay at the time of sale, he or she signs the SF 44 and gives a copy to the seller to use as an invoice. That's it! There's not much red tape with this process.

POs, however, are becoming endangered, thanks to the government-wide commercial purchase card.

Government-wide Commercial Purchase Card

A government-wide commercial purchase card is a credit card. What does this mean for your business? If your company doesn't accept credit cards, you could be missing out on quick sales opportunities. These cards are typically used to buy supplies and services that are under the micropurchase threshold.

More than 140,000 government employees currently hold one of these credit cards. During FY2006, the federal government purchased over $27 billion worth of products and services using credit cards. Federal agencies typically use MasterCard and Visa for their purchases.

Anyone in possession of a government purchase card has procurement authority to use it, based on the fact that he or she has the card. If you want additional verification that a buyer is eligible to use the card, ask to see his or her government identification card.

Blanket Purchase Agreement

Blanket purchase agreements (BPAs) are charge accounts set up with qualified vendors. Contracting officers typically issue BPAs to several different vendors for the same types of supplies or services. This gives the contracting officers greater flexibility and choice when making purchase decisions.

The BPA may be limited to specific items, or it may cover all the products a vendor can furnish. Each BPA includes information about personnel who are authorized to place orders with the vendor, invoicing and payment procedures, delivery requirements, and fixed price(s) of the covered items. When a vendor establishes a BPA, it agrees to fill orders at or below the lowest price paid by the supplier's most favored private sector customer.

A BPA may be established under the following circumstances:

■ The agency purchases a wide variety of items in a broad class of supplies or services but does not know the exact quantities and delivery requirements in advance.

■ Using the BPA would eliminate numerous purchase orders.

■ There are no existing contract requirements for the same supply or service that the contracting activity is required to use.

BPAs may be established with:

■ Multiple vendors for the same types of supplies or services to provide maximum practicable competition

■ A single vendor from which numerous individual purchases (below the simplified acquisition threshold) will likely be made.

BPAs are usually established with local sources so that purchases can be made with minimal time and effort. Vendors are encouraged to contact buying offices to get their supplies and services listed on a BPA. Once a buying office issues the BPA, the vendor must provide the authorized items upon request. BPAs are usually issued for a one-year period. With advance written notice (e.g., 30 days), either party may cancel a BPA.

When a contracting officer makes a purchase using a BPA, he or she must comply with small business set-aside requirements. Therefore, if two or more small businesses can perform the contract at reasonable prices, only small business BPA vendors may be solicited. Standard form 1449, Solicitation/Contract/Order for Commercial Items, is typically used to place orders.

Imprest Fund Method

Most federal agencies use an imprest fund to purchase routine supplies. It is basically a petty cash account.

Fast Payment Procedure

The fast payment procedure allows a contractor to be paid before the government verifies that supplies have been received and accepted. This procedure improves a contractor's cash flow by speeding up the payment process. The government may use these procedures only for purchases that are less than $25,000.

Fast payment procedures require a contractor to submit an invoice with the following certifications:

■ The supplies were delivered to a post office, common carrier, or point of first receipt by the government.

■ The contractor is responsible for replacing, repairing, or correcting the supplies not received, damaged in transit, or not conforming to purchase agreements.

Title to the supplies passes to the government upon delivery to the post office. Not all federal agencies use the fast payment procedure.

■   ■   ■

This chapter detailed the various thresholds for simplified acquisition or small purchase procedures. You must know these thresholds so you will be aware of the policies and procedures that apply when you sell your supplies or services to the government.

■   ■   ■

Sealed Bidding

© 1998 Randy Glasbergen.

"This is my final offer, Fred. I'll give you a
15% discount on all orders, free shipping for
six months, two of my pickles, half of my fries
and my little packet of crackers."

What's in this chapter?

- The solicitation process
- The sealed bidding (IFB) process
- Solicitation methods
- Preparing your bid
- Late bids
- Bid opening
- Bid evaluations
- Bid award
- Two-step sealed bidding

Sealed bidding is a rigid procurement process designed to protect the integrity of the competitive bidding system. It typically is used to purchase noncommercial products or services that are estimated to exceed $100,000. Although there is no dollar limit on the use of sealed bidding procedures, the federal government is authorized to use them only when:

■ The government's specifications can be described clearly and accurately.

■ Two or more bidders are expected to compete for the contract.

■ There is adequate time to perform the sealed bidding process.

■ The award will be made on the basis of price and other price-related factors.

Without these conditions, the contracting officer must use negotiated procurement procedures (see Chapter 12). Price-related factors might include the costs or savings that could result from making multiple awards, taxes, inspection costs, and transportation differences. Sealed bidding procedures attempt to give all qualified contractors the opportunity to compete for government contracts while avoiding any favoritism.

THE SOLICITATION PROCESS

The sealed bidding process begins when a contracting officer publicizes a synopsis for a solicitation package, called an invitation for bid (IFB), in FedBizOpps. A synopsis briefly describes the desired products and services, and it is issued 15 days before the actual solicitation. Information about obtaining a copy of the solicitation is included in the synopsis. Most solicitations can be downloaded directly from the Internet.

Sealed Bidding (IFB) Process

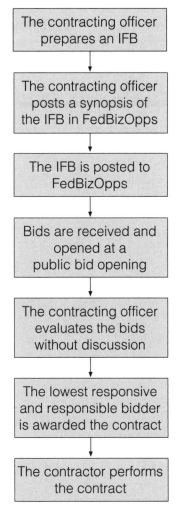

The contracting officer
prepares an IFB

↓

The contracting officer
posts a synopsis of
the IFB in FedBizOpps

↓

The IFB is posted to
FedBizOpps

↓

Bids are received and
opened at a
public bid opening

↓

The contracting officer
evaluates the bids
without discussion

↓

The lowest responsive
and responsible bidder
is awarded the contract

↓

The contractor performs
the contract

THE SEALED BIDDING (IFB) PROCESS

After the 15-day synopsis period, the contracting officer publicizes the actual IFB in FedBizOpps. The IFB contains everything a bidder must know to fulfill the contract, and it tends to be a sizable document. To be considered for an award, the bidder must agree to comply in all material respects of the IFB, at the bid price.

The IFB is divided into sections and subsections, and it includes a transmittal sheet and table of contents. The transmittal sheet usually shows the solicitation number, the items to be acquired, the contract period, and other pertinent information. Do not submit the transmittal sheet with your bid.

An IFB should always include the following information:

■ Description of supplies or services

■ Specifications or statement of work

■ Technical data

■ Packaging requirements

■ Inspection and acceptance criteria

■ Delivery or performance schedules

■ Deadline for submission of bids

■ Special contract requirements (if necessary).

The contracting officer must allow at least 30 days between the IFB's issuance and the bid opening, unless "Combined Synopsis/Solicitation" procedures are used. Sealed bidding always results in a fixed-price-type contract (see Chapter 14).

SOLICITATION METHODS

A contracting officer uses one of four formats in preparing an IFB: (1) Solicitation/Contract/Order for Commercial Items (SF 1449), (2) Combined Synopsis/Solicitation, (3) Uniform Contract Format (UCF), or (4) Simplified Contract Format (SCF).

Solicitation/Contract/Order for Commercial Items

Standard Form 1449 is typically used for purchases under this solicitation method. In fact, the contracting officer must use SF 1449 when:

■ The commercial items being acquired are expected to exceed the simplified acquisition threshold, which is $5.5 million for commercial items.

■ A paper solicitation or contract will be issued.

■ Procedures for Combined Synopsis/Solicitation are not being used.

Combined Synopsis/Solicitation

To reduce the time required to solicit and award commercial item contracts, the Combined Synopsis/Solicitation method is often used. It combines the synopsis and solicitation issuance into a single document. This format is being used more and more because it allows for greater flexibility in preparing and organizing the IFB. The combined synopsis/solicitation is appropriate only for a relatively simple acquisition.

When this method is used, there are no prescribed times specified between the publication of the synopsis and the issuance of the solicitation, nor is a time prescribed for how long the solicitation should remain open. The FAR only states that potential bidders should be afforded a reasonable opportunity to respond.

Uniform Contract Format

For most major purchases, the contracting officer uses the Uniform Contract Format (UCF). In fact, all IFBs for noncommercial products and services must use the UCF unless:

■ The simplified contract format is used.

SOLICITATION/CONTRACT/ORDER FOR COMMERCIAL ITEMS OFFEROR TO COMPLETE BLOCKS 12, 17, 23, 24, & 30				1. REQUISITION NO. 06-06PP00323		PAGE 1 OF 17
2. CONTRACT NO.	3. AWARD/EFFECTIVE DATE		4. ORDER NO.	5. SOLICITATION NO. DE-RP06-06PP00323		6. SOLICITATION ISSUE DATE 5/18/2008

7. FOR SOLICITATION INFORMATION CALL ▶

a. NAME Pat Thorn	b. TELEPHONE NO. *(No collect calls)* 202-426-8568	8. OFFER DUE DATE/LOCAL TIME 6/18/2008 5 pm

9. ISSUED BY   CODE MA-541

U.S. Department of Energy

HQ Procurement Services/MA-541

1000 Independence Ave., SW

Washington, DC 20585

10. THIS ACQUISITION IS
- ■ UNRESTRICTED
- ☐ SET ASIDE: ____ % FOR
- ☐ SMALL BUSINESS
- ☐ SMALL DISADV. BUSINESS
- ☐ 8(A)

NAICS: 517410
SIZE STD: 12.5 mil

11. DELIVERY FOR FOB DESTINATION UNLESS BLOCK IS MARKED
☐ SEE SCHEDULE

☐ 13a. THIS CONTRACT IS A RATED ORDER UNDER DPAS (15 CFR 700)
13b. RATING   N/A

14. METHOD OF SOLICITATION
☐ RFQ   ■ IFB   ☐ RFP

12. DISCOUNT TERMS

15. DELIVER TO   CODE

U.S. Department of Energy

16. ADMINISTERED BY   CODE

See Clause B.3

17a. CONTRACTOR/OFFEROR   CODE   FACILITY CODE

E-Watch, Inc.
401 West Peachtree St.
Atlanta, GA 30365
404-331-5159

☐ 17b. CHECK IF REMITTANCE IS DIFFERENT AND PUT SUCH ADDRESS IN OFFER

18a. PAYMENT WILL BE MADE BY   CODE

U.S. Department of Energy

18b. SUBMIT INVOICES TO ADDRESS SHOWN IN BLOCK 18a UNLESS BLOCK BELOW IS CHECKED   ☐ SEE ADDENDUM

19. ITEM NO.	20. SCHEDULE OF SUPPLIES/SERVICES	21. QUANTITY	22. UNIT	23. UNIT PRICE	24. AMOUNT
	See Clause B.5 and Statement of Work. Cable/Broadcast television and radio news/commentary monitoring service for energy-related news. *(Attach Additional Sheets as Necessary)*	See B.5	See B.5		

25. ACCOUNTING AND APPROPRIATION DATA	26. TOTAL AWARD AMOUNT *(For Govt. Use Only)*

■ 27a. SOLICITATION INCORPORATES BY REFERENCE FAR 52.212-1, 52.212-4. FAR 52.212-3 AND 52.212-5 ARE ATTACHED. ADDENDA ■ ARE ☐ ARE NOT ATTACHED.

☐ 27b. CONTRACT/PURCHASE ORDER INCORPORATES BY REFERENCE FAR 52.212-4. FAR 52.212-5 IS ATTACHED. ADDENDA ☐ ARE ☐ ARE NOT ATTACHED.

28. ■ CONTRACTOR IS REQUIRED TO SIGN THIS DOCUMENT AND RETURN ____ COPIES TO ISSUING OFFICE. CONTRACTOR AGREES TO FURNISH AND DELIVER ALL ITEMS SET FORTH OR OTHERWISE IDENTIFIED ABOVE AND ON ANY ADDITIONAL SHEETS SUBJECT TO THE TERMS AND CONDITIONS SPECIFIED HEREIN.	29. ☐ AWARD OF CONTRACT: REFERENCE ____ OFFER DATED ____. YOUR OFFER ON SOLICITATION (BLOCK 5), INCLUDING ANY ADDITIONS OR CHANGES WHICH ARE SET FORTH HEREIN, IS ACCEPTED AS TO ITEMS:

30a. SIGNATURE OF OFFEROR/CONTRACTOR	31a. UNITED STATES OF AMERICA *(SIGNATURE OF CONTRACTING OFFICER)*
30b. NAME AND TITLE OF SIGNER *(TYPE OR PRINT)*	30c. DATE SIGNED	31b. NAME OF CONTRACTING OFFICER *(TYPE OR PRINT)*	31c. DATE SIGNED

32a. QUANTITY IN COLUMN 21 HAS BEEN _____ ACCEPTED, AND CONFORMS TO THE ☐ RECEIVED ☐ INSPECTED ☐ CONTRACT, EXCEPT AS NOTED	33. SHIP NUMBER ☐ PARTIAL ☐ FINAL	34. VOUCHER NUMBER	35. AMOUNT VERIFIED CORRECT FOR
32b. SIGNATURE OF AUTHORIZED GOVT REPRESENTATIVE	32c. DATE	36. PAYMENT ☐ COMPLETE ☐ PARTIAL ☐ FINAL	37. CHECK NUMBER
		38. S/R ACCOUNT NO.	39. S/R VOUCHER NO.	40. PAID BY

41a. I CERTIFY THIS ACCOUNT IS CORRECT AND PROPER FOR PAYMENT		42a. RECEIVED BY *(Print)*
41b. SIGNATURE AND TITLE OF CERTIFYING OFFICER	41c. DATE	42b. RECEIVED AT *(Location)*
		42c. DATE REC'D *(YY/MM/DD)*	42d. TOTAL CONTAINERS

AUTHORIZED FOR LOCAL REPRODUCTION Computer Generated	SEE REVERSE FOR OMB CONTROL NUMBER AND PAPERWORK BURDEN STATEMENT	STANDARD FORM 1449 (10-95) Prescribed by GSA - FAR (48 CFR) 53.212

Sample SF 1449

■ The solicitation is for construction, shipbuilding, ship repairs and maintenance, architect/engineering services, or items that require special contract forms.

See Chapter 13 for more detailed information about the UCF.

Simplified Contract Format

Because an IFB uses only fixed-price contracts, a contracting officer is eligible to use the simplified contract format (SCF). The SCF should include the following information to the maximum practical extent:

■ *SF 1447, Solicitation/Contract.* SF 1447 is the cover page. It includes the solicitation number, the issue date, the contracting activity, and a place for the signature of the contractor and the contracting officer.

■ *Contract schedule.* The contract schedule includes the following: (1) contract line item number; (2) supplies or services description; (3) unit price and amount; (4) packaging requirements; (5) performance requirements; and (6) other information.

■ *Clauses.* The clauses include those required by the FAR and those considered necessary by the contracting officer.

■ *List of documents and attachments.*

■ *Representations and instructions.* These typically are divided into (1) representations and certifications; (2) instructions, conditions, and notices; and (3) award evaluation factors.

PREPARING YOUR BID

Responding to a solicitation requires considerable time and effort. Generally, the cost of preparing a winning proposal is 3% to 5 % of the contract's total dollar value. Prospective bidders should examine each solicitation carefully to decide whether preparing a bid is worth the effort.

SOLICITATION/CONTRACT BIDDER/OFFEROR TO COMPLETE BLOCKS 11, 13, 15, 21, 22 &27		1. THIS CONTRACT IS A RATED ORDER UNDER DPAS (15 CFR 350) N/A	RATING N/A	PAGE 1 OF 1

2. CONTRACT NO.	3. AWARD/EFFECTIVE DATE	4. SOLICITATION NUMBER DE-FB01-06AD66850	5. SOLICITATION TYPE [X] IFB [ ] RFP	6. SOLICITATION ISSUE DATE 11/10/08

7. ISSUED BY   CODE HR-541

U.S. Department of Energy
1000 Independence Ave., SW
Washington, DC 20585

8. THIS ACQUISITION IS:
[ ] UNRESTRICTED   [ ] LABOR SURPLUS AREA CONCERNS
                                    [ ] COMBINED SMALL BUSINESS &
[X] SET ASIDE: 100% FOR [ ] LABOR SURPLUS AREA CONCERNS
[X] SMALL BUSINESS   [ ] OTHER

NAICS: 561720   SIZE STANDARD: $ 14 Million

9. (AGENCY USE)

10. ITEMS TO BE PURCHASED (BRIEF DESCRIPTION)
[ ] SUPPLIES [X] SERVICES   Janitorial Services

11. IF OFFER IS ACCEPTED BY THE GOVT BY ____, THE CONTRACTOR AGREES TO HOLD ITS OFFERED PRICES FIRM FOR THE ITEMS SOLICITED HEREIN AND TO ACCEPT ANY RESULTING CONTRACT SUBJECT TO THE TERMS AND CONDITIONS STATED HEREIN.	12. ADMINISTERED BY CODE HR-541 U.S. Department of Energy 1000 Independence Ave., SW Washington, DC 20585
13. CONTRACTOR OFFEROR CODE: N/A FACILITY _____ Joe's Janitorial Services 1500 East Bannister Rd. Kansas City, MO 64131 TELEPHONE NO. (816) 926-7203 [ ] CHECK HERE IF REMITTANCE IS DIFFERENT & PUT ADDRESS IN OFFER	14. PAYMENT WILL BE MADE BY CODE CR-541-2 U.S. Department of Energy P.O. Box 500 Germantown, MD 20874 SUBMIT INVOICES TO ADDRESS SHOWN IN BLOCK 7
15. PROMPT PAYMENT DISCOUNT N/A	16. AUTHORITY FOR USING OTHER 10 USC 2304 41 USC 253 THAN FULL & OPEN COMPETITION [ ] (c) ( ) [ ] (c) ( )

17. ITEM NO.	18. SCHEDULE OF SUPPLIES/SERVICES	19. QUANTITY	20. UNIT	21. UNIT PRICE	22. AMOUNT
0001	Provide the U.S. Department of Energy with janitorial services in accordance with the Statement of Work found in Clause B.10 for the DOE Forrestal Complex and Child Development Center.				

23. ACCOUNTING AND APPROPRIATION DATA SEE SECTION G	24. TOTAL AWARD AMOUNT (FOR GOVT USE ONLY)

25. CONTRACTOR IS REQUIRED TO SIGN THIS DOCUMENT AND RETURN ALL COPIES TO ISSUING OFFICE. CONTRACTOR AGREES TO FURNISH AND DELIVER ALL ITEMS SET FORTH OR OTHERWISE IDENTIFIED ABOVE AND ON ANY CONTINUATION SHEETS SUBJECT TO THE TERMS AND CONDITIONS SPECIFIED HEREIN.	26. AWARD OF CONTRACT: YOUR OFFER ON SOLICITATION NUMBER SHOWN IN BLOCK 4 INCLUDING ANY ADDITIONS OR CHANGES WHICH ARE SET FORTH HEREIN, IS ACCEPTED AS TO ITEMS:
27. SIGNATURE OF OFFEROR/CONTRACTOR	28. UNITED STATES OF AMERICA (SIGNATURE OF CONTRACTING OFFICER

NAME AND TITLE OF SIGNER (TYPE OR PRINT)	DATE SIGNED	NAME OF CONTRACTING OFFICER	DATE SIGNED

NSN 7540-01-218-4366 Prescribed by GSA	1447-101	STANDARD FORM 1447 (5-88) FAR (48 CFR 53.215-1(g))

Sample SF 1447

If your company decides to bid, you should start to work on your bid immediately upon receipt of the IFB. This is particularly important if the contract is large or if you must obtain and read several documents before bidding. Carefully examine the IFB's specifications, including all instructions and clauses. Questions about the IFB should be directed to the contracting officer named in the solicitation. Make no assumptions without authorized clarification.

The solicitation package should indicate where to obtain essential specifications and standards. If it doesn't, the contracting officer will provide that information. Bidders must meet the requirements of all the documents cited in the package.

Once you have read the IFB and the required documentation carefully, you should prepare a work plan and a delivery schedule. The work plan should detail the time and material costs of fulfilling the contract—information you'll need in determining your bid price. The delivery schedule should detail distances to the locations to which you'll ship the products.

Some solicitations require bidders to submit a work plan and a delivery schedule as part of the offer. They might also require bidders to submit information about the company's financial stability and relevant experience. Your proposal must address performance and delivery at least equal to the IFB's minimum standards.

Bidders should not substitute items that they deem just as good as the specified items. A bid must meet the exact specifications called for in the bid request, or the bid may be declared nonresponsive. Because price is the primary evaluation factor in sealed bidding, it is to your advantage to determine the price that the government paid for similar supplies and services in the past. Among the best sources are past bids.

After a contracting activity issues an IFB, but before bid opening, it may make changes to the IFB. Typical changes involve quantities, specifications, delivery schedules, or opening dates. Such changes are made through an IFB amendment (SF 30, Amendment of Solicitation/ Modification of Contract).

Any amendments that a contracting officer makes to an IFB must be sent to each contractor that was sent a solicitation package. Upon submission of the IFB, bidders must acknowledge all issued amendments. Failure to do so may cause the bid to be declared nonresponsive.

Once you have completed your bid, review it for clarity, consistency, and accuracy. Compare your work plan, budget, and schedule to ensure that they agree. Double-check cost figures and computations to be sure that all information has been included.

If everything checks out, the next step is to submit your bid. Be sure to review the submission instructions and verify the address to which the bid should be sent to allow enough time to meet the deadline. Keep in mind that an IFB is a contractual document. If a prospective bidder submits an erroneous bid and is awarded a contract on that basis, the result could be little or no profit, or even serious financial loss.

LATE BIDS

If you receive a solicitation, the first thing to do is to note the date and time your bid is due. This is extremely important because the government will not accept bids that are even five seconds late.

This rule has a few exceptions. Late bids may be considered if the bid was:

- Mishandled by the government

- Sent by U.S. Postal Service Express Mail Next Day, no later than 5:00 P.M. at the place of mailing, two working days before the bid opening date

- Sent by registered or certified mail, postmarked no later than the fifth calendar day before the deadline

■ Sent electronically and received by the government no later than 5:00 P.M. one working day before the bid opening date

■ The only offer received.

The government may also, at any time, consider late modifications to an otherwise successful bid that make its terms more favorable to the government.

If hand delivering the bid, be sure that you include the room number and meet any other special requirements for hand delivery. Security concerns can delay hand delivery of a bid, so be sure to allow extra time or use a bonded courier. When a bid is received late and it cannot be considered, the government notifies the bidder and holds the bid unopened.

BID OPENING

All bids in response to an IFB are secured until the bid opening, which takes place in a public location at the time specified on the IFB. Anyone may attend a bid opening. At the time designated for opening, a bid opening officer publicly opens all unclassified bids.

A bidder may withdraw its bid at any time before the bid opening date. Once the bids have been opened, the contracting officer will allow withdrawals or corrections to bids only if the bidder substantiates a mistake, the manner in which it occurred, and the intended bid. An obvious clerical error, for example, may be corrected and the bid considered with the other offers if the contractor verifies the error and the intended bid.

BID EVALUATIONS

A bid opening officer, who is usually not the contracting officer, opens, announces, and records all the bids. They are recorded on a form called an *abstract of bids*. Interested parties may examine the bids at the time of recording but will be denied access to financial and other proprietary information of the bidders. Following the recording, the bid opening officer reveals the results to the contracting officer.

The contracting officer evaluates the bids, considering such items as price, options, economic price adjustments, transportation costs, and other areas controlled by regulations. Discounts, such as prompt payment discounts (see Chapter 17), are not considered during the evaluation of bids. Any discount that the bidder offers, however, becomes part of the contract award.

To be eligible for the award, the bidder must be both "responsive" and "responsible."

■ To be *responsive*, the otherwise successful bidder must not have taken exception to the IFB's specifications, work statement, or other terms. A bid usually will be rejected as nonresponsive if its prices are subject to change without notice.

■ To be *responsible*, the otherwise successful bidder must be able to produce the products or services, meet the delivery schedule, follow the terms and conditions, and have adequate financial capabilities.

The contracting officer uses the following "pre-award survey" to determine whether a bidder is both responsive and responsible:

■ Does the bidder have adequate financial resources to perform the contract or the ability to obtain them?

■ Can the bidder comply with the proposed delivery or performance schedule, considering all existing business commitments?

■ Does the bidder have a satisfactory performance record?

■ Does the bidder have a satisfactory record of integrity and business ethics?

■ Does the bidder have the necessary organization, experience, accounting controls, and technical skills?

■ Does the bidder have the necessary production, construction, technical equipment, and facilities?

■ Is the bidder qualified and eligible to receive an award under the applicable laws and regulations?

The pre-award survey may be informal or formal. The informal pre-award survey includes a review of the bidder's capabilities, performance records, and previous contracts and/or phone inquiries of previous customers. The informal survey typically is used for small and straightforward contracts.

The formal pre-award survey, on the other hand, involves the assistance of another federal agency, the Defense Contract Management Command (DCMC). DCMC is the contract administration branch of the Defense Logistics Agency. The contracting officer may ask DCMC to review all or some of the following items: technical capabilities, production capacity, quality assurance procedures, financial capability, transportation, security, environmental considerations, and any other areas of concern. Formal procedures typically are used for large contracts that involve a significant number of products or services.

If the apparent low or otherwise successful bidder is determined to be nonresponsive or nonresponsible and it is a small business, the findings must be referred to SBA for further investigation. SBA then performs its own investigation to determine whether the small business can perform the contract.

If SBA determines that the small business is competent, it issues a Certificate of Competency, which binds the contracting officer for that particular procurement (see Chapter 4).

BID AWARD

The lowest bidder that meets the IFB's evaluation criteria is awarded the contract. Each bidder must keep its bid open (or available) during the evaluation period. The contracting officer conducts these procedures based strictly on the sealed bids. There are no discussions with the bidders. When two or more equal low bids are received, the contract is awarded in the following order:

1. To a small business that is also in a Historically Underutilized Business Zone (HUBZone)

2. To another small business

3. To a business in a labor surplus area

4. To another business.

The contracting officer may reject all bids received if he or she believes that this action is in the government's best interest. For example, if the bids were submitted in bad faith or were calculated in collusion by the bidders, the contracting officer may reject them.

Finally, the successful bidder receives a properly executed award document, or Notice of Award (NOA). The NOA has no specified format, but it should include the contract number, the contract's effective date, the authorized funding, the initial tasks that the bidder will perform, and the contracting officer's approval (or signature). An NOA serves as the bidder's go-ahead.

The contracting officer notifies the unsuccessful bidders in writing or orally, usually within three days of contract award. If an unsuccessful bidder requests additional information, the government must provide the:

- Successful bidder's name and address

- Contract price

- Location of the abstract of bids that may be inspected.

Contracting officers must consider all contract award protests or objections, whether received before or after the award is issued. If a written protest is received, the contracting officer will not award the contract until the matter is resolved, unless the items being procured are urgent or the performance will be unduly delayed by failure to make the award promptly.

TWO-STEP SEALED BIDDING

Two-step sealed bidding combines sealed bidding procedures with negotiated procurements. This approach is designed to obtain the benefits of sealed bidding when adequate specifications are unavailable. It is especially useful for complex acquisitions requiring technical proposals.

The government uses two-step sealed bidding under the following conditions:

▪ The contracting officer can define the criteria for evaluating technical proposals.

▪ More than one technically qualified source is expected to bid.

▪ Sufficient time is available to apply the two-step method.

▪ A fixed-price-type contract will be used.

This solicitation method is more flexible than the IFB because it allows discussions to occur during step one, while maintaining the integrity of the bidding process in step two. Government personnel need to be well educated in this process to ensure that information does not leak inadvertently among vendors. The two-step sealed bidding method typically requires a long-term effort, usually several months.

Step One

During step one, each bidder submits a technical proposal describing its offered supplies or services, along with an explanation of its proposed approach. The solicitation document for this technical proposal is usually called a request for technical proposals (RFTP). No pricing is involved during this stage. Step one helps clarify the solicitation's technical requirements.

The RFTP includes:

■ A description of the supplies or services to be provided.

■ The technical proposal's requirements and evaluation criteria.

■ A statement that the technical proposal will not include prices or pricing information.

■ The date and time by which the proposals must be received.

■ A statement that, in the second step, only bids based on technical proposals determined to be acceptable will be considered for awards.

Any proposal that modifies or fails to conform to the essential requirements or specifications of the RFTP is considered nonresponsive and is categorized as unacceptable.

Step Two

Step two uses conventional sealed bidding procedures. However, the government issues IFBs only to those bidders that submitted adequate technical proposals in step one. Bidders submit a price, and the contracting officer evaluates those bids.

Step two is not synopsized in FedBizOpps or publicly posted as a new acquisition opportunity. FedBizOpps, however, lists bidders that submitted acceptable proposals in step one for the benefit of prospective subcontractors. Despite the use of negotiated procedures in step one, this method is still considered sealed bidding.

■ . ■   ■

Sealed bidding is perceived to be the fairest procurement method because it involves a public bid opening during which all prices and proposals are revealed and the contract is awarded based on the lowest overall cost. In general, the IFB allows for a shorter solicitation process, a fast evaluation, and a quick award at the lowest price.

The use of sealed bidding procedures requires the government to clearly articulate its product specifications. The government is less likely to procure state-of-the-art products because bidders can solicit older models that meet the specifications at a lower price than newer technology. The government must accept the low bid. Technical superiority and extra features cannot be evaluated.

■   ■   ■

12 Negotiated Procurements

© 1999 Randy Glasbergen.

GLASBERGEN

"Lemont is our finest negotiator. Perhaps you've read his book, *The Art of Pouting.*"

What's in this chapter?

- Exchanges with industry before proposal receipt
- Presolicitation notices
- The solicitation process
- Preparing your proposal
- Oral presentations
- Late proposals
- Proposal evaluation
- Source selection processes and techniques
- Changes and discussions
- Final proposal revision and award
- Debriefings
- Protests

When it is desirable to consider the technical superiority of a contractor's products or services, the federal government uses negotiated procurement procedures. Unlike sealed bidding procedures, negotiated procurements permit bargaining and discussions with offerors before making a final source selection. It is the federal government's most flexible acquisition method, but it is also the most complicated.

Negotiated procurement procedures take many forms. They may call for competitive proposals, involve restricted competition, or even be sole source. Eighty percent of the contracts that exceed the simplified acquisition threshold of $100,000 use negotiated procedures. They are frequently used for R&D projects, for which each contractor takes a different approach to meet the government's needs.

A request for proposal (RFP) is the solicitation document issued under negotiated procurement procedures. It contains the information necessary for prospective contractors to prepare proposals. A *bid set* includes all the documents that make up the RFP, including technical and cost matters.

The RFP, like an invitation for bid (IFB), is a request for an offer. A contractor's response to an RFP represents an offer, which the government may accept without change or negotiation, resulting in a binding contract. The solicitation, however, must state whether proposals will be evaluated and awarded (1) after discussions with offerors or (2) without discussions with offerors.

If the contracting officer intends to enter into discussions, he or she must conduct written or oral discussions with all responsible offerors that submit proposals within the competitive range. Price, technical requirements, performance, terms and conditions, and delivery schedules are all open to negotiation. During discussions, the contracting officer may also decide that the government's best interests might be better served by a contract that is significantly different from the original solicitation.

When a contracting officer uses negotiated procedures, the following conditions should be met:

■ The contract complies with federal regulations.

■ The contract gives the winning contractor incentive to perform the contract on time and at the lowest possible cost to the government.

■ The contract price is fair and reasonable.

EXCHANGES WITH INDUSTRY BEFORE PROPOSAL RECEIPT

The government encourages information exchanges among interested parties, from the earliest identification of a requirement through proposal receipt. These exchanges attempt to improve the understanding of government requirements and industry capabilities, thereby allowing potential offerors to determine whether or how to satisfy the requirements. Acquisition strategy, such as the proposed contract type and the feasibility of requirements, may also be addressed during the exchanges.

Interested parties typically include potential offerors, end users, acquisition personnel (such as the program manager), and others involved in the outcome of the procurement. The exchanges must be consistent with procurement integrity requirements. Some techniques that the government might use to promote these early exchanges include:

■ Industry or small business conferences.

■ Public hearings.

■ Market research.

■ One-on-one meetings with potential offerors.

■ Presolicitation notices.

■ Draft RFPs.

■ Requests for information (RFI), which may be used when the government currently does not intend to award a contract but wants market information for planning purposes. (RFI never result in a binding contract.)

■ Presolicitation or preproposal conferences.

■ Site visits.

Active participation in these early exchanges will give you a great head start on your competition. Once the solicitation is issued or released, the contracting officer will be the focal point of exchanges among potential offerors.

PRESOLICITATION NOTICES

Buying offices invite potential offerors to provide feedback on a presolicitation notice, thus allowing acquisition officials to identify and evaluate viable contractors. At a minimum, the presolicitation notice contains sufficient information to permit potential contractors to determine whether to participate in the acquisition. Federal agencies evaluate each response based on the criteria stated in the notice.

A presolicitation notice might request information on proposed technical concepts or might be limited to a statement of qualifications. Federal agencies notify the respondents in writing if they are invited to participate in the resultant acquisition or if, based on the information submitted, they are unlikely to be viable competitors.

THE SOLICITATION PROCESS

The process of negotiation starts in a way that is similar to sealed bidding. The contracting officer publishes a synopsis of an RFP in FedBizOpps 15 days before issuing the solicitation. After this 15-day period, the actual

RFP is published in FedBizOpps. If necessary, the contracting officer may hold a preproposal conference. (A preproposal conference is a briefing held by the contracting officer to explain complicated specifications and requirements to prospective offerors.)

Negotiated (RFP) Process

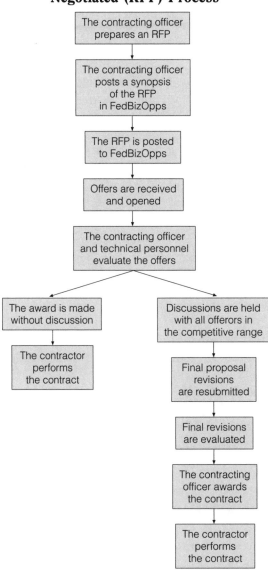

Solicitation Methods

The contracting officer uses one of the following formats to prepare RFPs:

- Solicitation/Contract/Order for Commercial Items (SF 1449)

- Uniform Contract Format (SF 33) (see Chapter 13)

- Simplified Contract Format (SF 1447).

At first glance, these solicitation methods look identical to those used for IFBs. Differences between IFBs and RFPs include the solicitation provisions, proposal preparation instructions, and evaluation factors. The quickest way to differentiate between them is to look at Block 4 of SF 33, Block 5 of SF 1447, or Block 14 of SF 1449 (see Chapter 11 and Chapter 13 for copies of these forms).

RFP Requirements

At a minimum, RFPs for competitive acquisitions must provide:

- The government's requirements.

- The contract's anticipated terms and conditions. (The solicitation may authorize offerors to propose alternative terms and conditions.)

- Information required for the offeror's proposal.

- Factors and significant subfactors that will be used to evaluate the proposal and their relative importance.

PREPARING YOUR PROPOSAL

Evaluation factors tell potential offerors what considerations will be used to evaluate and grade proposals compared to the requirements set forth in the statement of work (SOW). Price is always an evaluation factor in any source selection. Other evaluation factors may include:

■ Technical requirements

■ Management capabilities

■ Relevant experience and past performance.

The contracting officer tailors the evaluation factors to each acquisition's characteristics and requirements. This includes applying a relative order of importance or weight to the factors. Selected factors enable the contracting officer to determine, based on the proposal submitted, how well the offeror understands—and the degree to which the offeror could successfully meet—the RFP's requirements.

Cost/Price Proposal

Offerors develop cost and pricing data to convince the government purchaser of the reasonableness of their proposed costs. Cost and pricing data include estimates of the expected costs of performance and the offeror's expected profit or fee (i.e., cost + profit = total price). The cost/price evaluation criteria differ for fixed-price, incentive, and cost-reimbursement contracts. Part 5 of this book details the various contract types.

For a fixed-price contract, the offeror's total proposed price is the main evaluation factor. Incentive contracts, on the other hand, are structured and evaluated as a package of cost factors, including target cost, share ratio, ceiling price, or maximum/minimum fee. Finally, cost-reimbursement contracts require federal agencies to use estimates of expected costs (plus a fee or profit) to measure the cost realism of the proposed contract costs. The RFP states the contract type to be awarded and its applicable terms.

Cost/price evaluation factors include:

■ Proposed cost/price completeness

■ Proposed cost/price reasonableness

■ Proposed cost/price realism

■ Cost/price risk assessment.

Note: When an award is based on adequate price competition, the cost/price proposal may not be required.

Technical Proposal

The primary purpose of the technical proposal is to assure the government that you possess the know-how and resources to perform the contract requirements. The RFP details specific technical criteria that your proposal must meet. Technical proposals are generally prepared according to the Instructions to Offerors (section L) of the Uniform Contract Format (see Chapter 13).

In large, technically complex procurements, a representative from an agency's technical and operational areas might help develop the factors for award. In many cases, the technical proposal is the most significant evaluation factor. Technical evaluation factors might include:

■ Soundness of proposed technical approach

■ Innovativeness of proposed technical approach

■ Requirement compliance

■ Requirement understanding

■ Key personnel or other resources

■ Available facilities

■ Technical risk assessment.

Federal specifications and standards are a prescribed set of rules, conditions, and requirements established to achieve uniformity in materials and products. They specify performance requirements and the quality and construction of materials and equipment needed to produce acceptable goods. The General Services Administration (GSA) issues and controls federal specifications, which all federal agencies must use. The technical proposal may cover the RFP's management aspects, or the contracting activity may require separate technical and management proposals.

Management Proposal

A management proposal explains how the contractor intends to manage the proposed program if awarded the contract. The key element here is the description of your type of management. Specifically, your management proposal should explain the organizational structure, management capability, company controls, and assignment of key personnel to the contract. If you do not intend to form a specific management group, describe your overall operation method.

A management proposal is evaluated based on:

■ Soundness of the proposed management plan

■ Corporate resources for overseeing and performing the work

■ Logical, timely pursuit of work schedules

■ Quality plan

■ Management risk.

Developing the factors and determining their relative importance should be the joint responsibility of the requiring organization's contracting officer and the program manager or technical representative. Ideally, the evaluation factors should be developed as early as possible in the acquisition's planning phase.

ORAL PRESENTATIONS

To enhance or substitute portions of the written proposal, the government may request that offerors perform oral presentations. They may occur at any time during the acquisition process and are subject to the same restrictions as written information regarding timing and content. Oral presentations provide an opportunity for dialogue between the parties.

The solicitation may also require that offerors submit part of their proposals orally. The offeror's capabilities, past performance, work plans or approaches, staffing resources, and transition plans are all suitable topics. Substituting oral presentations for portions of a proposal streamlines the source-selection process.

Unless the RFP requires it, offerors do not have to discuss confidential information, such as technical approaches, during their oral presentations. Instead, offerors may provide the government with a written description of their planned approach for carrying out the work upon the completion of their presentation. Prerecorded videotaped presentations that lack real-time interactive dialogue are not considered oral presentations, although they may be included in an offeror's submission when appropriate.

When a solicitation calls for oral presentations, it describes:

- Types of information to be presented orally and the associated evaluation factors

- Qualifications of the personnel who will give the oral presentation

- Requirements for, and any limitations on, written material or other media to supplement the oral presentations

■ The oral presentation's location, date, and time

■ Time restrictions for each presentation

■ The scope and content of exchanges that may occur between the parties during the presentation, including whether discussions will be
permitted.

The contracting officer maintains records of the oral presentations and
documents the evaluation factors for the source-selection decision. The
source-selection authority determines the method and level of detail of
this record (e.g., videotaping, audiotape recording, written records).

LATE PROPOSALS

Negotiated procurement procedures have no formal public bid opening,
as with sealed bidding, but you must submit your proposal by the date
and time stated on the RFP, the closing date. Late proposals will be considered only if:

■ The government mishandled the proposal.

■ You sent the proposal by U.S. Postal Service Express Mail Next-Day no
later than 5:00 P.M. at the place of mailing, two working days before the
proposal opening date.

■ You sent the proposal by registered or certified mail, postmarked no
later than the fifth calendar day before the deadline.

■ You sent the proposal electronically and the government received it no
later than 5:00 P.M. one working day before the proposal closing date.

■ Only one proposal is received.

The government will also consider, at any time, late modifications to an
otherwise successful proposal that make the proposal's terms more favorable to the government. If you hand deliver the proposal, make sure you

have the right room number and meet any other special requirements for
hand delivery.

PROPOSAL EVALUATION

The time the government takes to perform an evaluation depends on the
number of proposals received and the complexity of the items being evaluated. The process of selecting the winning contractor is called *source selection*. The purpose of source selection is to select the contractor whose
proposal has the highest degree of credibility and whose performance is
expected to best meet the government's needs at a reasonable price.

The selection process must be fair and reflect a comprehensive evaluation
of each submitted proposal. Throughout the evaluation process, the contracting officer is designated as the source selection authority (SSA) and
the government's exclusive agent with the authority to enter into and
administer contracts. Price is always an evaluation factor in any source
selection.

The selection process typically includes the evaluation of technical and
cost/price proposals, negotiations between the various parties, and preparation and selection of a best and final offer. When certain evaluation factors affect the selection decision more than others, the solicitation should
clearly identify the weight of the factors and how the final scoring will be
done. It is the responsibility of the offerors to understand the basis on
which their proposals will be evaluated and how best to prepare them.

Contracting officers evaluate past performance in all RFPs that are
expected to exceed $100,000. Your past performance helps indicate your
ability to perform the contract requirements for which you submitted
your proposal. The RFP allows you to provide references for similar contracts you provided. Contractors that lack relevant past performance
information receive a neutral evaluation.

Technical proposals should not contain a total price reference; that way,
price doesn't influence the technical evaluation. They should, however,
include resource information, such as labor hours and categories, materi-

als, and subcontracts, so that the offeror's understanding of the scope of work can be evaluated. Technical representatives/personnel are often used to help evaluate technical proposals.

RFPs are not opened publicly, so the competitive position of the various offerors is not disclosed.

SOURCE SELECTION PROCESSES AND TECHNIQUES

The following are some of the more common acquisition processes and techniques.

Best Value Continuum

In negotiated acquisitions the contracting officer looks for the best over-all value to the government. If the contract requirements are clearly definable and the risk of unsuccessful performance is minimal, price dominates the source selection. When successful contract performance is less certain and more development work is required, technical and past performance considerations might play a more important role. The solicitation should clearly identify the source-selection factors.

Tradeoff Process

If simply comparing the prices of proposals that meet the solicitation's requirements will not result in the best value to government, a tradeoff process should be used. The tradeoff process gives the source-selection authority the flexibility to select the offer providing the best value, which might not be the lowest price or the highest technically rated offeror. This tradeoff must be consistent with the RFP.

The tradeoff process is appropriate where the government's requirements are difficult to define or complex. The perceived benefits of additional cost must merit a higher priced proposal, and the rationale for tradeoffs must be documented.

Technically Acceptable Low Dollar Process

The lowest priced, technically acceptable source-selection process is appropriate when the best value to the government is expected to result from selecting the technically acceptable proposal with the lowest evaluated price. For this method, the following requirements apply:

■ The solicitation must set forth the evaluation factors and significant subfactors that establish the requirements of acceptability.

■ Tradeoffs are not permitted.

■ Proposals are evaluated for acceptability but not ranked using the non-price factors.

CHANGES AND DISCUSSIONS

Unlike sealed bidding, negotiated procedures allow offerors to propose changes to the RFP's terms and conditions. It is common for offerors to propose changes to the statement of work, recommend alternative delivery schedules, or even suggest a different product or service. If, for example, a buying office issues a solicitation for red widgets, the offeror, for whatever reason, could submit a proposal for blue widgets.

The contracting officer must consider the proposal as long as it conforms to the material aspects of the RFP. In proposing changes to the RFP, however, you take the chance that the government will award the contract without discussion to a competitor.

When discussions are necessary, the regulations require the contracting officer to conduct written or oral discussions with all responsible offerors in the competitive range. Discussions may be as specific as pointing out particular proposal problems or as broad as complete negotiations. Information about competing proposals may not be disclosed during the discussions.

The competitive range consists of offerors that have a reasonable chance of winning the contract, based on the initial proposal evaluation. Such considerations include:

■ Strengths and weaknesses of each technical proposal

■ Past performance

■ The proposed price

■ Offeror's understanding of the contract requirements

■ Management proposal (if applicable) and any other special requirements of the RFP.

Offerors outside the competitive range are eliminated from further consideration.

FINAL PROPOSAL REVISION AND AWARD

At the conclusion of the discussions, the offerors that are still within the competitive range receive an opportunity to revise their proposals. The government then notifies all offerors to submit their final proposal revision (previously called the best and final offer) by a certain time and date. A final proposal revision is, in effect, an opportunity to enhance your proposal. Be sure to submit your final proposal revision on time.

A contracting officer will not reopen discussions with contractors after receiving the final proposal revisions unless it benefits the government. For example, additional discussions would be necessary if it is clear to the contracting officer that the final proposal revisions received are inadequate to justify contractor selection and award.

The final source selection (or contract award) is based on the content of the final proposal revisions. Just as in sealed bidding, however, an offeror must be deemed "responsible" to receive the contract (see Bid Evaluations, Chapter 11). The contract is usually awarded in one of three ways:

- By sending the successful offeror a copy of the award contract. (If SF 33, Solicitation, Offer and Award [see Chapter 13], is used as the cover sheet for the RFP, the contracting officer would complete and sign the award section of this form.)

- By notifying the successful offeror by phone with written confirmation.

- By notifying the successful offeror by letter.

The contracting officer usually notifies unsuccessful offerors within three business days of contract award.

Sealed Bidding versus Negotiated Procedures		
Characteristics	**Sealed Bidding**	**Negotiated Procedures**
Initial solicitation document	IFB	RFP
Response (offer)	Bid	Proposal
Specification or requirements	Must be precise	Less precise (discussions allowed)
Minimum prospective bidders	Two	May be sole source
Amendments to solicitation after closing	Not allowed	Allowed

Selection criteria	Lowest bidder	Award is made in accordance with the stated evaluation criteria
Types of contracts (see Part 5)	Fixed-price only	Fixed-price or cost-reimbursement may be used

DEBRIEFINGS

Once the contract is awarded, unsuccessful offerors may request a debriefing with the acquisition officials. During a debriefing the contracting officer, along with other government personnel involved in the evaluation, discusses with the unsuccessful offeror why its proposal was not chosen for award. The debriefing should occur within five days after receipt of the written request. (Debriefings are conducted with only one offeror at a time.)

Successful offerors can also request a debriefing and I encourage it. Why? Because if you're the winner, it's valuable information to know what you did right and for future proposal submissions, what you could have done to improve your proposal.

As part of the discussions, the contracting officer may provide details on the number of offers solicited and received, the name and address of each firm receiving an award, the quantities and prices of each award, and (in general terms) the reasons their proposals were not accepted. Offerors excluded from the competitive range during the evaluation process may also request a preaward debriefing.

The debriefing should foster an open, nonadversarial environment. Please use this opportunity to learn what did and didn't work with your proposal! At a minimum, the debriefing should provide:

■ Government's evaluation of the significant strengths and weaknesses of the offeror's proposal

- Overall evaluated price and technical rating, if applicable, of the successful offeror

- Overall ranking of all offerors

- Summary of the rationale for award

- For acquisitions of commercial items, a description of the make and model of the item to be delivered by the successful offeror

- Reasonable responses to concerns about source-selection procedures and applicable regulations.

The contracting officer will not provide point-by-point comparisons of the proposals. Also, the debriefing should not disclose proprietary information about other offerors, including:

- Trade secrets and confidential manufacturing processes and techniques

- Confidential financial information

- The names of individuals who provided past performance information.

Don't expect to be completely satisfied with the debriefing results. Debriefings tend to be ineffective because government evaluators are naturally inhibited by the fear of triggering a protest. Briefings that clearly explain the SSA's rationale for the source selection decision mitigate the possibility of protests.

PROTESTS

Protests are written objections by interested parties to a solicitation, proposed award, or award of a contract. Interested parties include actual or prospective offerors whose direct economic interest would be affected by the award of or failure to award a particular contract.

The contracting officer must consider all protests, whether submitted before or after contract award. Successful protests can change a planned award, cause cancellation of an award already made, require reimbursement to the protester of the cost of the protest or the bid preparation effort, or result in some combination of these outcomes. Protests are usually initiated by filing a written protest with the Government Accountability Office (GAO).

A protest may also be filed directly with the contracting activity or, in some cases, the U.S. Claims Court. Protests should be filed no later than ten days after the date on which the basis for the protest was known or should have been known.

Once a protest has been filed, the protester must provide a copy of it to the contracting officer no later than the next day. GAO's Office of General Counsel then requests a report on the matter from the contracting officer. When this report is received, a copy is provided to the protester, who is given the opportunity to comment.

Many times, GAO holds an informal conference to give the contractor an opportunity to present its views. GAO then considers the facts and issues raised by the protest and adjudicates a decision in the name of the Comptroller General. Decisions are usually made within 100 days of initial receipt of the protest.

Both the protester and the contracting officer receive a copy of the decision. If a protester disagrees with the GAO's decision, it may appeal the decision to the federal district court. If the protester disagrees with that decision, it may appeal the matter all the way to the Supreme Court. FAR 33.1 provides detailed information on protests.

In government contracting, protests are par for the course. Sooner or later, you will probably have to file a protest. If you feel you have a valid claim, do whatever it takes to protect your interests.

■   ■   ■

Negotiated procurement procedures enable the government to evaluate desirable features and technical superiority. RFPs allow the government and industry to correct errors in understanding and specifications by permitting discussions and negotiations.

On the down side, RFPs usually require a long-term effort. Vendors often learn who their competitors are. Multiple final proposal revisions tend to erode the integrity of the procurement process.

■   ■   ■

13 The Uniform Contract Format

© 1997 Randy Glasbergen.

"I haven't read your proposal yet, Bob,
but I already have some great ideas
on how to improve it."

What's in this chapter?

- Part I: The schedule
- Part II: Contract clauses
- Part III: List of documents, exhibits, and other attachments
- Part IV: Representations and instructions
- Amendments to the solicitation
- Typical proposal weaknesses
- Procurement instrument identification numbers
- Unsolicited proposals
- Contingent fees

The Uniform Contract Format (UCF) is a blank solicitation package that the contracting officer sends out to prospective contractors. It is the most common solicitation format used by the federal government. During FY2006, the federal government issued the UCF for more than 100,000 solicitations. It is used for both invitations for bid (IFBs) and requests for proposal (RFPs). A completed solicitation package can be anywhere from 20 to 10,000 pages in length, depending on the complexity of the procurement.

Prospective contractors tend to be intimidated by the sheer volume or size of the UCF. Don't be! Once you become familiar with the UCF's organization, you will be able to anticipate and understand its content. Careful attention to the entire solicitation package is crucial to your success.

The four parts and 13 sections of the UCF are shown below.

Uniform Contract Format

Part I—The Schedule

Section A	Solicitation/contract form
Section B	Supplies or services and prices/costs
Section C	Description/specifications/statement of work
Section D	Packaging and marking
Section E	Inspection and acceptance
Section F	Deliveries or performance
Section G	Contract administration data
Section H	Special contract requirements

Part II—Contract Clauses

Section I	Contract clauses

Part III—List of Documents, Exhibits, and Other Attachments

Section J	List of attachments

Part IV—Representations and Instructions

Section K	Representations, certifications, and other statements of offerors or respondents
Section L	Instructions, conditions, and notices to offerors or respondents
Section M	Evaluation factors for award

The UCF may not be used for the following acquisitions:

■ Construction and architect-engineering contracts

■ Shipbuilding, ship overhaul, and ship repair

■ Subsistence contracts

■ Product or service contracts requiring special contract formats

■ Letter requests for proposals

■ Contracts exempted by the agency head

■ Firm-fixed-price or fixed-price with economic price adjustment acquisitions that use the simplified contract format.

Contracting officers are encouraged to use the UCF to the maximum extent practicable. One of its primary benefits is that it ensures that the same general information appears in the same order in most federal solicitations. This familiar format enables the reader to focus on the proposal's content rather than its form. Federal agencies must ensure that the various sections of the solicitation are in agreement.

Any section of the UCF that does not apply to the particular solicitation may be deleted. Part IV, Representations and Instructions, is usually not included in the resulting contract, but the contracting officer retains it in the contract file. Each solicitation package includes all the necessary forms, along with the date and time proposals must be received.

PART I: THE SCHEDULE

The purpose of the schedule is to explain the products or services being acquired, along with contractual requirements and specifications. The schedule provides details on the items being solicited; technical information about production, packaging, delivery, and inspection; and other information necessary to meet the contract requirements.

Section A—Solicitation/Contract Form

Standard Form 33 (SF 33), Solicitation, Offer, and Award, is typically the first page and serves as the cover sheet of the solicitation package. It contains information about the time and place at which offerors should submit proposals. It also itemizes a table of required contents that each offeror must provide.

The offer section of this form, which the offeror completes, constitutes a legally binding offer. The award section is completed by the contracting officer after making the source selection or award decision. Once the contractor receives this signed solicitation package, the package becomes an executed contract.

If the contracting officer does not use SF 33, the cover sheet of the UCF must include the following:

■ Name, address, and location of issuing activity (including room and building where proposals must be submitted)

■ Solicitation type

■ Solicitation number (each federal agency uses its own contract numbering system)

■ Issuance date

■ Closing date and time

■ Number of pages

■ Requisition or other purchase authority

■ Brief description of item or service

■ Requirement for the offeror to provide its name and complete address

■ Offer expiration date.

SOLICITATION, OFFER AND AWARD	1. THIS CONTRACT IS A RATED ORDER UNDER DPAS (15 CFR 700)		RATING	PAGE OF PAGES

2. CONTRACT NUMBER	3. SOLICITATION NUMBER	4. TYPE OF SOLICITATION	5. DATE ISSUED	6. REQUISITION/PURCHASE NUMBER
DE-AC06-98FD00036	DE-RP06-98FD00036	[X] SEALED BID (IFB) [ ] NEGOTIATED (RFP)	3/17/08	01-98FD00036.000

7. ISSUED BY	CODE HR-541	8. ADDRESS OFFER TO (If other than Item 7)
U.S. Department of Energy 1000 Independence Ave., SW Washington, DC 20585		

NOTE: In sealed bid solicitations "offer" and "offeror" mean "bid" and "bidder".

SOLICITATION

9. Sealed offers in original and   2   copies for furnishing the supplies or services in the Schedule will be received at the place specified in Item 8, or if handcarried, in the depository located in Room 505, Building A until 04:30 local time 6/15/08

(Hour)   *(Date)*

CAUTION - LATE Submissions, Modifications, and Withdrawals: See Section L, Provision No. 52.214-7 or 52.215-1. All offers are subject to all terms and conditions contained in this solicitation.

10. FOR INFORMATION CALL:	A. NAME	B. TELEPHONE (NO COLLECT CALLS)			C. E-MAIL ADDRESS
	Sam Mills, Contract Officer	AREA CODE 202	NUMBER 426-0150	EXT.	

11. TABLE OF CONTENTS

(X)	SEC.	DESCRIPTION	PAGE(S)	(X)	SEC.	DESCRIPTION	PAGE(S)
		PART I - THE SCHEDULE				PART II - CONTRACT CLAUSES	
X	A	SOLICITATION/CONTRACT FORM	1	X	I	CONTRACT CLAUSES	52-62
X	B	SUPPLIES OR SERVICES AND PRICES/COSTS	2-20			PART III - LIST OF DOCUMENTS, EXHIBITS AND OTHER ATTACH.	
X	C	DESCRIPTION/SPECS./WORK STATEMENT	21-28	X	J	LIST OF ATTACHMENTS	63
X	D	PACKAGING AND MARKING	29			PART IV - REPRESENTATIONS AND INSTRUCTIONS	
X	E	INSPECTION AND ACCEPTANCE	30-31	X	K	REPRESENTATIONS, CERTIFICATIONS AND OTHER STATEMENTS OF OFFERORS	64-80
X	F	DELIVERIES OR PERFORMANCE	32				
X	G	CONTRACT ADMINISTRATION DATA	33-36	X	L	INSTRS., CONDS., AND NOTICES TO OFFERORS	81-95
X	H	SPECIAL CONTRACT REQUIREMENTS	37-51	X	M	EVALUATION FACTORS FOR AWARD	96-98

OFFER (Must be fully completed by offeror)

NOTE: Item 12 does not apply if the solicitation includes the provisions at 52.214-16, Minimum Bid Acceptance Period.

12. In compliance with the above, the undersigned agrees, if this offer is accepted within _____ calendar days (60 calendar days unless a different period is inserted by the offeror) from the date for receipt of offers specified above, to furnish any or all items upon which prices are offered at the price set opposite each item, delivered at the designated point(s), within the time specified in the schedule.

13. DISCOUNT FOR PROMPT PAYMENT (See Section I, Clause No. 52.232-8)	10 CALENDAR DAYS (%)	20 CALENDAR DAYS (%)	30 CALENDAR DAYS (%)	CALENDAR DAYS (%)

14. ACKNOWLEDGMENT OF AMENDMENTS (The offeror acknowledges receipt of amendments to the SOLICITATION for offerors and related documents numbered and dated):	AMENDMENT NO.	DATE	AMENDMENT NO.	DATE

15A. NAME AND ADDRESS OF OFFEROR	CODE 8711	FACILITY	16. NAME AND TITLE OF PERSON AUTHORIZED TO SIGN OFFER (Type or print)
TechNet 450 Garden Gate Ave. Denver, CO 80225			Scott Turner, President

15B. TELEPHONE NUMBER			15C. CHECK IF REMITTANCE ADDRESS IS [ ] DIFFERENT FROM ABOVE - ENTER SUCH ADDRESS IN SCHEDULE.	17. SIGNATURE	18. OFFER DATE
AREA CODE 303	NUMBER 867-5301	EXT. 123			05/30/2009

AWARD (To be completed by Government)

19. ACCEPTED AS TO ITEMS NUMBERED	20. AMOUNT	21. ACCOUNTING AND APPROPRIATION

22. AUTHORITY FOR USING OTHER THAN FULL AND OPEN COMPETITION: [ ] 10 U.S.C. 2304(c) ( ) [ ] 41 U.S.C. 253(c) ( )	23. SUBMIT INVOICES TO ADDRESS SHOWN IN (4 copies unless otherwise specified)	ITEM
24. ADMINISTERED BY (If other than Item 7) CODE	25. PAYMENT WILL BE MADE BY	CODE

26. NAME OF CONTRACTING OFFICER (Type or print)	27. UNITED STATES OF AMERICA	28. AWARD DATE
	(Signature of Contracting Officer)	

IMPORTANT - Award will be made on this Form, or on Standard Form 26, or by other authorized official written notice.

AUTHORIZED FOR LOCAL REPRODUCTION
Previous edition is unusable

STANDARD FORM 33 (REV. 9-97)
Prescribed by GSA - FAR (48 CFR) 53.214(c)

Sample SF 33

SF 33 also has a section for any price discounts you're willing to offer.

The Prompt Payment Act (see Chapter 17) requires the government to make payments within 30 days of receipt of a properly prepared invoice. If, however, a contractor wants a faster payment turnaround, it may offer the government a prompt-payment discount. For example, the contractor may offer a 1% discount on the invoice amount if the government makes payment within 15 days. Prompt-payment discounts are not considered in determining the low offeror.

An authorized company representative must complete and sign the requested information above. Do not use a transmittal letter to forward an offer unless the contracting officer specifically requires you to do so. Any such letter attached to an offer will be considered part of the offer. Stock phrases, such as "prices subject to change without notice" or even letterhead slogans, could invalidate an offer.

Section B—Supplies or Services and Prices/Costs

Section B is basically the government's ordering form. Anything the government intends to buy should show up here, along with the bid price. Contractors must include a brief description of the offered supplies and services, including item number; stock/part number, if applicable; and quantities. It may also include information about the contract type, renewal options, delivery requirements, ordering procedures, and other considerations.

The Federal Acquisition Regulation (FAR) lists no specific structure requirements for this section, but the Department of Defense (DOD), the General Services Administration (GSA), and the Department of Energy (DOE) all have specific formats for their purchases. DOD, for example, would use the following format to purchase 30 office desks:

DOD Price/Cost Format					
ITEM NO.	SUPPLIES/ SERVICE	QUANTITY	UNITS	UNIT PRICE	AMOUNT
0001	Office Desk	30	EA	$1,000.00	$30,000.00

DOD uses a four-digit contract line item number (CLIN). If chairs were also purchased with this solicitation, CLIN 0002 would be the item number.

When the purchased item has separate parts, different prices, or different delivery schedules, they are further subdivided. The following shows a breakdown for a computer system being purchased by DOD.

DOD Computer System Purchase					
ITEM NO.	SUPPLIES/ SERVICE	QUANTITY	UNITS	UNIT PRICE	AMOUNT
0001	Computer System				
0001AA	Monitor	5	EA	$300.00	$1,500.00
0001AB	Keyboard	5	EA	$50.00	$250.00
0001AC	CPU	5	EA	$800.00	$4,000.00
0002	Setup	As Reqd			$500.00
0003	Maintenance	As Reqd Agreement			$1,000.00

Subline items receive a two-digit alphanumeric identifier, such as 0001AA. This further CLIN breakdown helps in monitoring or administering contract performance.

Section B usually requires price lists, catalogs, or GSA schedule contracts to justify prices/costs for the commercial items solicited. Service contracts, on the other hand, are based on estimated costs. This section requires a detailed breakdown of costs for labor, overhead, general and administrative services, subcontracts, and materials (with fee or profit expressed as a cost percentage). Part 5 of this book details various costing methods.

Section C—Description/Specifications/Statement of Work

Section C provides detailed information about the supplies and services being purchased and addresses what the seller must do to perform the contract. The FAR provides no specific structure requirements for this section. Section C also describes minimum or mandatory requirements. If a contractor fails to satisfy any of the stated requirements, the government may reject the proposal as nonresponsive. Please read this section carefully!

The description of the products or services may reference specifications, standards, technical data packages, or other descriptive resources. If the contract is for products, Section C includes purchase descriptions or specifications that the products must meet. For services, the statement of work describes the tasks to be performed.

Procurements with a large number of specifications may be grouped together and listed in Section J as an exhibit. Section J is typically used to inventory large documents or attachments.

Section D—Packaging and Marking

This section is pretty self-explanatory. Contractors must preserve, pack, and mark all items in accordance with standard commercial practices or other special requirements if the products are subject to a more hostile environment. Packaging and marking requirements may exceed the cost of the unit itself, so be sure to include these costs in your proposal or bid price. If there are no packaging and marking requirements, as in service contracts, this section is omitted from the proposal.

Section E—Inspection and Acceptance

Before any product is accepted, the government verifies that the materials meet all contractual requirements. Section E contains the contractor inspection and acceptance instructions, as well as quality assurance and reliability requirements. The standard inspection requirement directs the contractor to maintain an inspection system that is acceptable to the government, maintain records of inspections conducted, and allow the government to make its own inspections.

This section may also identify specific tests that the contractor must conduct during the manufacturing process or, if the contract is for services, during specific phases of the work. The government has the right to require a contractor to replace or correct defective products. Rejections, late deliveries, and other performance failures are recorded in the contract file. Contracting officers review this file before making new awards to the contractor.

Section F—Deliveries or Performance

For products, the delivery (or performance) schedule usually states the calendar date or a specified period after the contract has been awarded. It also lists the place of delivery, usually stated as F.O.B. (free-on-board) origin or F.O.B. destination. Service deadlines are usually specified by a contractual period (or period of performance).

An F.O.B. origin contract requires the government to pay shipping costs and to assume the risk of loss or damage to the goods en route. The contractor is responsible only for delivering the goods to a common carrier or to the U.S. Postal Service. Delivery is complete once this occurs.

With F.O.B. destination, the contractor is responsible for the arrival of goods to the location specified in the contract. The contractor pays all shipping costs and retains the risk of loss or damage to the goods until they arrive at their destination.

Section G—Contract Administration Data

Section G supplements the administrative information contained in section A. This information typically includes:

- The contracting officer's name and address, the contract's technical representative, and the administrative officer

- Accounting and appropriation data

- Procedures for preparing and submitting invoices

- Seller's payment address

- Contract administration office instructions.

This section becomes important as a company tries to collect payment.

Section H—Special Contract Requirements

Customized clauses that do not fit elsewhere in the UCF are contained in Section H. Policies concerning placement of these clauses vary among federal agencies and even among the buying offices within an agency. Such clauses might include:

- Option terms

- Economic price adjustment provisions

- Government-furnished property or facilities

- Foreign sources

- Multiyear provisions

- Limitations on the federal government's obligations

- Service Contract Act wage determinations

- Payment of incentive fees

- Technical data requirements.

The contracting officer has several hundred clauses and provisions to choose from when drafting section H. Every clause included in this section must be there for a reason—either a regulation requires it or the administration of the contract necessitates it. Careful judgment should be used when selecting clauses because they add to the contract cost and tend to raise objections by contractors.

PART II: CONTRACT CLAUSES

Part II of the UCF contains a variety of contract clauses.

Section I—Contract Clauses

The circumstances of the proposed contract predetermine the clauses in this section, although the contracting officer may include any additional clauses that he or she expects to apply to the resulting contract. As a general rule, only clauses included in FAR Part 52 (and a federal agency's FAR supplement, Part 52) are included in this section.

These laws or regulations are commonly referred to as *boilerplate clauses*. The contracting officer has little or no leeway in preparing this section. Each clause derives its authority from the FAR or from a public law, statute, or executive order.

Most clauses included in this section are referenced by the clause number, title, date, and regulation source. Instead of printing an entire clause within a contract, an agreement may merely refer to the clause, e.g., FAR 52.203-3, Gratuities. Contractors are still liable for the legal consequences of the clause's terms, even if the clause is not expressly quoted or spelled out.

Clauses must be written out or incorporated in full text if:

■ The FAR or an agency regulation specifically requires full text

■ The seller must complete the clause

■ The contracting officer's boss directs it.

Most clauses included in section I must "flow down" to subcontractors. In other words, the same clauses that apply to the prime contractor also apply to the subcontractor. If you are unfamiliar with a referenced clause, be sure to obtain a copy of it so you will know exactly what the government requires of you.

The easiest way to obtain a copy of a referenced clause is to download it directly from the FAR at:

www.arnet.gov/far

Provisions do not typically appear in this section. How does a provision differ from a clause? A *clause* is a term or condition that is used in both contracts and solicitations that can apply *before and after* the contract award, such as a clause requiring a contractor to maintain a drug-free workplace. A *provision* is used only in solicitations and applies only *before* contract award, such as procedures for handling late proposals. Provisions provide direction to the seller and are typically found in section K, L, or M.

PART III: LIST OF DOCUMENTS, EXHIBITS, AND OTHER ATTACHMENTS

Part III contains a variety of attachments.

Section J—List of Attachments

Requirements that do not fit into any other sections of the UCF appear in section J. It's essentially an inventory of documents. The FAR provides little guidance on the format or content of these attachments. The contracting officer, however, is directed to provide a list of the title, date, and number of pages for each attached document. Attachments might include:

■ System requirements and specifications

■ Architectural drawings

■ Exhibits

■ Work statements

■ Government-furnished property.

When you receive an IFB or RFP, be sure that it includes all the attachments listed in this section.

PART IV: REPRESENTATIONS AND INSTRUCTIONS

This part includes instructions for preparing your bid, along with questions you must answer (or a questionnaire you must fill out) for your bid to be considered. Items ranging from definitions of contracting terms to statements about contract conditions are contained in this section.

Part IV is not included in the final contract award, but the contracting officer retains the winning contractor's representations and certifications. Be sure to fill in and sign all sections as required; if you don't, you might be considered nonresponsive and your bid might be rejected.

Section K—Representations, Certifications, and Other Statements of Offerors or Respondents

In section K, the offeror provides information about itself and certifies that it complies with all applicable laws and regulations. The contracting officer typically uses FAR 52.3 as a guide for selecting the provisions that apply to the contract.

- Is the offeror's workplace drug-free?

- Is the offeror a small business?

- Is the offeror minority-owned?

- Has the offeror performed the requirements for Certification of Procurement Integrity?

These representations and certifications (sometimes called reps and certs) usually require several pages of fill-in-the-blank answers. If your government contracting background is limited, some questions might be difficult to answer. Check with the small business specialist at the contracting activity issuing the solicitation if you're not sure how to answer a question.

Be sure to complete all the representations, certifications, and other statements in this section. Contracting officers will generally accept a contractor's self-certification, unless there is a reason to challenge it (such as a competitor request). If an offeror makes a false representation or certification, the contract may be terminated for default.

ORCA: Online Representations and Certifications Application

Effective January 2005, the FAR requires that as part of the solicitation process, you need to submit an online representations and certifications application— known as ORCA. Prior to ORCA, vendors were required to submit reps and certs for each individual contract award over $100,000.

ORCA is a web-based system that aggregates and standardizes the collection of representations and certifications found in solicitations. This site not only benefits contractors by allowing them to maintain accurate records, but also benefits contracting officers because as they can view records, including archives, with a click of the mouse. ORCA records are considered public information, meaning anyone with your DUNS number can search your records. For more information, visit:

https://orca.bpn.gov

Section L—Instructions, Conditions, and Notices to Offerors or Respondents

Section L spells out how the proposal should be prepared. Each evaluation factor outlined in the source-selection plan stated in section M should have a corresponding instruction in section L. The instructions are designed to facilitate the evaluation process.

Section L also contains information on the various conditions and circumstances that might affect the proposal, such as:

■ Whether the proposal is set aside for small businesses

■ The expected contract type

■ Procedures for handling late proposals.

In general, section L should include information that allows you to submit your best possible proposal, while providing the source-selection team with sufficient data to make an award decision. This section, for example, might specify a limitation on the number of pages or volumes in the proposal, require that a certain font size and margins be used, and lay out the order of presentation.

Section M—Evaluation Factors for Award

The federal government's criteria for evaluating proposals and selecting the winning contractor are identified in this section. Section M must include and adequately describe all factors the government will consider in making the selection. The solicitation also informs offerors of minimum requirements that apply to particular evaluation factors, such as the requirement that the contractor's proposal be technically sound.

In sealed bidding, the evaluation criteria are limited to price and price-related factors. Cost/price data are always an evaluation factor in any source selection. However, negotiated procurements allow the contracting officer to evaluate price, terms and conditions, technical requirements, delivery schedules, and management proposals.

Section M often shows each factor's relative weight in the evaluation process. The technical requirements, for example, might be twice as important as the management proposal. If no relative order is stated, the evaluation factors are of equal importance. Prospective offerors should carefully examine section M before developing a proposal. The government will consider only the factors specified in this section.

> To help ensure that your proposal addresses all the elements of section C, section L, and section M, you might consider preparing a compliance matrix that identifies where each item is addressed in the proposal.

AMENDMENTS TO THE SOLICITATION

In many cases, the contracting officer will issue amendments to a solicitation. An amendment might, for example, clarify ambiguities or add or delete requirements to the statement of work. Amendments should be taken very seriously because their content could dictate significant changes to the original solicitation, as well as the time allowed for performance. Now that most procurements are available on the Internet, contractors should be sure to check the solicitation daily for any forthcoming amendments.

To amend a solicitation, the contracting officer must furnish an SF 30, Amendment of Solicitation/Modification of Contract, to all prospective offerors who received a copy of the original. (The sample shows an amendment to extend the date that proposals are due from April 5, 2010, to April 19, 2010.) Each prospective offeror must acknowledge receipt of the amendment by:

■ Completing Blocks 8 and 15 on SF 30 and returning the form with the bid.

■ Identifying receipt of the amendment on each copy of the offer. You will need to enter the amendment date and number in the spaces provided on Block 14 of SF 30.

■ Submitting a separate letter or fax (if permitted) that includes the solicitation number and the amendment's number and date, as well as your company's name, address, and phone number.

If the offeror does not acknowledge or sign the amendment, its bid may be disqualified as nonresponsive.

> Don't confuse amendments to a solicitation with modifications to a contract. Amendments generally add new requirements, change requirements, clarify discrepancies in the solicitation, or delete something before the proposal's due date. Modifications, on the other hand, are changes to an awarded contract.

TYPICAL PROPOSAL WEAKNESSES

Government evaluators are supposed to make decisions based solely on what appears in your proposal. It's imperative to include all pertinent information about your company. Common proposal weaknesses include:

■ Noncompliance with the solicitation's specifications and requirements

AMENDMENT OF SOLICITATION/MODIFICATION OF CONTRACT		1. CONTRACT ID CODE		PAGE OF PAGES 1 / 1
2. AMENDMENT/MODIFICATION NO. 0001	3. EFFECTIVE DATE 3/19/2008	4. REQUISITION/PURCHASE REQ. NO. 01-06NN63100.000		5. PROJECT NO. (If applicable)

6. ISSUED BY   CODE   MA-542   **7. ADMINISTERED BY** (If other than Item 6)   CODE

U.S. Department of Energy
Headquarters Office of Procurement Services
1000 Independence Ave., SW
Washington, DC 20585

8. NAME AND ADDRESS OF CONTRACTOR (No., street, county, State, and Zip Code)

Happy's Office Furniture
850 Taylor St.
Fort Worth, TX 76102

(x) **X**

9A. AMENDMENT OF SOLICITATION NO.
DE-RP01-06NN63100

9B. DATED (SEE ITEM 11)
March 3, 2008

10A. MODIFICATION OF CONTRACT/ORDER NO.

10B. DATED (SEE ITEM 13)

CODE   FACILITY CODE

11. THIS ITEM ONLY APPLIES TO AMENDMENTS OF SOLICITATIONS

[X] The above numbered solicitation is amended as set forth in Item 14. The hour and date specified for receipt of Offers [X] is extended, [ ] is not extended.

Offers must acknowledge receipt of this amendment prior to the hour and date specified in the solicitation or as amended, by one of the following methods:
(a) By completing Items 8 and 15, and returning __2__ copies of the amendment; (b) By acknowledging receipt of this amendment on each copy of the offer submitted; or (c) By separate letter or telegram which includes a reference to the solicitation and amendment numbers. FAILURE OF YOUR ACKNOWLEDGEMENT TO BE RECEIVED AT THE PLACE DESIGNATED FOR THE RECEIPT OF OFFERS PRIOR TO THE HOUR AND DATE SPECIFIED MAY RESULT IN REJECTION OF YOUR OFFER. If by virtue of this amendment you desire to change an offer already submitted, such change may be made by telegram or letter, provided each telegram or letter makes reference to the solicitation and this amendment, and is received prior to the opening hour and date specified.

12. ACCOUNTING AND APPROPRIATION DATA (If required)

**13. THIS ITEM APPLIES ONLY TO MODIFICATIONS OF CONTRACTS/ORDERS,
IT MODIFIES THE CONTRACT/ORDER NO. AS DESCRIBED IN ITEM 14.**

(x)

A. THIS CHANGE ORDER IS ISSUED PURSUANT TO: (Specify authority) THE CHANGES SET FORTH IN ITEM 14 ARE MADE IN THE CONTRACT ORDER NO. IN ITEM 10A.

B. THE ABOVE NUMBERED CONTRACT/ORDER IS MODIFIED TO REFLECT THE ADMINISTRATIVE CHANGES (such as changes in paying office, appropriation date, etc.) SET FORTH IN ITEM 14, PURSUANT TO THE AUTHORITY OF FAR 43.103(b).

C. THIS SUPPLEMENTAL AGREEMENT IS ENTERED INTO PURSUANT TO AUTHORITY OF:

D. OTHER (Specify type of modification and authority)

E. IMPORTANT: Contractor [ ] is not, [ ] is required to sign this document and return ____ copies to the issuing office.

14. DESCRIPTION OF AMENDMENT/MODIFICATION (Organized by UCF section headings, including solicitation/contract subject matter where feasible.)
The purpose of this amendment is to extend the date that proposals are due from April 5, 2008 to April 19, 2008. Accordingly, Part II, Section L, Provision L.8 – Time, Date and Place Bids/Proposals are Due is revised to reflect the following: 1:00 p.m. on April 19, 2008

15A. NAME AND TITLE OF SIGNER (Type or print) Happy Gilmore, CEO		16A. NAME AND TITLE OF CONTRACTING OFFICER (Type or print) David J. Smith Contracting Officer	
15B. CONTRACTOR/OFFEROR	15C. DATE SIGNED March 19, 2008	16B. UNITED STATES OF AMERICA BY	16C. DATE SIGNED March 19, 2008
(Signature of person authorized to sign)		(Signature of Contracting Officer)	

NSN 7540-01-152-8070
PREVIOUS EDITION UNUSABLE   30-105   **STANDARD FORM 30** (Rev. 10-83)
Prescribed by GSA
FAR (48 CFR) 53.243

Sample SF 30

■ Unrealistic cost estimates (either too high or too low)

■ Insufficient understanding of the contract's requirements

■ Poor proposal organization

■ Wordiness or unclear writing style and grammatical errors

■ Unsubstantiated rationale for the proposed approach

■ Insufficient resources to accomplish the contract's requirements

■ Incomplete response to the solicitation.

To avoid these problems, set up a checklist of solicitation requirements as you read the IFB or RFP. Use the checklist in your final proposal review.

PROCUREMENT INSTRUMENT IDENTIFICATION NUMBERS

Each solicitation/contract issued by the government receives a procurement instrument identification number (PIIN), which typically consists of 13 digits (or positions). The first six digits identify the contracting activity (or buying office) issuing the solicitation/contract. For example, here are a few PIINs used by DOD buying offices:

Major Army Buying Offices:

U.S. Army Industrial Operations Command	DAAA09
U.S. Army Research Laboratory	DAAD17

Major Navy Buying Offices:

Office of Naval Research	N00014
Naval Air Warfare Center	N68936

Defense Logistics Agency Supply Centers:

Defense Industrial Supply Center   DLA500

Defense Electronic Supply Center   DLA900

The next two digits in the PIIN identify the fiscal year. The ninth character identifies the solicitation type being used, such as an invitation for bid
(B) or a request for proposal (R). The remaining digits identify the particular solicitation or contract. The following is the PIIN for a request for
proposal issued in FY2010 by the Office of Naval Research.

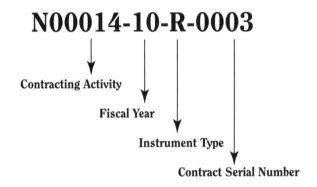

N00014-10-R-0003

Contracting Activity

Fiscal Year

Instrument Type

Contract Serial Number

UNSOLICITED PROPOSALS

If you or your company has a new and innovative idea that might benefit
the government, why not prepare an unsolicited proposal? An unsolicited
proposal is a written offer submitted to a federal agency on the contractor's initiative to obtain a government contract. It is not submitted in
response to a formal or informal solicitation request.

The government typically encourages the submission of new and innovative ideas in response to Broad Agency Announcements and Small Business
Innovation Research topics. In many cases, such ideas are actually "solicited" by technical personnel rather than by contracting personnel.

Each federal agency uses different procedures for handling unsolicited
proposals. To get information on an agency's submission procedures, contact the Small Business Specialist at the agency of interest to you. A major

advantage of submitting an unsolicited proposal is that your offer is typically one of a kind. That is, you probably won't have competition.

Federal agencies are not, however, responsible for costs incurred in proposal preparation. It is always a good idea to consult with appropriate agency officials before starting on an unsolicited proposal. A valid unsolicited proposal must:

■ Be innovative and unique

■ Be independently originated and developed by the contractor

■ Be prepared without government supervision, endorsement, or direction, although detailed discussions with government personnel about the need often encourage the contractor to prepare and submit the proposal

■ Include sufficient detail to determine that government support could be worthwhile and the proposed work could benefit the agency

■ Not be an advance proposal for a known federal agency requirement that can be acquired by competitive methods.

Advertising material, commercial item offers, contributions, or routine correspondence on technical issues are not considered unsolicited proposals. Unsolicited proposals should contain the following basic information to permit objective and timely consideration:

■ The offeror's name, address, and organization type (such as profit, nonprofit, educational, small business)

■ Names and phone numbers of technical and business personnel to be contacted for evaluation or negotiation purposes

■ Identification of proprietary (or confidential) data to be used only for evaluation purposes

■ Submission date

■ Signature of a person authorized to represent and contractually obligate the contractor

■ A title and an abstract of the proposed effort (which should be approximately 200 to 300 words, stating the basic purpose and expected end result)

■ A report or narrative that discusses the activity's objectives, approach, and anticipated results

■ Key personnel names and bios

■ Type of support needed from the agency (such as facilities, equipment, or materials)

■ Proposed price or total estimated cost

■ Time period for which the proposal is valid (a six-month minimum is suggested)

■ Preferred contract type

■ Brief description of the organization and relevant experience.

Federal agencies have procedures and contact points for controlling the receipt, evaluation, and timely disposition of unsolicited proposals. If the agency determines that it doesn't need the services, it returns the unsolicited proposal to the offeror, citing the reasons.

Government personnel are prohibited from disclosing restrictively marked information included in an unsolicited proposal. Also, unless the contractor is notified of and agrees to the intended use, the government should not use any data, concept, idea, or other part of an unsolicited proposal as the basis for a solicitation or in negotiations with other firms.

CONTINGENT FEES

Contingent fee arrangements are a very complicated area of government contracting. Simply stated, a contingent fee means any commission, percentage, brokerage, or other fee that is contingent on the success that a person or concern has in securing a government contract award. For example, if a company hires a consultant to help prepare a proposal for a government contract and the agreement states that payment is contingent upon the company's winning, the agreement would be considered a contingent fee arrangement.

Arrangements to pay contingent fees for soliciting or obtaining government contracts have long been considered contrary to public policy because they might lead to attempted or actual exercise of improper influence. In every negotiated contract, the government requires the contractor to provide a certification that it has not paid contingent fees to secure the contract. If the contractor fails to provide this documentation, the government may annul the contract without liability or deduct from the contract price the full amount of the contingent fee.

There is, however, an exception to this certification requirement. If contingent fee arrangements are made between contractors and "bona fide employees," they are permitted. A *bona fide employee* is a person employed by a contractor who is subject to the contractor's supervision and control with respect to time, place, and manner of performance. Therefore, this person neither exerts improper influence to obtain government contracts nor holds himself or herself out as being able to obtain them through improper influence.

Federal regulations also allow this same type of bona fide employee relationship on a part-time basis to small businesses because they typically do not have the resources to employ salespeople full-time. If a small business hires a consultant to help prepare price proposals, the consultant would be considered a bona fide employee if he or she is supervised by the company's president and performs the company's services two days a week throughout the year. A bona fide employee may represent more than one firm but should not bid for more than one firm in the same line of work.

Contingent fee arrangements are complex. Be sure to obtain legal advice if you have questions or concerns about any of your contractual arrangements.

■　■　■

In the world of government contracting, proposals represent the "point of sale" for companies looking to do business with the federal government. Effective and efficient proposal development, preparation, management, and design are essential to your company's success. If any part of the solicitation is unclear, you're far better off asking the contracting officer to clarify than taking a guess and hoping for the best!

■　■　■

PART 5

What Are the Contract Types and Administrative Requirements?

> "Show me a good loser and I'll show you a man playing golf with his boss."
>
> —*Unknown*

There is a perception in government contracting that the lowest bidder always wins the contract. Sealed bidding procedures, for example, enable the bidder with the lowest priced proposal to win the contract. Low bids, however, do not apply to federal supply schedule orders, best-value procurements, or sole-source acquisitions. How comfortable would you be riding on the space shuttle if you knew it was built by the bidder with the lowest-priced proposal?

The federal government contracts for products and services at fair and reasonable prices, but no set of standard rules defines a "fair and reasonable price." Eventually, no matter how the problem is approached, the decision comes down to a matter of good personal judgment.

The contracting officer chooses a procurement method that best fits the contract's requirements (see Part IV). To purchase an item that can be clearly and accurately described, such as office furniture, sealed bidding procedures would probably be used. If the contracting officer is unsure of a contractor's ability to provide acceptable items, negotiated procedures might be a better alternative. No matter which solicitation method is used, price must always be part of the evaluation criteria.

The selection of a contract type requires negotiation and the exercise of good judgment. A contracting officer usually considers several factors, including:

■ Contract's expected length (or period of performance)

■ Price competition

■ Contract's technical complexity

■ Urgency of the need

■ Dollar value of the contract

■ Contract's performance risks

■ Market conditions

■ Contractor's motivation to perform the contract.

The contractor may also propose an alternative contract type.

The federal government uses two basic types of contracts: fixed-price and cost-reimbursement. The primary differences between the contract types are the amount of responsibility placed on the contractor and the amount of profit incentive offered to the contractor for achieving or exceeding specified standards or goals.

With fixed-price contracts, the contractor assumes the risk of contract performance (or cost risk), and its performance determines its profit. Cost-reimbursement contracts, on the other hand, place the risk of contract performance on the government because it reimburses the contractor for the expenses incurred during the contract's performance. The solicitation document always indicates the contract type.

The other contract types available (discussed in Chapter 16) are variations of fixed-price or cost-reimbursement contracts:

■ Indefinite-delivery contracts

■ Time and materials

■ Labor-hour contracts

■ Letter contracts

■ Basic ordering agreements.

Fixed-Price
Contracts

14

Berry's World

"Remember, money can't buy happiness, but in Washington it CAN BUY access, jobs and influence."

11-5-96

What's in this chapter?

- Firm-fixed-price contract
- Fixed-price contract with economic price adjustment
- Fixed-price incentive contract
- Fixed-price contract with prospective price redetermination
- Fixed-ceiling-price contract with retroactive price redetermination

Under a fixed-price contract, the government agrees to pay a specific price (which includes the contractor's profit) for completed work and delivered products. Fixed-price contracts are used primarily to acquire commercial items but are being increasingly used for acquiring services. When a contract is fixed-price, acceptable performance by the contractor is the basic criterion for payment. (A contractor's bill under a fixed-price contract is called an invoice.)

The government prefers fixed-price contracts because the contract price is not subject to adjustment on the basis of the contractor's cost experience in performing it. If a contractor wins a fixed-price government contract, it must perform the contract at the award price, even if its actual costs of performance exceed the award price.

Fixed-price contracts place the cost risk on the contractor. However, there is no statutory limit on the profits that can be earned under fixed-price contracts. Maximum profit can be earned by managing fixed-price contracts aggressively and identifying, understanding, and controlling risk. Fixed-price contracts are typically used when:

■ Price competition is adequate.

■ Reasonable price comparisons with past purchases of the same or similar products or services made on a competitive basis are available.

■ Available cost or pricing information permits realistic estimates of the probable performance costs.

■ Performance uncertainties can be identified, and reasonable estimates of their cost impact can be made.

The government uses fixed-price contracts in simplified acquisition and sealed bidding procedures. They are used in 80% of negotiated procurements as well.

Both fixed-price and cost-reimbursement contracts may contain incentives that increase or decrease a contractor's profit or fee on the basis of performance. An incentive contract, for example, might award contractors for holding down costs, improving technical performance, or making prompt deliveries.

FIRM-FIXED-PRICE CONTRACT

In a firm-fixed-price (FFP) contract, the government agrees to pay a specific amount (or price) when a contractor's performance has been completed and accepted. The contract price does not change, regardless of the contractor's actual cost experience. A contractor accepts full cost responsibility when agreeing to this type of contract. FFP contracts are typically used when:

■ The statement of work can be clearly and accurately described. (FFP contracts are generally used for purchasing commercial items and standard services.)

■ A fair, accurate, and reasonable contract price can be established before contract award.

The government prefers this contract type because the contractor bears all the risk and the government's administrative burden is minimal. If the contracting officer determines that the agreed-upon prices are based on adequate price competition, FFP contracts require no cost or pricing data. (See the Truth in Negotiations Act in Chapter 2.)

The government establishes the "firm" contract price and performance requirements during the pre-award negotiation phase. Suppose three contractors were awarded contracts to supply office furniture.

	RJC Furniture	Joe's Office Supplies	All Office, Inc.
	100 Executive Chairs	5 Conference Tables	20 Office Desks
Contract value	$ 75,000	$ 150,000	$ 200,000
Actual costs	$ 50,000	$ 185,000	$ 200,000
Profit (or loss)	$ 25,000	($ 35,000)	$ —

In this example, RJC Furniture made a profit of $25,000, which the government will pay once the chairs are delivered and accepted. Joe's Office Supplies incurred unexpected costs during contract performance and lost $35,000. It must fulfill the contract requirements in spite of its loss. All Office, Inc., broke even.

Most FFP solicitations over $100,000 include FAR provision 52.203-2, Certificate of Independent Price Determination. This provision requires contractors to certify that they have not prepared their price proposals in collusion with another person or firm. A contractor's failure to submit a certificate (or submission of a false certificate) may be grounds for rejection of its proposal.

FFP Advantages

■ You can obtain a higher profit under an FFP contract if you control your costs.

■ Because the government awards most FFP contracts under adequate price competition, your reporting requirements are minimal.

■ FFP contracts require less administration for both the government and the contractor.

FFP Disadvantages

■ FFP contracts offer little flexibility. (Price cannot be adjusted.)

■ If you do not control your costs, you can lose money.

FIXED-PRICE CONTRACT WITH ECONOMIC PRICE ADJUSTMENT

Suppose the U.S. Treasury Department awarded a contract to Coppermine, Inc., to supply copper for minting pennies for two years. Because the price of copper tends to fluctuate over time, the contracting officer makes its price subject to an economic price adjustment. The price index for metals is used to reflect market changes to copper. Coppermine, Inc., delivers 5,000 pounds of copper each year.

	Year 1	Year 2
5,000 pounds of copper	$ 250,000	$ 275,000*
Labor costs	$ 50,000	$ 50,000
Shipping costs	$ 75,000	$ 75,000
Profit	$ 25,000	$ 25,000
Total contract value	$ 400,000	$ 425,000

* Per examination of the price index for metals, the price of 5,000 pounds of copper went up $25,000 in Year 2. This contract has a 10% ceiling, so the fluctuation could not exceed $40,000 (400,000 x 10% = $40,000).

In this contract, the price of copper is isolated to provide for a foreseeable economic price adjustment, but the other requirements remain the same. Labor, shipping, and profit are handled as an FFP contract. Allowance for increased profit never justifies an economic price adjustment.

A fixed-price contract with economic price adjustment (FP/EPA) is designed to protect against contingencies that threaten multiyear contracts. It is basically an FFP contract with a clause that allows the contract price to be revised (either upward or downward) in case of economic uncertainties. The contracting officer chooses an FP/EPA contract that meets the government's requirements for the supply or service being purchased, including elements subject to cost fluctuations.

The government generally allows for three types of economic price adjustments:

■ *Adjustments based on established prices.* Price adjustments are based on increases or decreases of an agreed-upon published or otherwise established price.

■ *Adjustments based on actual costs of labor or material.* Price adjustments are based on increases or decreases in specified costs of labor or material that the contractor actually experiences during contract performance.

■ *Adjustments based on cost indexes of labor or material.* Price adjustments are based on increases or decreases in labor or material cost indexes that the contract specifically identifies. The indexes are largely dependent on two series of publications put out by the Department of Labor: (1) *The Wholesale Price Index for Material—Industrial Commodities*; (2) *The Wage and Income Series by North American Industry Classification System.*

Economic price adjustments usually are restricted to industry-wide contingencies. If the price adjustment is based on labor and material costs, it should be limited to contingencies beyond the contractor's control. Usually a ceiling on the upward adjustments is set at 10% of the unit price. There is never a floor on downward adjustments.

The price that may be adjusted is typically determined in three steps:

1. The government accepts a contract free of contingencies.

2. The contracting officer identifies the items subject to adjustment before contract performance. A ceiling is set for contingencies and the ground rules for adjustments are made.

3. The contracting officer revises the prices up or down during the contract's performance as defined by market conditions. Support must be provided for these adjustments.

As with an FFP contract, FP/EPA contracts must include FAR provision 52.203-2.

FP/EPA Advantages

■ The contract price can be revised to reflect the effects of economic aberrations or changes in the marketplace.

■ FP/EPA contracts offer many of the same benefits as FFP contracts.

> ## FP/EPA Disadvantages
>
> ■ Price adjustments are limited to contingencies beyond the contractor's control.
>
> ■ There is usually a ceiling on upward adjustments but no floor for downward adjustments.

FIXED-PRICE INCENTIVE CONTRACT

Whereas a fixed-price contract does not allow for profit adjustment, a fixed-price incentive (FPI) contract does. The government offers incentive contracting in the belief that a contractor will be motivated to enhance its performance if there is a chance of increased profits (kind of like a tip). Thus, by achieving better performance results and controlling contract costs, the contractor can earn higher profits. A fixed-price incentive contract is typically used for a development contract, such as a highway construction contract.

FPI contracts are appropriate when:

■ The government and the contractor can negotiate at the outset (1) a firm target cost, target profit, and profit adjustment formula that offer a fair and reasonable incentive and (2) a ceiling to ensure that the contractor assumes an appropriate share of the risk.

■ The contractor assumes a major share of the cost responsibility under the adjustment formula, which is reflected in the target profit.

The contracting officer calculates the final contract price (with the profit or loss) by applying a formula based on the relationship of total actual cost of performance to total target cost. To understand this formula, you need to be familiar with the following terms:

■ *Target cost* is the estimated cost to complete the contract. Both parties agree to the target cost after analysis and negotiation. A contractor usually has an equal chance of overrunning or underrunning the total estimated cost.

■ *Target profit* is the profit a contractor would earn if its costs equaled the target costs. The profit must be fair and reasonable.

■ *Target price* is the sum of the target cost and the target profit.

■ *Ceiling price* is the maximum amount the government will pay for the contract. When the contract costs reach this point, the contractor's profit is zero and it assumes responsibility for any additional costs.

■ *Sharing formula* apportions the cost overruns or underruns between the government and the contractor. There may be two separate formulas—one for the overrun and one for the underrun—or the same formula may be used for both expressions. The share ratio is typically between 50/50 and 75/25.

Let's assume a contractor had an overrun of $50,000 and the sharing formula was 75/25.

The Government's Portion:	
Overrun	($ 50,000)
Sharing formula	x 75%
	($ 37,500)
The Contractor's Portion:	
Overrun	($ 50,000)
Sharing formula	x 25%
	($ 12,500)

Here's an illustration of how the FPI contract works: Suppose the Department of Transportation (DOT) awarded Street Works, Inc., a contract to add a ramp to an existing highway. Street Works, Inc., negotiated the following contract cost projections:

Target cost	=	$ 6,000,000
Target profit	=	$ 500,000
Target price	=	$ 6,500,000
Ceiling price	=	$ 6,750,000
Sharing formula	=	60/40

The contracting officer used a sharing formula of 60/40 to strongly encourage Street Works, Inc., to perform the contract for less than the cost projections. Therefore, if Street Works, Inc., actually incurred $5,750,000 in contract costs, it would make the following profit on the contract:

Actual cost	$ 5,750,000
Less: target cost	$ 6,000,000
Contract underrun	$ 250,000
Contractor sharing %	40%
Total underrun profit	$ 100,000
ADD: target profit	$ 500,000
Total profit	**$ 600,000**
ADD: actual cost	$ 5,750,000
Total contract value	**$ 6,350,000**

If Street Works, Inc., had actually incurred $6,800,000 in contract costs, its profit on the contract would be:

Actual cost	$ 6,800,000
Less: target cost	$ 6,000,000
Contract overrun	$ (800,000)
Contractor sharing %	40%
Total overrun profit	$ (320,000)
ADD: target profit	$ 500,000
Total profit	**$ 180,000**
ADD: actual cost	$ 6,800,000
Total contract value	**$ 6,980,000**

In this second example, Street Works, Inc., exceeded the projected target cost, so its total profit was reduced. However, it also exceeded the contract ceiling price of $6,750,000. The sharing formula changes from 60/40 to 0/100 once Street Works, Inc., reaches the ceiling price. The ceiling price is also referred to as the point of total (cost) assumption.

Street Works, Inc., must absorb the portion of the contract cost that exceeded the ceiling price:

Total contract value	**$ 6,980,000**
Ceiling price	**$ 6,750,000**
Additional loss to contractor	**($ 230,000)**

There are two types of FPI contracts, firm target and successive target. This chapter discusses only the FPI firm target contract. Successive target contracts are used only when available cost or pricing data are *not* sufficient to permit the negotiation of a realistic firm target cost and profit before award. Because of the uncertainties involved with successive target contracts, they are rarely used. (See FAR 16.403-2 for information on successive target contracts.)

FPI Advantages

■ FPI contracts combine the sharing incentive feature and the FFP feature into one contract type.

■ The government shares in any cost overrun (up to the ceiling price).

FPI Disadvantages

■ The contractor is responsible for all costs beyond the ceiling price.

■ The government shares in cost savings.

FIXED-PRICE CONTRACT WITH PROSPECTIVE PRICE REDETERMINATION

Suppose the Department of Justice (DOJ) awarded Make It Shine, Inc., a five-year contract to provide janitorial services. This contract originally was awarded at $100,000 a year, starting on January 1, 2010, and it has a redetermination date of January 1, 2013.

Contract Year	Contract Amount
2010	$ 100,000
2011	$ 100,000
2012	$ 100,000
2013	$ 125,000 *
2014	$ 125,000
Total contract value	**$ 550,000**

* On January 1, 2013, the contracting officer approved a price redetermination of $125,000 a year for this contract. In this example, the annual contract amount was increased; in many cases, however, the contract amount is lowered on the redetermination date.

A fixed-price contract with prospective price redetermination provides for a firm-fixed price for the initial period of contract performance and a redetermination of the contract price (either up or down) at a stated date during performance. The initial period should be the longest period for which it is possible to negotiate a fair and reasonable firm-fixed price. Each subsequent pricing period should be at least 12 months.

This contract type is used when:

■ Negotiations have established that neither an FFP contract nor an FPI contract is appropriate.

■ The contracting officer can provide reasonable assurance that price redetermination actions will take place promptly at the specified times.

The contract may establish a ceiling price based on uncertainties involved in the contract's performance and their possible cost impact. This ceiling price helps ensure a reasonable amount of risk is given to the contractor.

Prospective Price Redetermination Advantages

■ This contract type allows for a price redetermination during contract performance.

> **Prospective Price Redetermination Disadvantages**
>
> ■ This contract type is typically used for multiyear contracts only.
>
> ■ Price redetermination periods should be at least 12 months apart.

FIXED-CEILING-PRICE CONTRACT WITH RETROACTIVE PRICE REDETERMINATION

The Environmental Protection Agency (EPA) awarded Virus Tech, Inc., a six-month contract to develop software to protect against computer viruses. The contracting officer determined the contract's estimated cost of $80,000, with a ceiling of $100,000, to be fair and reasonable.

Contract Period	Contract Amount
Jan. 1, 2012, through June 30, 2012	$ 80,000
Redetermination date July 20, 2012	($ 5,000)
Total contract value	**$ 75,000**

On July 20, 2012, the contracting officer redetermined the total contract value, reducing it to $75,000.

A fixed-ceiling-price contract with retroactive price redetermination allows for a price redetermination (either up or down) after the contract is completed. The negotiated ceiling price ensures that the contractor assumes a reasonable amount of risk. This contract type is used only when:

■ The contract is for research and development (R&D) and the estimated cost is $100,000 or less. The contract period of performance should be no longer than 12 months.

■ The contracting officer can provide reasonable assurance that the price redetermination will take place promptly at the specified time.

■ The head of the contracting activity approves the use of this contract type in writing.

The contracting officer considers the contractor's management effectiveness and ingenuity when the contract price is redetermined retroactively.

Retroactive Price Redetermination Advantages

■ This contract type allows for a price redetermination once the contract is completed.

Retroactive Price Redetermination Disadvantages

■ Estimated contract costs must be $100,000 or less.

■ The contract period is typically less than 12 months.

■   ■   ■

The government uses fixed-price contracts for most of its purchases. They tend to be the simplest contract type to administer and evaluate. Fixed-price contracts place the maximum amount of cost risk on the contractor. Why should the government bear the risk if it can make you bear it? Once the government signs a fixed-price contract, it must pay the full amount, even if it subsequently determines the price to be too high.

■   ■   ■

15 Cost-Reimbursement Contracts

© 1999 Randy Glasbergen.
www.glasbergen.com

**"Paying close attention to every detail.
That's the key to my success, Bob!"**

What's in this chapter?

- Determining your contract cost
- Calculating contract cost
- Understanding rates
- Fee/profit
- Types of cost-reimbursement contracts

For many government projects it is almost impossible to estimate the costs to actually perform and complete the job. Goal-directed R&D work, such as finding a cure for AIDS, is such an example. In these cases, the government prefers to enter into cost-reimbursement contracts.

With cost-reimbursement contracts, the government reimburses the contractor for the reasonable, allocable, and allowable costs it incurs under the terms and conditions of the contract. The government essentially carries all the risk. Because there is little incentive for contractors to control costs, contracting officers are hesitant to use this type of contract.

If a contracting officer insists on using a fixed-price contract for a job that would be better suited for a cost-reimbursement contract, the contractor has to inflate the proposed contract price to protect itself from the uncertainties involved in performing the contract. Anytime a cost-reimbursement contract is used, it must be solicited using negotiated procedures (see Chapter 12).

A cost-reimbursement contract establishes a total cost estimate for the purpose of obligating funds and establishing a ceiling that the contractor may not exceed (except at its own risk). The contractor agrees to put forth its best effort to get the job done within a mutually agreed-upon cost estimate. The contracting officer closely monitors the contractor's performance to ensure that it performs the contract effectively and efficiently.

The contractor must notify the contracting officer when its expenditure rate reaches a specified percentage of the agreed-upon cost estimate. If the estimated cost to complete becomes greater than the originally agreed-upon cost estimate, the contractor is required to submit a revised cost estimate. The contract is then modified to reflect the revised estimate or brought to an end.

If the contractor completes the job for less than the estimated cost, the excess funds can be used for other projects. A contractor's bill under a cost-reimbursement contract is called a public voucher.

DETERMINING YOUR CONTRACT COST

Before the government issues a cost-reimbursement contract, it must determine whether the contractor's accounting system can accumulate costs by contract (commonly referred to as a job cost accounting system). The systems also must have the ability to segregate direct costs from indirect costs.

Direct costs are costs that can be specifically identified with a particular contract, such as labor costs incurred to build a warehouse for a construction contract.

Indirect costs are expenses incurred by a contractor that cannot be attributed to any one particular contract. Heat or air-conditioning in a manufacturing area that houses the work of several contracts would be considered an indirect cost because it benefits all the contracts. Indirect costs are allocated to a contract during the period in which they are incurred.

Indirect costs are further classified as either overhead (O/H) expenses or general and administrative (G&A) expenses.

O/H expenses are general in nature, such as indirect labor, rent, supplies, insurance, and depreciation. O/H expenses are distinct from the costs necessary for the overall business operation. By charging each customer for part of these O/H expenses, the contractor recoups enough money to meet its total O/H expenses. This is sometimes called *burden* or *loading*.

G&A expenses are any organizational, financial, or other expenses incurred by a company for the general management and administration of the business as a whole. The salary of a company's president is generally considered a G&A expense. A contractor recovers these expenses by including a portion of them in the charges made to each customer.

The total operating cost of a company for a period, such as a year, is the sum of all the direct and indirect costs the company incurs. In ascertaining what constitutes a cost, the contractor may use any generally accepted method of determining or estimating costs that is equitable and consistently applied. Costs applied to a cost-reimbursement contract must therefore be reasonable, allocable, and allowable.

Don't let all of this "accountant-speak" scare you. This chapter has several easy-to-follow examples that will help clarify how this works!

Reasonable Costs

A cost is accepted as reasonable if, by its nature and amount, it does not exceed that which would be incurred by a prudent person in the conduct of a competitive business. Determining cost reasonableness is mostly a matter of common sense. When a contractor's business is in a highly competitive industry, its costs are probably reasonable because the business must keep its costs competitive. If the government contracts for specially designed products or services in a business market that is not highly competitive, it needs to ensure that the proposed costs are reasonable. If a specific cost is challenged, the contractor bears the burden of proving its reasonableness.

Allocable Costs

Contractors accumulate indirect expenses into logical cost groupings to permit the distribution of expenses in relation to benefits received by the contracts (or cost objectives). An indirect cost is allocable to a government contract if:

■ It is incurred specifically for the contract.

■ It benefits the contract and can be distributed in reasonable proportion to the benefits received.

■ It is necessary to the overall operation of the business, although a direct relationship to any particular cost objective cannot be shown.

Each contractor must allocate its indirect costs to contracts in an equitable, logical, and consistent way. The FAR does not suggest or require the use of any particular cost distribution base. Instead, it allows for the use of alternative distribution bases that will bring about a substantial matching of the indirect costs with the appropriate cost objectives. The illustration below uses direct labor to allocate O/H expenses (see Calculating Contract Cost later in this chapter).

Determining what is equitable should be objective, but often it is not. If a contractor hires a security guard for a specific contract but the guard's services are allocated to all contracts, the allocation probably wouldn't be considered equitable. On the other hand, if the security guard provides services for the entire company, this could be considered a benefit to each contract, in which case allocating such costs to all contracts would be appropriate if done in an equitable manner.

Allowable Costs

An allowable cost meets the tests of reasonableness and allocability, is in agreement with generally accepted accounting principles, and otherwise conforms to specific limitations or exclusions set forth in the FAR (Part 31). If the government determines a cost to be unallowable, the law prohibits its payment. This is a very hard concept for many contractors to understand because many of these unallowable costs are legitimate business expenses in the eyes of the Internal Revenue Service.

Bad debt expenses are not allocable to government contracts because the government always pays its debts. The reason for the apparent inconsistency of these unallowable costs is that the government pays the contractor for only those costs from which the government benefits. The decision for determining the allowability of a particular cost ultimately rests with the contracting officer.

Common unallowable costs include:

■ **Public relations and advertising costs.** Public relations includes all functions and activities dedicated to maintaining, protecting, and enhancing the image of a company or its products. Advertising, the most common means for promoting public relations, includes conventions, exhibits, samples, magazines, direct mail, displays, radio, and television.

The only allowable advertising costs are those that the contract specifically requires or that arise from government contract requirements and are exclusively for (1) recruiting personnel required for performing contractual obligations, (2) acquiring scarce items for contract performance, and (3) disposing of surplus materials acquired for contract performance.

Allowable public relations costs include costs specifically required by contract and costs of (1) responding to inquiries on company policies and activities; (2) communicating with the public, press, stockholders, creditors, and customers; (3) conducting general liaison with news media and government public relations officers; (4) participating in community service, such as blood bank drives, charity drives, and disaster assistance; and (5) conducting plant tours and holding open houses.

All other advertising and public relations costs are unallowable.

■ **Bad debts.** Bad debts, including actual or estimated losses arising from uncollectible accounts receivable due from customers and any directly associated costs, such as collection and legal costs, are unallowable.

■ **Contributions or donations.** Gifts made to charities, including cash, property, and services are unallowable.

■ **Entertainment costs.** Costs of amusement, such as tickets to shows or sporting events, meals, lodging, transportation, and gratuities, are unallowable. Membership costs to country clubs are also unallowable, regardless of whether the cost is reported as taxable income to the employees. Moreover, the government expressly prohibits its employees from accepting contractor-provided gratuities or entertainment. The rationale behind this provision is that entertaining with government-provided funds is against public policy.

■ *Fines and penalties.* Costs of fines and penalties resulting from the contractor's violations of or failure to comply with federal, state, local, or foreign laws and regulations are unallowable. The only exception is when the penalty is incurred as a result of compliance with specific terms and conditions of the contract or written instructions from the contracting officer.

■ *Interest and other financial costs.* Interest on borrowings, bond discounts, costs of financing and refinancing capital, legal and professional fees paid in connection with preparing a prospectus, costs of issuing stock rights, and directly associated costs are unallowable. However, interest assessed by state or local taxing authorities is allowable.

■ *Organizational costs.* Unallowable organizational costs include (1) costs for planning or executing the organization or reorganization of the business's corporate structure (including mergers and acquisitions); (2) costs associated with raising capital; and (3) incorporation fees and the costs of attorneys, accountants, brokers, promoters, management consultants, and investment counselors (regardless of whether they are company employees).

■ *Alcoholic beverages.* Don't even think about it!

The above list does not cover all the unallowable costs, just those most common to commercial contractors. See Part 31 of the FAR for a complete listing of unallowable costs.

The contract itself also contains a variety of terms and conditions that will affect cost allowability. It cites the requirements and deliverables, which will define the scope of work to be performed. Other contract clauses will address cost-associated matters.

You will find, for example, clauses dealing with such topics as reimbursement for travel and other advance agreements peculiar to that specific contract. Such items are often referred to as Other Direct Charges (ODCs) and it is not uncommon for the government to specify that these charges are reimbursable on a cost basis only, meaning that no fee is applied.

As a contractor, you must maintain your cost records in enough detail for the government to audit. Auditors will seek to identify unallowable costs, including directly associated costs incurred in the contract performance. This requirement enables the government to identify and eliminate unallowable costs from your billing, claim, or proposal.

CALCULATING CONTRACT COST

The following is a simple example of how to calculate the total contract cost for each cost-reimbursement contract owned by a company. Suppose Microhard, Inc., an engineering firm, incurred the following direct and indirect costs as of December 31, 2010:

Direct Costs:

Direct labor	$ 700,000
Direct materials	$ 650,000

Indirect Costs:

Overhead:		General and Administrative:	
O/H labor	$110,000	G&A labor	$126,000
O/H vacation expense	25,000	Marketing labor	5,000
O/H sick leave	15,000	G&A vacation expense	28,000
Holidays	12,000	G&A sick leave	18,000
FICA expense	8,000	Holidays	14,000
Unemployment taxes	700	FICA expense	9,000
Workers compensation	500	Unemployment taxes	1,000
Disability insurance	1,200	Workers comp.	800
Group health insurance	10,000	Disability insurance	1,500
Conferences & seminars	500	Group health insurance	11,500
Consultants	850	Bank service charges	8,000
Depreciation	20,000	Conferences & seminars	3,000
Dues & subscriptions	700	Consultants	8,000
Copy charges	5,450	Postage & shipping	750
Equipment rentals	2,000	Depreciation	3,500
Recruiting	400	Dues & subscriptions	2,000
Repairs & maintenance	700	Copy charges	2,800
Postage & shipping	200	Equipment rental	850

Rent	80,000	Legal costs	6,500
Office supplies	5,500	Recruiting	1,500
Travel costs	520	Office supplies	3,600
Misc. expenses	2,780	Rent	15,000
		Repairs & maintenance	3,500
		Taxes	1,000
		Travel	2,400
		Misc. expenses	2,800
Total O/H claimed	**302,000**	**Total G&A expenses**	**280,000**

These accumulated costs are referred to as "pools." Microhard, Inc., has an overhead pool and a G&A pool. (If applicable, bid and proposal [B&P] and other business development costs are included in the G&A pool.)

The first step in determining your total cost for a cost-reimbursement contract is to calculate your O/H and G&A rates. An O/H rate is typically determined by dividing your indirect O/H expenses by your total direct labor.

> Note: Any allocation base (or denominator) can be used if you can establish and defend a causal/beneficial relationship, such as labor hours, square footage, or units of production.

Microhard, Inc., had the following rates:

O/H Rate Calculation:
Indirect O/H costs = $ 302,000 = **43%**
Total direct labor = $ 700,000*

* Microhard, Inc., uses direct labor dollars for its allocation base.

Microhard, Inc., calculates its G&A rate by dividing its G&A expenses by all other costs (total cost input).

G&A Rate Calculation:
Indirect G&A costs = $ 280,000 = **17%**
Total cost input* = $ 1,652,000

* In this example, Microhard's total cost input consisted of:

Direct labor	$ 700,000
Direct materials	$ 650,000
O/H costs	$ 302,000
Total cost input	$ 1,652,000

Now that Microhard, Inc., has determined its rates, the next step is to apply them to its various contracts.

Microhard, Inc.
Analysis of Incurred Costs
For the Year Ending 12/31/10

O/H Contract No.	Direct Labor	Rate 43%	Direct Materials	Subtotal	G&A Rate 17%	Total Contract Cost
Cost-Reimbursement Contracts:						
6000	150,000	64,710	125,000	339,710	57,580	397,290
6001	200,000	86,300	175,000	461,300	78,185	539,485
Time and Materials (T&M) Contracts (see Chapter 16):						
6200	100,000	43,140	50,000	193,140	32,735	225,875
Fixed-Price (FP) Contracts (see Chapter 14):						
6300	150,000	64,710	150,000	364,710	61,815	426,525
Commercial Fixed-Price (FP) Contracts:						
6301	100,000	43,140	150,000	293,140	49,685	342,825
Totals	**700,000**	**302,000**	**650,000**	**1,652,000***	**280,000**	**1,932,000**

* This subtotal balance ties to Microhard's G&A base (total cost input).

This schedule details the allocation of the O/H rate and the G&A rate to Microhard's various contracts (both government and commercial).

UNDERSTANDING RATES

Rates are typically calculated yearly because O/H and G&A costs tend to fluctuate from month to month. For example, rent might be paid quarterly. Most businesses establish temporary or proposed rates, commonly referred to as *billing* or *provisional* rates, at the beginning of each business year. The government compares proposed rates with the actual rates incurred in previous years to determine their reasonableness.

By establishing provisional rates at the beginning of each business year, a contractor can seek government reimbursement using these rates at interim dates. The government and the contractor establish final indirect cost rates after the contractor's business year closes. The provisional rates are then adjusted as necessary by the contractor.

Settlement of final indirect cost rates is a lengthy process. The contractor submits a proposed set of final indirect cost rates for the year. In many cases, the approval process will require an audit from the Defense Contract Audit Agency (DCAA). Once these final indirect cost rates are approved, they are not subject to change. The contractor needs to prepare a schedule to recognize any differences between the final indirect cost rates and the provisional rates.

Suppose PharmCo, a pharmaceutical company, determined its provisional (or billing) rates as follows:

Provisional (or Billing) Rates:

O/H rate	**44%**
G&A rate	**18%**

The government approved these rates for the business year beginning January 1, 2010. On August 30, 2011, PharmCo and the government determined the final indirect cost rates to be:

Final Indirect Cost Rates:

O/H rate	**43%**
G&A rate	**17%**

As a result, PharmCo had to reimburse the government for the rate differences. This difference was calculated as follows for contract number 6001:

		Final Provisional Rates		Indirect Rates	Difference
Direct labor		200,000		200,000	—
O/H	44%	88,000	43%	86,300	1,700
Direct materials		175,000		175,000	=
Subtotal		463,000		461,300	1,700
G&A	18%	83,340	17%	78,185	5,155
Total billed		546,340		539,485	6,855

PharmCo owes the government $6,855 for this contract. If PharmCo's final indirect cost rates had exceeded its provisional rates, it would be entitled to reimbursement for the difference (up to any ceiling rates stated in the contract).

Cost Calculation Recap

The FAR contains no specific requirements for the allocation of indirect costs. It merely dictates that indirect costs be allocated to provide for logical cost groupings that permit the costs to be distributed to the cost objectives receiving the corresponding benefits. The FAR does indicate, however, that manufacturing overhead costs, selling costs, and G&A costs are usually accounted for separately.

Most small- to medium-sized contractors use two cost pools: one for O/H and one for G&A. The use of a fringe benefits pool is becoming increasingly popular, probably because it creates the appearance of lower O/H rates. Fringe benefit costs typically include vacation, health insurance, bonuses, retirement plans, and payroll taxes.

If a contractor performs work at more than one location, including government sites, it might be advisable to use multiple O/H pools. These additional O/H pools enable the contractor to better associate its O/H costs with the specific activities receiving the corresponding benefits.

Contractors are always concerned about their rates because they express a percentage relationship between their indirect costs and their direct (base) costs. Having consistently low rates tends to enhance a contractor's competitiveness. The problem with examining a contractor's rates for competitiveness is that the rates themselves do not show the whole picture.

A manufacturing company that uses old, fully depreciated equipment might have a low O/H rate but be very inefficient, while a company that uses modern equipment might have a high O/H rate but be very efficient at manufacturing products at a low overall cost.

A contracting officer must look at the total cost of a proposal, as well as the individual cost elements, to make an accurate evaluation. An O/H rate is simply a device for allocating indirect costs. A rate by itself is meaningless!

FEE/PROFIT

The government defines *profit* as that element of the total remuneration that contractors may receive for contract performance over and above allowable costs. In laymen's terms, profit is whatever monies are left after all costs are paid. When talking about a particular contract, profit is the amount a contractor receives above its out-of-pocket costs. It is the reward for undertaking the contract in the first place. All contractors, except the narrow category of not-for-profit institutions, are primarily interested in profit.

Although the government wants to see businesses make a profit, that margin of profit is carefully examined to verify the contract's fairness. The government looks at various factors to justify the profit percentages, including risk, the economy, the time involved in the project, previous R&D expenditures, and the contractor's professional expertise.

The government puts statutory limitations on the amount of profit that can be earned on cost-reimbursement contracts. Profit on a cost-reimbursement contract is termed *fee*. The profit is a percentage of the total estimated (not actual) cost.

Cost-plus R&D contract profits may not exceed 15% of the agreed-to cost estimate. Most cost-plus-fixed-fee contracts have a profit ceiling of 10%. Federal law always limits the fee to some dollar amount on cost-reimbursement. There is no limit on the profit you may include in your price on fixed-price contracts, but it must be reasonable. Many government procurements are so competitive that contractors will use absurdly small fees in an attempt to lower the overall proposal cost to win the contract.

Federal law also prohibits the use of cost-plus-a-percentage-of-cost contracting. This contracting method encourages contractors to spend, not to manage costs, because profit is tied to increased expenditures and not to cost control or reduction. The more a contractor spends, the greater the profit it receives. The government requires all prime contracts (other than firm-fixed-price contracts) to prohibit cost-plus-a-percentage-of-cost subcontracts.

TYPES OF COST-REIMBURSEMENT CONTRACTS

The following are some common cost-reimbursement contract types.

Cost Contract

A cost contract is a cost-reimbursement contract in which the government reimburses the contractor for all allowable costs incurred during the contract's performance. The contractor receives no profit. This contract type is typically used for R&D, particularly with nonprofit organizations.

Cost-Sharing Contract

When the government agrees to reimburse a contractor for a predetermined portion of the allowable and allocable costs of contract performance, it uses a cost-sharing contract. With this contract type, the contractor agrees to absorb a portion of the contract costs, in expectation of substantial compensating benefits. These benefits might include enhancing the contractor's operational capabilities and expertise or enhancing its position for follow-on work. A contractor would be in an ideal position for obtaining additional work on a development contract if the jobs are awarded in stages or phases. The contractor receives no profit/fee for its efforts.

Sample Cost-Sharing Contract

Rockwell Collins, Inc., Cedar Rapids, Iowa, was awarded a $6.5 million cost-sharing contract ($4 million, government portion; $2.5 million, contractor portion) to provide for R&D to produce the next-generation security cards for programs employing GPS technology. Nine firms were solicited and eight proposals were received. The expected contract completion date is December 31, 2011. The solicitation issue date was April 10, 2010, and the negotiation completion date was June 16, 2010. The Space and Missile Systems Center, California, is the contracting activity.

Cost-Plus-Fixed-Fee Contract

The cost-plus-fixed-fee (CPFF) contract is the most commonly used cost-reimbursement contract. Under this contract type, the government pays all of the contractor's allowable costs, in addition to a fixed fee (or profit). The fixed fee does not vary with the costs of performing the contract. The terms of the contract determine the allowability of costs.

A CPFF takes two basic forms, the completion form and the term form. The completion form describes the scope of work by stating a definite goal or target and specifying an end product. It normally requires the contractor to complete and deliver the specified end product, such as a final report, within the estimated cost.

The term form describes the scope of work in general terms and obligates the contractor to devote a specified level of effort for a stated time. Under this form, if the government considers the contractor's performance satisfactory, it pays the fixed fee at the expiration of the agreed-upon period. This form may be used only if the contractor is obligated by the contract to provide a specific *level of effort* within a definite time period.

Both completion and term types are used primarily when the contract price is significant, the work specifications cannot be precisely defined, and the uncertainties involved in performing the contract are significant. Normally, the government prefers the completion form over the term form because of the differences in obligation assumed by the contractor.

Sample Completion Form

Suppose the government awarded First Aid, Inc., a CPFF contract to perform a study on AIDS. The contract requires First Aid to submit a report detailing its findings when the study is complete. The contract has an estimated cost of $500,000 and a fixed fee of $50,000. Assuming that First Aid had the following actual costs, it would be paid the following:

	Scenario 1	Scenario 2	Scenario 3
Actual costs	$ 450,000	$ 500,000	$ 550,000*
Fixed fee	$ 50,000	$ 50,000	$ 50,000
Total paid	$ 500,000	$ 550,000	$ 600,000

Notice that the fixed fee is not affected by the actual costs of contract performance.

* This example assumes that the contracting officer gave the contractor permission to exceed the estimated contract value/cost.

Sample Term Form

The government awarded Joe's Security a CPFF contract for guard services. The contract is in the term form and requires Joe's Security to provide 10,000 staff-hours at an estimated cost of $200,000. The contract has a fixed fee of $20,000.

Period of Performance	Level of Effort	Guard Rate	Actual Costs	
01/01–12/31/10	10,000 staff-hours	$20.00/hr.	$ 200,000	
			$ 20,000	Fixed Fee
			$ 220,000	Total Paid

In this example, the contractor certified that the level-of-effort hours (10,000 hours) specified in the contract were expended in performing the work.

If a contractor is in jeopardy of exceeding the level-of-effort hours during contract performance, the contracting officer may amend the contract or issue a new procurement for the remaining work. More than likely, the contracting officer will amend the contract before its expiration to avoid having to issue a new procurement, which tends to be time-consuming and costly.

The problem with CPFF contracts is that they give the contractor little incentive to control costs because the fee remains the same regardless of the actual costs. The government assumes all the cost risk. However, a contractor's costs may not exceed the contract's estimated cost unless the contracting officer approves the deviation.

CPFF Advantages

■ CPFF contracts offer little risk to the contractor.

■ Fee/profit is fixed, despite actual performance costs.

■ All allowable performance costs are reimbursed.

CPFF Disadvantages

■ Amount of profit or fee is limited (usually to 10%).

■ For the government, CPFF contracts give the contractor little incentive to control costs.

■ CPFF contracts are costly for the government to administer.

Cost-Plus-Incentive-Fee Contract

A cost-plus-incentive-fee (CPIF) contract is a cost-reimbursement contract that allows for an initially negotiated fee that is adjusted by a formula based on the relationship of total allowable costs to total target costs. It specifies a target cost, a target fee, minimum/maximum fees, and a fee adjustment formula. After contract performance, the fee payable to the contractor is determined in accordance with the formula.

This contract type bears the basic incentive-sharing features of an FPI contract in terms of an expressed sharing formula. A CPIF contract does not, however, contain a total price ceiling. Instead, it contains a provision for a minimum/maximum fee. At predetermined points above and below the target cost (the point of maximum or minimum fee), the contract converts into a CPFF contract.

This means that a contractor is eligible for a minimum fee, no matter what its actual contract costs turn out to be. The maximum fee is usually limited to 10% of the target cost. A CPIF contract is typically used when realistic incentives can be negotiated and the government can establish reasonable performance objectives.

Sample CPIF Contract

Suppose the Department of Agriculture awarded Pest Control, Inc., a contract to develop a pesticide for cornfields. It negotiated the following contract cost projections:

Target cost	=	$ 6,000,000
Target fee	=	$ 500,000
Maximum fee	=	$ 600,000
Minimum fee	=	$ 400,000
Sharing formula	=	70/30 (government/contractor)

The contracting officer used a sharing formula of 70/30 to ensure that Pest Control, Inc., is not unfairly penalized for contract overruns. If Pest Control, Inc., actually incurred $6,250,000 in contract costs, it would make the following profit:

Actual cost	$ 6,250,000*
Less: target cost	$ 6,000,000
Contract overrun	($ 250,000)
Contractor sharing %	30%
Total overrun profit	($ 75,000)
ADD: target profit	$ 500,000
Total profit	**$ 425,000**
ADD: actual cost	$ 6,250,000
Total contract value	**$ 6,675,000**

* This example assumes the contracting officer gave Pest Control, Inc., permission to exceed the target cost.

If Pest Control, Inc., had actually incurred $5,500,000 in contract costs, its profit would be:

Actual cost	$ 5,500,000
Less: target cost	$ 6,000,000
Contract underrun	$ 500,000
Contractor sharing %	30%
Total underrun profit	$ 100,000*
ADD: target profit	$ 500,000
Total profit	**$ 600,000**
ADD: actual cost	$ 5,500,000
Total contract value	**$ 6,100,000**

* Pest Control, Inc., is not entitled to the complete contract underrun ($500,000 x 30% = $150,000) because the maximum fee is limited to $600,000.

CPIF contracts are more likely to be used in situations where the cost reduction can be identified (e.g., energy contracts) and where the government and the contractor share in the reduction.

CPIF Advantages

■ If the contractor performs the job at less than the target cost, it accrues additional fee or profit (rewards for good management).

■ All allowable costs of performance are reimbursed.

CPIF Disadvantages

■ CPIF contracts are costly for the government to administer.

■ The amount of profit or fee is limited (usually to 10%).

Cost-Plus-Award-Fee Contract

A cost-plus-award-fee (CPAF) contract is a cost-reimbursement contract that provides for base fee at the inception of the contract and an award amount that the contractor earns in whole or in part during contract performance. The contractor receives the base fee provided it satisfactorily completes the contract. The award fee is designed to motivate the contractor to achieve excellence in such areas as quality, timeliness, technical ingenuity, and cost-effective management.

A base fee is paid in the same manner as the fixed fee in a CPFF contract—independent of the award criteria. Not all CPAF contracts, however, have a base fee. Some firms forgo a base fee as a demonstration of their commitment to lower costs and their confidence that they will succeed and make it up in the award fee.

The amount of the award fee to be paid is determined by the contracting officer's evaluation of the contractor's performance in terms of the criteria stated in the contract. The government makes this determination unilaterally, and it cannot be appealed by the contractor.

Sample CPAF Contract

Suppose Harvey's Moving Company was awarded a contract to move office furniture from the General Services Administration office in Washington, D.C., to the GSA office in Kansas City, Missouri. The contract states that the award fee paid to Harvey's Moving Company will be based on the following items:

■ Estimated cost—the job should be completed at or below the estimated cost.

■ Deadline—the job should be completed within two weeks.

■ Packaging requirements—the furniture should be properly packaged.

■ Proper distribution—the furniture should be delivered to the proper office locations in the new building.

This contract has the following features:

Estimated cost	$ 1,500,000
Base fee	$ 75,000
Award fee	$ 50,000

Let's assume that Harvey's Moving Company met most of these requirements, except that some furniture was delivered to the wrong office locations. It was paid the following:

Actual cost	$ 1,475,000
Base fee	$ 75,000*
Award fee	$ 45,000
Total paid	$ 1,595,000

* The base fee is not affected by the actual contract performance costs.

Evaluation summaries are typically given to the contractor to allow for comments and observations on the government's findings. This practice gives the contractor an opportunity to appeal the award fee recommendation. The contractor must qualify or justify actions taken during contract performance.

After considering the contractor's comments, the contracting officer (or the evaluation official) makes a unilateral award fee decision. That decision is not subject to further discussions, and the contractor may not appeal the decision.

CPAF Advantages

■ The fee is made up of a fixed portion and an award fee portion. The fixed fee is guaranteed; the award fee is based on performance.

■ All allowable performance costs are reimbursed.

CPAF Disadvantages

■ The base fee is typically small (usually around 3% of the target cost).

■ The total fee (base fee plus award fee) cannot exceed 10%.

■ ■ ■

Cost-reimbursement contracts are the government's least favorite contracting method because they place all, or essentially all, of the cost risk on the government. The government is prohibited from using cost-reimbursement contracts for acquiring commercial items. Once a cost-reimbursement contract is signed, the government must closely monitor the work to ensure that it is done in an effective and efficient manner.

■ ■ ■

16 Other Contract Types

Berry's World

SO BUSINESS IS REALLY GREAT, EH?

NOT REALLY! THAT'S MY PAY PACKAGE.

CEO

© 1996 by NEA, Inc

What's in this chapter?

- Indefinite-delivery contracts
- Time and materials contracts
- Labor-hour contracts
- Letter contracts
- Basic ordering agreements
- Performance-based contracting
- Multiyear contracts
- Options
- Life-cycle costing

Contracts come in all shapes and sizes. This chapter highlights many of the other contract types you are likely to run into. Don't be intimidated by these "other contract types." If you look closely, you'll notice they are all special modifications or variations of fixed-price or cost-reimbursement contracts. They are used to provide the government with greater flexibility in a number of different contracting situations.

INDEFINITE-DELIVERY CONTRACTS

Frequently, a buying office can specify accurately what it intends to purchase but cannot define the exact delivery dates and/or quantity that will be required. In that case, it uses indefinite-delivery contracts to procure such items. Indefinite-delivery contracts typically result in a fixed-price contract.

The actual delivery of these commonly used supplies and services is made when the contracting officer places an order. One of the primary advantages of this contract type is that it permits contractors to maintain a limited stock of the supplies that are being purchased in storage depots. It also permits direct shipment by the contractor to federal agencies.

Indefinite-delivery contracts come in two varieties: requirements contracts and indefinite-quantity contracts.

Requirements Contracts

This contract type typically is used for acquiring supplies or services when the government anticipates recurring requirements but cannot specify the precise quantities it will need during the specified contract period. The delivery or performance is scheduled when orders are placed with the contractor. These are also known as *call contracts*.

The contracting officer determines a realistic estimate of the total quantity required in the solicitation and the resulting contract. Records of previous requirements and consumption are used to develop the estimate. This estimate is not, however, a representation to the contractor that the estimated quantity will be required or ordered.

The contract also may place limits on the contractor's obligation to deliver and the government's obligation to order. In fact, most requirements contracts do not guarantee that a contractor will receive any orders. The contract guarantees only that the government will purchase all of its requirements for the supplies and services in the contract from the contractor during the contract term.

Buying offices use two types of requirements contracts: delivery order contracts and task order contracts. A delivery order contract is used to issue orders for the delivery of products or supplies, such as furniture and equipment, during the contract period, but it does not specify firm quantities (other than a minimum or maximum quantity). A task order contract, on the other hand, is used for services performed during the contract period, such as repairs and maintenance.

Indefinite-Quantity Contracts

Indefinite-quantity contracts provide for an indefinite quantity, within stated limits, of supplies or services to be furnished during a fixed period. These contracts are also referred to as indefinite-delivery/indefinite-quantity (ID/IQ) contracts. This contract type should be used only when a recurring need is anticipated. Delivery or performance is scheduled on the basis of orders placed with the contractor.

The government encourages buying offices to make multiple awards of indefinite-quantity contracts for the same or similar supplies or services. When multiple-award contracts are used, the contracting officer ensures that each awardee is given a fair opportunity to be considered for each order in excess of $3,000.

Each federal agency designates an ombudsman, who reviews contractor complaints and helps ensure that all contractors are afforded a fair opportunity to be considered for orders, consistent with the contract. The ombudsman must be a senior agency official who is independent of the contracting officer.

TIME AND MATERIALS CONTRACTS

Time and materials (T&M) contracts tend to be the contract vehicle of choice for specialized or high-tech services, such as engineering and accounting. Basically, a T&M contract combines the features of a cost-reimbursement contract and a fixed-price contract. T&M contracts are typically used when estimating the costs or extent of the work is almost impossible at the time of contract award.

Direct labor is provided at specified fixed hourly rates that include wages, O/H expenses, G&A expenses, and profit. This combined direct labor rate is referred to as a loaded labor rate. The contractor provides materials, at cost, including, if appropriate, material-handling costs.

Sample T&M Contract

Let's assume Joe Smith, a senior systems engineer, receives a T&M contract to provide technical assistance to the Department of the Navy. Joe's annual salary is $83,200; therefore, he has the following hourly rate:

Annual wage: $83,200/2,080 hours = $40.00
(52 weeks x 40 hours/week = 2,080 hours*)

* The government often requires the contractor to use a figure much lower than 2080 hours/year to break out holidays, vacation, and sick leave. The remaining hours are referred to as *productive hours*. Productive hours are often figured at 1,920 hours/year.

Hourly Direct Rate	O/H Rate 40%	G&A Total Subtotal	Fee on Rate 22%	Total Total Cost	Cost 10%	Bill Rate/ Hour
40.00	16.00	56.00	12.32	68.32	6.84	$75.16*

* This balance represents the loaded labor rate.

Joe's next step is to determine his total billing. If this job took 200 hours to complete and required the purchase of a new computer, the total bill would be calculated as follows:

	Total Hours	Loaded Labor Rate	Amount Billed
Senior Systems Engineer	200	$75.16	$15,032.00
Total labor			$15,032.00
Materials: Computer			$5,500.00*
Total billing			**$20,532.00**

* This computer was billed at actual cost.

Because T&M contracts give contractors an incentive to increase costs to increase profit, they are closely monitored by government officials. All T&M contracts have a ceiling price that the contractor may not exceed, expect at its own risk.

LABOR-HOUR CONTRACTS

A labor-hour contract is simply a variation of the T&M contract. The only difference is that the contractor does not supply materials.

LETTER CONTRACTS

If there is a national emergency, such as an earthquake or a hurricane (like Katrina), the government issues letter contracts to contractors to help provide immediate relief. A letter contract (or a letter-of-intent contract) is a written preliminary contractual instrument that authorizes a contractor to begin manufacturing products or performing services immediately. Depending on the circumstances, the letter contract should be as complete and definite as possible.

For its convenience, the government issues letter contracts without a firm contract price, but they do contain standard contract clauses and a limitation on the government's liability. Each letter contract must contain a negotiated definitization schedule that includes:

■ Dates for submission of the contractor's price proposal, required cost or pricing data, and, if required, subcontracting plans

■ Start date for negotiations

■ Agreement between the government and the contractor on the date by which definitization is expected to be completed.

Note: *Definitization* means the agreement on, or determination of, contract terms, specifications, and price, which converts the letter contract into a definitive/standard contract.

The target date for definitization should be within 180 days of the date the letter contract is issued or before completion of 40% of the work, whichever occurs first. The contracting officer may, in extreme cases and according to agency procedures, authorize an additional period. Contractors are reimbursed for only 80% of expenditures and receive no fee while under a letter contract, which gives the contractors a great incentive to get the contract definitized.

If, after exhausting all reasonable efforts, the parties fail to reach an agreement on price and fee, the contracting officer may unilaterally establish a reasonable price and fee. The contractor may appeal this determination in accordance with the disputes clause (see Chapter 17). Because of the uncertainties involved with letter contracts, they may be used only after the contracting officer determines in writing that no other contract is suitable.

BASIC ORDERING AGREEMENTS

A basic ordering agreement (BOA) is not a contract; it is a written instrument of understanding, negotiated between the government and a contractor. BOAs allow the government to expedite the procurement of products or services when specific items, quantities, and prices are unknown at the time of the agreement. If the government purchases a high-resolution printer, for example, it may establish a BOA for future toner purchases.

BOAs typically are used when past experience or future plans indicate the need for a contractor's particular products or services during the forthcoming year. They may be issued with fixed-price or cost-reimbursement contracts, but the contracting officer must still use competitive solicitations whenever possible. The BOA also lists the buying offices that are authorized to place orders under the agreement.

At a minimum, a BOA must contain:

■ Terms and clauses applying to future contracts (orders) that might be awarded to the contractor

■ Description of products or services

■ Methods for pricing, issuing, and delivering future orders.

Each BOA specifies the point at which an order becomes a binding contract. The agreement, for example, may state that the issuance of an order gives rise to an immediate contract.

PERFORMANCE-BASED CONTRACTING

Performance-based contracting methods attempt to base the total amount paid to a contractor on the performance quality levels achieved and standards met on the contract (i.e., they motivate the contractor to perform at optimal levels). Each performance-based contract should:

■ Describe the work in terms of what is to be the required output, rather than how the work is to be accomplished

■ Use measurable performance standards, such as terms of quality, timeliness, and quantity

■ Specify procedures for reductions of fee or for reductions to the price of a fixed-price contract when services are not performed or do not meet contract requirements

■ Include performance incentives (where appropriate).

Contracting activities should also develop quality assurance surveillance plans when acquiring services. These plans should recognize the responsibility of the contractor to carry out its quality control obligations, and they should contain measurable inspection and acceptance criteria.

The contract type most likely to motivate the contractor to perform at optimal levels should be chosen. Fixed-price contracts are generally appropriate for services that can be objectively defined and for which the risk of performance is manageable.

MULTIYEAR CONTRACTS

In 1972 the Commission on Government Procurement recommended that Congress authorize all federal agencies to enter into multiyear contracts that are based on clearly specified requirements. A multiyear contract is for the purchase of products and services for more than one year, but not more than five years. This recommendation was based on the Commission's findings that the use of multiyear contracts would result in significant savings to the government because they enable contractors to offer better overall prices while maintaining a steady workload.

Congress was reluctant to approve multiyear contracts because it has no authority to approve programs that future congresses must fund. It was also reluctant to approve contracting arrangements that are difficult to change in subsequent years. Congress did, however, recognize that one-

or two-year planning and funding horizons are generally too short for many of the government's larger procurements.

The FAR encourages the use of multiyear contracts to achieve:

■ Lower costs and reduced administrative burdens

■ Continuity of production and, thus, avoidance of annual start-up costs

■ Stabilization of the contractor workforce

■ A broader competitive base, resulting from greater opportunity for participation by firms that might not otherwise be willing or able to compete for lesser quantities—particularly for contracts involving high start-up costs

■ Greater incentive for contractors to improve productivity through investment in capital facilities, equipment, and advanced technology.

Federal agencies that propose to use multiyear contracts must seek advance approval during the budget process.

Multiyear-Basis Contracts

If the government awards the contract on a multiyear basis, it obligates only the contract funds for the first-year requirement, with succeeding years' requirements funded annually. If the funds do not become available to support the succeeding years' requirements, the federal agency must cancel the contract, including the total requirements of all remaining program years.

Because of this cancellation risk, the contract often contains a contract provision that allows for reimbursement of unrecovered nonrecurring costs. These costs might include special tooling and test equipment; preproduction engineering; and costs incurred for the assembly, training, and transportation of a specialized workforce.

For each program year subject to cancellation, the contracting officer establishes a cancellation ceiling price by estimating the nonrecurring costs. The cancellation ceiling price is reduced each program year in direct proportion to the remaining requirements subject to cancellation.

Suppose a contracting officer in the General Services Administration awarded a multiyear contract to Security Experts, Inc., to install a new security system in its Washington, D.C., office. The contract is for three years, and the estimated cancellation ceiling price is 10% of the total multiyear contract price.

Total multiyear contract price	$5,000,000
	10%
Cancellation ceiling price	$500,000

The cancellation ceiling price is then reduced by the contracting officer over the three-year contract period.

Cancellation ceiling price	$500,000
Year 1: 30% x 500,000	($150,000)
	$350,000
Year 2: 30% x 500,000	($150,000)
	$200,000
Year 3: 40% x 500,000	($200,000)
	0

The contracting officer also establishes cancellation dates for each program year's requirements.

Although multiyear-basis contract requirements are budgeted and financed for only the first program year, the government solicits prices for both the current-year program requirement alone and the total multiyear requirements. By obtaining dual proposals, the contracting officer is better able to establish the total job requirements and the contracting period. A 10% savings in favor of multiyear contracting has typically been used as an evaluation benchmark.

Either sealed bidding or negotiated procedures may be used when soliciting for multiyear contracts. Multiyear contracts typically result in a fixed-price contract. In any multiyear contract, the government must indicate the evaluation period.

OPTIONS

Let's assume Computer Learning Center was awarded an option contract to provide computer training services to the Department of Commerce. The contract has a one-year base period and four option periods.

	Beginning Date	Ending Date	Maximum Labor Costs	Contract Exercised
Base year	01/01/11	12/31/11	$1,800,000	Yes
Option I	01/01/12	12/31/12	$1,900,000	Yes
Option II	01/01/13	12/31/13	$2,000,000	Yes
Option III	01/01/14	12/31/14	$2,000,000	Yes
Option IV	01/01/15	12/31/15	$2,100,000	Pending
Total Contract Value			**$9,800,000**	

An option gives the government a unilateral right to purchase additional products or services called for by the contract. Option contracts are not the same as multiyear contracts, which require the government to purchase the entire multiyear procurement (unless the requirement is canceled or the funds are made unavailable). To exercise an option, a contracting officer must determine that funds are available and the need for the option exists.

The presence of an option is no guarantee that the government will exercise the option and purchase additional items. The contracting officer considers price and other related factors when determining whether to exercise the option. If a new solicitation fails to produce a better price or more advantageous offer than that provided by the option, the government generally exercises an option.

The solicitation states the basis on which the options will be evaluated. Anticipated market conditions should never be a basis for deciding whether to exercise an option. To exercise an option, the contracting officer must provide a written notice to the contractor within the period specified in the contract.

If the contracting officer decides to exercise the option, he or she must certify that all administrative requirements have been met by the contractor for the base year. This certification is filed with the original contract. The contract is then modified to incorporate the option, citing the appropriate contract clause as the authority.

When soliciting for option contracts, the contracting officer may use sealed bidding or negotiated procedures.

LIFE-CYCLE COSTING

Suppose the Department of Homeland Security is acquiring a satellite dish, the life of which is determined to be four years. Because satellite dishes tend to have high support costs, the contracting officer seeks costs that apply to the:

■ Outright purchase of the satellite dish

■ Total leased price/costs

■ Total leased price/costs with an option to purchase.

Now let's assume that Satellites "R" Us submits the following prices/cost estimates to the government:

Total purchase price: $500,000

Estimated maintenance costs (by year):
2011	$15,000
2012	$18,000
2013	$21,000
2014	$24,000

Leased price/costs (by year):

2011 ($10,000 per month)	$120,000
2012 ($12,000 per month)	$144,000
2013 ($14,000 per month)	$168,000
2014 ($16,000 per month)	$192,000

Purchase option: The government has the option of purchasing the satellite dish for $375,000 at the beginning of 2013.

This satellite dish will also incur the following operating costs:

Electricity:	$ 3,000 ($250 a month)
Rent:	$ 12,000 ($1,000 a month)

The next step is to calculate the total cost of each purchase option.

1. Outright purchase of the satellite dish:

	2011	2012	2013	2014	Totals
Purchase price	$ 500,000	—	—	—	$ 500,000
Maintenance costs	15,000	18,000	21,000	24,000	78,000
Electricity costs	3,000	3,000	3,000	3,000	12,000
Rent	12,000	12,000	12,000	12,000	48,000
Totals	**530,000**	**33,000**	**36,000**	**39,000**	**$ 638,000**

2. Lease price/costs of the satellite dish:

	2011	2012	2013	2014	Totals
Lease costs	$ 120,000	144,000	168,000	192,000	$ 624,000
Maintenance costs	—	—	—	—	—
Electricity costs	3,000	3,000	3,000	3,000	12,000
Rent	12,000	12,000	12,000	12,000	48,000
Totals	**135,000**	**159,000**	**183,000**	**207,000**	**$ 684,000**

3. Total cost when the purchase option is exercised:

	2011	2012	2013	2014	Totals
Lease costs	$ 120,000	144,000	—	—	$ 264,000
Purchase option	—	—	375,000	—	375,000
Maintenance costs	—	—	—	—	—
Electricity costs	3,000	3,000	3,000	3,000	12,000
Rent	12,000	12,000	12,000	12,000	48,000
Totals	**135,000**	**159,000**	**390,000**	**15,000**	**$ 699,000**

In this example, the contracting officer would purchase the satellite dish outright because that option offers the lowest overall cost to the government. This illustration is designed to provide a basic understanding of life-cycle costing (LCC). Many other costs and factors could apply to the acquisition and operation of a satellite dish.

LCC is the estimation and analysis of the total cost of acquiring, developing, operating, supporting, and (if applicable) disposing of an item or system being acquired. Both direct and indirect costs make up the total LCC of the system. LCC enhances the decision-making process in system acquisitions and is used as a management tool throughout the process.

The government is concerned about a system's LCC because of the rapidly increasing cost of supporting the system once it is placed into operation. In fact, for many system acquisitions, the cost of operating and supporting the system over its useful life is greater than the acquisition cost. The LCC program is designed to reduce these operating and support costs by analyzing design alternatives.

When a federal agency determines that LCC could be an important aspect of a particular program, it decides on the degree and method of implementation. The solicitation states the requirements as they relate to the proposal and source-selection process.

An LCC model comprises one or more systematically arranged mathematical calculations that formulate a cost methodology to arrive at reliable cost estimates. The General Services Administration makes its LCC program, called BARS, available to agencies at no charge and to vendors for a nominal cost. Various commercial packages are also in widespread government and commercial use.

To get more detailed information on LCC, contact:

National Technical Information Service (NTIS)
Technology Administration
U.S. Department of Commerce
Phone (800) 553-6847

www.ntis.gov

■   ■   ■

Selection of the contract type should not be based on either the government's or the contractor's individual biases. Rather, the selection should be based on an objective analysis of all factors involved and of the contract type that fits the particular procurement.

■   ■   ■

Contract
Administration

© Randy Glasbergen.

"Our billing system was perfect until the boss put in his two-cents worth. Now all of our figures are off by two cents."

What's in this chapter?

- Contract administration office
- Contract financing
- Getting paid
- Changes clause
- Contract modifications
- Constructive changes
- Government-furnished property
- Inspection and acceptance
- Contractor data rights
- Record retention
- Audits/examination of records
- Contract Disputes Act
- Alternative dispute resolution
- Termination for convenience
- Termination for default
- Contract closeout

You've followed many of the recommendations in this book, and the contracts are pouring in. Champagne toasts all around! So what happens after the contract is awarded?

A contractor must be prepared to deal with the responsibilities associated with the contract's performance. These include complying with applicable labor laws, preparing budgets and status reports, performing inspections, and preparing invoices, to name a few. All requirements are spelled out in the contract. This chapter highlights many of the administrative responsibilities your contract will have.

Both the government and the contractor are responsible for the contract's administration. The government acts through its agent, typically the administrative contracting officer (ACO), to perform or oversee contract-related functions. The ACO's degree of involvement depends on the type and nature of the contract.

CONTRACT ADMINISTRATION OFFICE

Many federal agencies use contract administration offices (CAOs), located throughout the country, to administer contract functions. Each CAO assists in such areas as correcting administrative errors, explaining special clauses and requirements, ensuring on-time performance, inspecting/accepting final products, and ensuring payment. FAR 42.3 details the CAO's functions.

CONTRACT FINANCING

Government financing is available to contractors in certain circumstances. A contractor with a large fixed-price contract that has a long lead time would be a good candidate for contract financing. (The contracting officer may not treat the need for financing as a handicap during source selection.) The government typically uses three methods to finance a contract: progress payments, guaranteed loans, and advance payments.

Progress Payments

The contractor receives progress payments as work progresses on the contract. Payments are typically based on the costs incurred by the contractor during contract performance. They do not relate to any contract milestones or completion stages.

Contracting activities customarily apply a standard progress payment rate to the contract performance costs. This standard rate ranges from 75% to 85% of the incurred costs for large businesses and 80% to 95% for small businesses. Progress payments are used only with fixed-price contracts.

Let's assume Office Store received a firm-fixed-price contract from the Department of State for the production of 400 executive desks on January 1, 2010. The contract's value is $400,000, and it is expected to be completed over a one-year period. The contracting officer determines that Office Store is eligible for progress payments, which will be made quarterly.

QTR	Costs Incurred Y-T-D	Standard Rate	Payment
1st	100,000	90%	$ 90,000
2nd	90,000	90%	$ 81,000
3rd	80,000	90%	$ 72,000
4th	80,000	90%	$ 72,000
		Total Payments	**$ 315,000**

Office Store receives the remaining balance of $85,000 upon contract completion.

Before a contracting officer authorizes progress payments, he or she determines whether the contractor's accounting system can reliably segregate and accumulate contract costs and properly administer the progress payments.

Note: Percentage-of-completion payments are usually treated as a method of payment, not as contract financing.

Guaranteed Loans

Guaranteed loans are essentially the same as conventional loans made by private financial institutions. The only difference is that the government shares in any losses up to its guaranteed percentage (usually 90% or less). The private lending institution handles all administrative aspects of the loan. The contractor makes the principal and interest payments to the lending institution and pays a fee to the government for the privilege of the guarantee.

Guaranteed loans may be made by the following federal agencies:

■ Department of Defense

■ Department of Energy

■ Department of Commerce

■ Department of the Interior

■ Department of Agriculture

■ General Services Administration

■ National Aeronautics and Space Administration

■ Small Business Administration.

For more information on guaranteed loans, see FAR 32.3.

Advance Payments

Suppose the Department of Agriculture (DOA) awarded a firm-fixed-price contract on July 1, 2010, to The Sky's the Limit, Inc., to design and build a satellite. The contract's total value is $6 million, and the estimated contract period is three years. Because of the satellite's high cost, the contracting officer agrees to advance the contractor $1.5 million each year of the contract.

Advance Payment	Amount
Year 1	1,500,000
Year 2	1,500,000
Year 3	1,500,000
Total advance payments	**4,500,000**

The Sky's the Limit, Inc., completes the satellite on August 15, 2013, at which time DOA pays the contract balance.

Total advance payments	**4,500,000**
Total contract value	**6,000,000**
Final payment	**1,500,000**

To obtain advance payments, the contracting officer must determine it is in the government's best interests and the contractor must post adequate security (bank accounts or other significant assets). These payments are then liquidated or applied against the contract amount owed the contractor upon the delivery of the contracted products or the performance of the contracted services.

Because advance payments are not measured by contract performance, they differ from partial, progress, or other payment loan types. Prime contractors also may obtain advance payments to use with subcontractors.

GETTING PAID

Every contract or purchase order has specific instructions for preparing and submitting invoices. Information on where to send the invoice (or bill), number of copies to send, and required government codes is generally included on the contract's cover page. If the instructions are incomplete or unclear, call the contracting officer immediately.

To be paid in a timely manner, you must prepare your invoice according to the contract's instructions! Each invoice submitted to the government must contain:

■ Contractor's name and address

■ Invoice date (as close as possible to the mailing date)

■ Contract number (including order number and contract line item number)

■ Price of supplies delivered or services performed

■ Shipping and payment terms (e.g., shipment number and date, prompt-payment discount terms)

■ Name and address of the contractor official to whom payment is sent (must be the same as that in the contract)

■ Name, title, phone number, and mailing address of the person to be notified in the event of a defective invoice

■ Any other information or documentation required by the contract (such as evidence of shipment).

Contractors are strongly encouraged to assign an identification number to each invoice.

The contractor must support all of its invoices with an approved receiving report or any other government documentation authorizing payment. The Department of Defense uses DD Form 250, Material Inspection and Receiving Report, to demonstrate government inspection and acceptance. Any receiving report authorizing payment must, at a minimum, include:

■ Contract number for products delivered or services performed

■ Description of product delivered or services performed

■ Quantities of products received and accepted or services performed

■ Date products were delivered or services performed

■ Date products or services were accepted by the designated government official

■ Signature or electronic equivalent (when permitted), and printed name, title, mailing address, and phone number of the designated government official responsible for acceptance or approval.

The agency receiving official should forward the receiving report to the designated payment office by the fifth working day after government acceptance or approval.

Payments will depend on the contract type, its terms and conditions, and the allowability of those costs. Under fixed-price contracts, final payment is typically due when the government accepts the completed contract. The contractor obtains final payment by submitting a proper voucher or invoice, with appropriate backup, such as DD Form 250.

For cost-reimbursement contracts, the normal payment procedure is to invoice the government for allowable costs and fees incurred as work progresses. Most contracting activities allow contractors to submit invoices monthly. Contractors typically use SF 1034, Public Voucher, to bill the government. The voucher should be accompanied by appropriate backup documentation, such as the number of labor hours expended by labor category.

Prompt Payment Act

In 1982 Congress passed the Prompt Payment Act to require federal agencies to pay interest on contractor invoices that are not paid in a timely manner. The bill was enacted because contracting activities were chronically tardy in making payments, which caused many contractors to have cash flow problems, even putting some out of business.

MATERIAL INSPECTION AND RECEIVING REPORT

Form Approved
OBM No. 0704-0248

The public reporting burden for this collection of information is estimated to average 30 minutes per response, including the time for reviewing instructions, searching existing data sources, gathering and maintaining the data needed, and completing and reviewing the collection of information. Send comments regarding this burden estimate or any other aspect of this collection of information, including suggestions for reducing this burden, to Department of Defense, Washington Headquarters Services, Directorate for Information Operations and Reports, (0704-0248), 1215 Jefferson Davis Highway, Suite 1204, Arlington, VA 22202-4302. Respondents should be aware that notwithstanding any other provision of law, or person shall be subject to any penalty for failing to comply with a collection of information it does not display a currently valid OMB control number.

PLEASE DO NOT RETURN YOUR COMPLETED FORM TO EITHER OF THESE ADDRESSES.
SEND THIS FORM IN ACCORDANCE WITH THE INSTRUCTIONS CONTAINED IN THE DFARS, APPENDIX F-401.

1. PROCUREMENT INSTRUMENT IDENTIFICATION (CONTRACT) NO. SP0600-YY-D-0000	(ORDER) NO. AB01	6. INVOICE NO./DATE	7. PAGE 1 OF 1	8. ACCEPTANCE POINT D

2. SHIPMENT NO. ABC-0001	3. DATE SHIPPED 10/30/08	4. B/L Prepaid Rail Road Company TCN	5. DISCOUNT TERMS Net 30 Days

9. PRIME CONTRACTOR CODE	10. ADMINISTERED BY CODE
Coal Diggers, Inc. 490 West Point Street Columbus, OH 43216-5000	DESC-AC Defense Fuel Supply Center 8725 John J. Kingman Rd., Ste 2941 Ft. Belvoir, VA 22060-6222
11. SHIPPED FROM (If other than 9) CODE	12. PAYMENT WILL BE MADE BY CODE
Coal Diggers, Inc. 490 West Point Street Columbus, OH 43216-5000	DESC-AC Defense Fuel Supply Center 8725 John J. Kingman Rd., Ste 2941 Ft. Belvoir, VA 22060-6222
13. SHIPPED TO CODE	14. MARKED FOR CODE
DLA Stream Plant 700 Robbins Ave. Philadelphia, PA 19111-5096	

15. ITEM NO.	16. STOCK/PART NO. (Indicate number of shipping container -type of container – container number) DESCRIPTION	17. QUANTITY SHIP/REC'D*	18. UNIT	19. UNIT PRICE	20. AMOUNT
0001	" x " Bituminous Coal Total Cars Shipped 12	1,000	TONS	$ 500	500,000

21. CONTRACT QUALITY ASSURANCE

a. ORIGIN	b. DESTINATION	22. RECEIVER'S USE
■ CQA ☐ ACCEPTANCE of listed items	☐ CQA ☐ ACCEPTANCE of listed items	Quantities shown in column 17 were received in apparent good condition except as noted.
Has been made by me or under my supervision and they conform to contract, except as noticed herein or on supporting documents.	Has been made by me or under my supervision and they conform to contract, except as noticed herein or on supporting documents.	DATE RECEIVED / SIGNATURE OF AUTHORIZED GOVERNMENT REPRESENTATIVE
DATE / SIGNATURE OF AUTHORIZED GOVERNMENT REPRESENTATIVE	DATE / SIGNATURE OF AUTHORIZED GOVERNMENT REPRESENTATIVE	TYPED NAME:
TYPED NAME:	TYPED NAME: TITLE:	TITLE: MAILING ADDRESS:
TITLE: MAILING ADDRESS:	MAILING ADDRESS:	COMMERCIAL TELEPHONE NUMBER:
COMMERCIAL TELEPHONE NUMBER:	COMMERCIAL TELEPHONE NUMBER:	* If quantity received by the Government is the same as quantity shipped, indicate by (X) mark, if different, enter actual quantity received below quantity shipped and encircle.

23. CONTRACTOR USE ONLY

I certify that on October 30, 2006, Coal Diggers, Inc. shipped the materials called for by contract SP0600-YY-D-0000 CLIN0001 via Railway Inc. in railcars on 12 bills of lading in accordance with the applicable requirements for shipment. I further certify that the supplies are of the quality specified and are in all respects in conformance with the contract requirements, including specifications, size consist, item description, and in the quantity shown on this acceptance document and the attached mine analysis.

Date: October 30, 2008   Title: Joe Smith, President   Signature:

DD FORM 250, AUG 2000   PREVIOUS EDITION IS OBSOLETE.

Sample DD Form 250

Standard Form 1034 Revised October 1987 Department of the Treasury 1 TFM 4-2000 1034-122		**PUBLIC VOUCHER FOR PURCHASES AND SERVICES OTHER THAN PERSONAL**	VOUCHER NO. 0005
U.S.DEPARTMENT, BUREAU, OR ESTABLISHMENT AND LOCATION		DATE VOUCHER PREPARED 10/31/08	SCHEDULE NO.
U.S. Department of Energy 1000 Independence Ave., SW Washington, DC 20585		CONTRACT NUMBER AND DATE DE-AC05-98AD63275	PAID BY
		REQUISITION NUMBER AND DATE 01-99PP00323.000 6/15/08	

PAYEE'S NAME AND ADDRESS	Safety Shuttle, Inc. 450 Sharp Street Albuquerque, NM 87103	DATE INVOICE RECEIVED
		DISCOUNT TERMS
		PAYEE'S ACCOUNT NUMBER
SHIPPED FROM	TO WEIGHT	GOVERNMENT B/L NUMBER

NUMBER AND DATE OF ORDER	DATE OF DELIVERY OR SERVICE	ARTICLES OR SERVICES (Enter description, item number of contract or Federal supply schedule, and other information deemed necessary)	QUAN- TITY	UNIT PRICE		AMOUNT
				COST	PER	(¹)
0001AB	10/16/08	Shuttle bus service				
	To	For detail, See SF1035 – total amount of claim				6,000.00
	10/31/08	transferred from page 1 of 1 SF 1035				
		Cost-Reimbursement – Provisional Payment				

(Use continuation sheets if necessary)   (Payee must NOT use the space below)   **TOTAL**   6,000.00

PAYMENT: ☐ PROVISIONAL ☐ COMPLETE ■ PARTIAL ☐ FINAL ☐ PROGRESS ☐ ADVANCE	APPROVED FOR Provisional Pmt =$ Subject to Audit BY² Joel J. Hunt, Auditor Defense Contract Audit Agency (DCAA) TITLE 123 Anyplace, Any City, State 00000 (703) 555-1111	EXCHANGE RATE =$1.00	DIFFERENCES
			Amount verified; correct for
			(Signature or initials)

Pursuant to authority vested in me, I certify that this voucher is correct and proper for payment.

_____   _____   _____
(Date)   (Authorized Certifying Officer)³   (Title)
                           ACCOUNTING CLASSIFICATION

CHECK NUMBER	ON ACCOUNT OF U.S. TREASURY	CHECK NUMBER	ON (Name of bank)
CASH $	DATE	PAYEE³	

¹ When stated in foreign currency, insert name of currency.
² If the ability to certify and authority to approve are combined in one person, one signature only is necessary; otherwise the approving officer will sign in the space provided, over his official title.
³ When a voucher is receipted in the name of a company or corporation, the name of the person writing the company or corporate name, as well as the capacity in which he signs, must appear. For example: "John Doe Company, per John Smith, Secretary" or "Treasurer", as the case may be.

Previous edition usable

PER
TITLE

NSN 7650-00-634-4206

PRIVACY ACT STATEMENT
The information requested on this form is required under the provisions of 31 U.S.C. 82b and 82c, for the purpose of disbursing Federal money. The information requested is to identify the particular creditor and the amounts to be paid. Failure to furnish this information will hinder discharge of the payment obligation.

Sample SF 1034

If a contractor is not paid within 30 days of receipt of a properly prepared invoice, the paying office (or contracting activity) must pay interest on the overdue bills, at a rate periodically set by the Treasury Department. The interest penalty begins the day after the required payment date and ends on the date when payment is made. The temporary unavailability of funds needed to make timely payments does not excuse the contracting activity from obligations to pay interest penalties.

The contracting activity must notify the contractor within seven days of receiving an erroneous invoice to explain any defects or improprieties. This act also prohibits contracting activities from taking prompt-payment discounts after the discount period has expired. The burden of completing formal acceptance and making payments on time to qualify for the discount falls on the government.

CHANGES CLAUSE

The changes clause allows the contracting officer to make unilateral changes to a contract in one or more of the following areas:

■ Drawings, designs, or specifications

■ Shipment or packaging methods

■ Place of inspection, delivery, or acceptance.

A unilateral change occurs when the government orders the contractor to change the performance requirements without prior contractor approval. The changes, however, must be within the scope of the original contract. The contracting officer, for example, cannot direct a construction contractor to perform R&D services. The changes clause depends on the contract type.

The contracting officer is the only person authorized to make these changes. A change order, SF 30 (Amendment of Solicitation/Modification of Contract), is the document used to implement the change. If the change order requires the contractor to incur additional costs, the contracting officer must equitably adjust the contract to compensate the contractor.

CONTRACT MODIFICATIONS

Contract modifications are written changes to an existing contract. These changes may be accomplished by unilateral action under a contract provision or by bilateral (or mutual) action of the contracting parties. Modifications are typically used to:

■ Make administrative changes

■ Issue change orders

■ Make changes authorized by clauses other than a change clause (such as property clause, options clause, or suspension of work clause)

■ Issue termination notices

■ Definitize letter contracts.

Bilateral changes, also called *supplemental agreements,* must be in writing and signed by both parties.

Only contracting officers, acting within the scope of their authority, may execute modifications on the government's behalf. As with change orders, SF 30 (Amendment of Solicitation/Modification of Contract) is used for making contract modifications.

Modifications to contracts, including those issued unilaterally, are priced before they are executed if it can be done without adversely affecting the government's interest. If the modification could result in a significant cost increase, a new ceiling price is negotiated.

CONSTRUCTIVE CHANGES

Constructive changes, also known as *de facto* changes, are actions (or failures to act) by the government that cause the contractor to perform additional or different responsibilities from those expressed in the contract. These changes are not accompanied by a formal change order. The following constitute constructive changes:

■ Defective specifications

■ Requirements to adhere to delivery schedules when a contractor is entitled to an extension (e.g., weather-related delays)

■ Excessive inspection requirements

■ Unwarranted rejection of products following inspection

■ Acceleration of the contract's performance requirements

■ Interference with the contractor's performance by government personnel.

The contractor should notify the contracting officer in writing when a government action affects the contract terms and conditions. This notification or claim should be sent as soon as the change is identified. Upon claim receipt, the contracting officer investigates the circumstances of the alleged change.

If the contracting officer agrees with the claim, the alleged government action is confirmed as a legitimate change and appropriate written directions are issued. Contractors should be certain they receive written authorization before proceeding with a constructive change.

On the other hand, if the contracting officer feels the action is "within the scope of the contract," he or she may reject the claim. In that case, the contractor must file a claim under the disputes clause (see FAR 52.233-1).

GOVERNMENT-FURNISHED PROPERTY

For most government contracts, the contractor furnishes all property or equipment necessary to perform the requirements. However, the government allows contractors to use government property when its use results in significant savings, standardization, or expedited contract production. Common types of government-furnished property include facilities, materials, special tooling, and special test equipment.

Contractors must segregate the government-furnished property and equipment from their own. They must also maintain adequate control records, such as inventory documents and maintenance records. The government identifies all government-furnished property in the solicitation and resulting contract.

INSPECTION AND ACCEPTANCE

Inspection and acceptance requirements help protect the government's interests. For purchases at or below the simplified acquisition threshold ($100,000) and commercial purchases, the government typically relies on the contractor to test whether the items conform to the contract quality requirements. The contractor must keep complete records of its inspection work and make them available to the government.

For all other product purchases, the contractor has the following inspection requirements:

■ The contractor must maintain an acceptable system for the inspection.

■ The contractor must maintain records that completely document the inspections it conducts during contract performance.

■ The government may inspect and test all products at any time prior to acceptance. The government may also inspect subcontractors' plants.

■ The government may require replacement or correction of products that fail to meet contract requirements. If the contractor fails to replace or fix rejected items, the government may have another contractor provide them and charge any additional costs to the defaulting contractor.

If the government fails to conduct inspections or tests, the contractor still must furnish the products specified by the contract.

Acceptance is the government's acknowledgment that the products meet the contractual requirements, as evidenced by the signature of the government's authorized representative (typically, the contracting officer). The government typically uses three forms for inspection and receiving documentation:

■ DD Form 250, Material Inspection and Receiving Report

■ DD Form 1155, Order for Supplies and Services

■ SF 44, Purchase Order-Invoice-Voucher.

Each contract specifies the point of acceptance for the products. Title to the items passes to the government upon acceptance.

FIRST ARTICLE APPROVAL

First article testing is a specialized type of government inspection required for some contracts. A first article is a preproduction sample of products prepared for the contract. This inspection procedure ensures that the contractor can furnish a product that conforms to the contract requirements. Commercial purchases and R&D contracts are usually not subject to first article testing.

First article testing may be appropriate when:

■ The contractor has not previously furnished the product to the government.

> ■ The government requires assurance that the product is appropriate for its intended use.
>
> ■ An approved first article will serve as a manufacturing standard.
>
> The contract may require the government, the contractor, or both to perform first article testing; upon successful completion, the contractor may begin production.
>
> A first article should not be confused with a bid sample. Bid samples are used by contractors to demonstrate their products' characteristics. First articles, in contrast, are actual samples of the items required by the contract.

CONTRACTOR DATA RIGHTS

One of the most complex and misunderstood areas in federal contracting is determining the owner of data produced or used under a contract. Do the data rights belong to the government or to the contractor? Both have valid and specific interest in data.

The government has extensive needs for technical data, such as research results, engineering drawings, and manuals. Therefore, in most contracts, the government exerts its authority to acquire data rights. Contractors, on the other hand, have an economic interest in the data components or processes that they have developed at their own expense. Public disclosure of these data could jeopardize their competitive advantage.

Each contract arrangement includes provisions to balance the government's need for data rights against the contractor's interest in protecting proprietary data. The government uses three types of data rights to protect its interests:

■ *Unlimited rights.* The government's right to use, duplicate, or disclose data for any purpose (and to have or permit others to do so).

■ *Limited rights.* Limited data rights may include restrictions on the data's being (1) released or disclosed outside the government, (2) used by the government for manufacture, or (3) in the case of computer software documentation, used for preparing the same or similar computer software.

■ *Government purpose license rights.* Rights to use, duplicate, or disclose data, in whole or in part and in any manner, for government purposes only, or to permit others to do so for government purposes only (such as for competitive procurements).

The source of funds used in developing data dictates the type of data rights clause in a contract. If the data were developed at the government's expense (i.e., the government paid the contractor for developing the product), the government holds unlimited rights. When the contractor develops the data wholly at its private expense and the information has not been made available to the public without restrictions, the government holds limited rights.

The limited rights protection is effective only if the contractor suitably identifies and marks the data to which the government asserts limited rights. Government purpose license rights typically apply to partially funded contracts (or contracts for which the contractor has contributed more than 50% of the development costs).

RECORD RETENTION

Contractors and subcontractors must retain and make available to the government certain books, records, documents, and other supporting evidence if the contract exceeds the simplified acquisition threshold. Generally, contractors must retain these records for three years after final contract payment.

Most accounting or financial records have a retention period of four years. The retention period is calculated from the end of the fiscal year during which the contractor entered a charge or allocated a cost to a government contract or subcontract. The contract itself may also specify a retention policy of its own.

Let's assume Urban Crisis, Inc., researched highway congestion in urban areas for the Department of Transportation and received the final contract payment on November 15, 2011. Urban Crisis, Inc., operates on a calendar-year basis (January 1 through December 31), and the contract requires a four-year retention period. In this case, the contractor must maintain the contract records until December 31, 2015.

Final payment date	November 15, 2011
Retention period	4 years
End of retention period	December 31, 2015

If the contractor operated on a fiscal-year basis (October 1 through September 30), the end of the retention period would be September 30, 2016.

Final payment date	November 15, 2011
Retention period	4 years
End of retention period	September 30, 2016

AUDITS/EXAMINATION OF RECORDS

The government can examine and audit books, records, and other data relating to claimed performance costs; cost/pricing data used to support proposals; and any status reports required under the contract. This audit requirement applies to virtually all contracts. However, because audits require significant time and expense to perform, they are typically not used for small purchases (under $100,000) or contracts awarded under sealed bidding procedures.

The government's right of examination includes the right to inspect a contractor's plants that are engaged in performing the contracts at all reasonable times. This right begins at the start of the contract and continues until the retention period expires. The Defense Contract Audit Agency (DCAA) performs the contract audit functions required by DOD and many civilian agencies.

Auditors act as the contracting officer's principal financial advisors on matters relating to contract cost/price. They express opinions on the allowability, allocability, and reasonableness of contract costs claimed by contractors for reimbursement. Auditors use applicable public laws, procurement regulations (the FAR), and cost accounting standards to determine contractor compliance.

CONTRACT DISPUTES ACT

The Contract Disputes Act of 1978 established procedures and requirements for asserting and resolving claims by (or against) contractors. This act allows contractors with a dispute to seek redress outside the judiciary system, thereby saving the government and the contractor time and money. The main provisions of this act include:

- Strengthening the authority and capabilities of the Board of Contract Appeals

- Giving contractors the option of direct appeal to the U.S. Claims Court, bypassing the Board of Contract Appeals

- Providing the government with the right to seek judicial review of adverse Board of Contract Appeals decisions

- Providing contracting activities with more flexibility in negotiating and settling contract disputes

- Establishing new Board of Contract Appeals procedures for handling small claims

- Establishing a requirement for certification of contractor claims.

The disputes clause applies to all government contracts, either expressed or implied. This clause requires the contractor to pursue resolution of its claims through the administrative procedures delineated in the Contract Disputes Act. Contractors are required to continue contract performance pending resolution of a dispute, unless the dispute arises outside the contract or in breach of the contract.

Claims and Disputes

Many times during contract performance, the government and the contractor differ on contractual issues. If the differences persist, the contractor should submit a written claim to the contracting officer. A claim is a written demand by one of the contracting parties seeking, as a matter of right, an adjustment to the contract terms, payment, or other relief arising under the contract. All disputes under government contracts begin with a claim submitted by a contractor.

For a claim to be valid, it must:

■ Be in writing. A voucher, invoice, or other routine request for payment does not, in itself, constitute a claim.

■ Seek the payment of a specific sum, adjustment of the contract terms, or other relief.

■ Be certified by the contractor, if the claim seeks relief in excess of $100,000. For example:

> I certify that the claim is made in good faith; that the supporting data are accurate and complete to the best of my knowledge and belief; that the amount requested accurately reflects the contract adjustment for which the contractor believes the government is liable; and that I am duly authorized to certify the claim on behalf of the contractor.

The government tries to resolve all claims by mutual agreement at the contracting officer's level and to avoid litigation if at all possible. Normally, the contracting officer reviews the pertinent facts of the claim and, after discussions with the contractor, reaches agreement and modifies the contract. Advice and assistance from legal and other advisors may be obtained, but ultimately the contracting officer is responsible for making the final decision.

The contracting officer is required to issue a decision on any claim of less than $100,000 within 60 days from receipt. If the claim exceeds $100,000, the contracting officer must either issue a decision or notify the contractor when a decision will be issued, within 60 days from receipt of a written request.

The final decision is furnished in writing. A decision statement, at a minimum, includes:

■ Description of the claim or dispute

■ References to pertinent contract provisions

■ Statements of the factual areas of agreement/disagreement

■ Statement of the contracting officer's decision, with supporting rationale.

If the contractor disagrees with the determination, it may appeal the decision to the Board of Contract Appeals within 90 days from receipt of the decision. The notice should indicate that an appeal is planned, reference the decision, and identify the contract by number.

Board of Contract Appeals

The Board of Contract Appeals hears and decides contract disputes. In performing its functions, the Board may issue subpoenas that are enforceable by the U.S. District Courts. It can also seek related facts and data through the discovery process and take depositions, as necessary.

Many federal agencies have established boards, such as the General Services Administration Board of Contract Appeals and the Department of Transportation Board of Contract Appeals. The Armed Services Board of Contract Appeals handles all DOD contract disputes. Some small agencies use GSA's Board of Contract Appeals.

For a claim of $50,000 or less, small claim or expedited procedures provide a decision within 120 days. Claims that are $100,000 or less come under accelerated procedures, which require a decision within 180 days, whenever possible. If the claim is for more than $100,000, the Board will conduct a formal hearing with no time limit on the decision.

Either the contractor or the government may appeal the Board's decision within 120 days to the U.S. Court of Appeals. If either party disagrees with the Court of Appeals decision, it must file an appeal with the Supreme Court within 60 days. Supreme Court decisions are final.

The Contract Disputes Act allows contractors to appeal a contracting officer's decision directly to the U.S. Claims Court, bypassing the Board of Contract Appeals. If a contractor chooses this route, it must file the appeal within one year of the contracting officer's final decision. There are no time limits on the court to make a decision. Most contractors favor using the Board of Contract Appeals because doing so tends to be less costly and time-consuming.

The Equal Access to Justice Act permits small businesses and individuals to recover attorney or agent fees if they prevail in administrative or court actions brought against the government. The contractor has 30 days from the decision date to submit an application for reimbursement to the government (or the agency involved in the dispute).

ALTERNATIVE DISPUTE RESOLUTION

Federal courts are swamped with cases. The average dispute takes more than a year to resolve. If a contractor wants an accelerated decision, it might look at alternative dispute resolution (ADR). The Administrative Disputes Act of 1990 authorizes the use of ADR to settle disputes brought to the Board of Contract Appeals. Each ADR must have:

■ An issue in controversy

■ A voluntary election by both parties to participate in the ADR process

■ An agreement on alternative procedures and terms to be used in lieu of formal litigation

■ Process participation by officials of both parties who have the authority to resolve the issue.

Requests to use ADR must be made jointly by the government and the contractor to the board or court that is responsible for hearing the dispute. The board then examines the issues involved with the dispute and determines whether ADR would be appropriate. If a contracting officer rejects a contractor's request for ADR, the contractor must be given a written explanation citing the reasons. Contractors that reject an ADR request must inform the agency of their objections in writing.

Alternative dispute resolution procedures may include, but are not limited to, mediation, fact-finding, minitrials, arbitration, and use of ombudsmen. Federal agencies are encouraged to use ADR procedures to the maximum extent practicable.

TERMINATION FOR CONVENIENCE

Each government contract contains a provision not found in commercial contracts—the ability to terminate the contract for any reason. The "termination for convenience" provision exists because of the government's need to end contracts when its requirements are eliminated, such as when a war ends or when Congress eliminates a program.

The government may terminate the entire contract or just part of it. Partial terminations can actually occur several times during the life of a contract. The contracting officer makes those decisions. When a contracting officer terminates a contract for the government's convenience, he or she provides the contractor with a written notice of termination stating:

■ That the contract is being terminated for the convenience of the government

■ The effective date of termination

■ The extent of termination

■ Any special instructions

■ The steps the contractor should take to minimize the impact of the termination on the company's personnel, if applicable.

If the government terminates a contract for convenience, it must pay the costs incurred by the contractor up to the termination date, plus a reasonable profit. The government uses several different termination clauses depending on the kind of contract.

TERMINATION FOR DEFAULT

The government holds the contractual right to terminate a contract in whole or in part if a contractor fails to perform its obligations under the contract. The government may exercise its right to terminate a contract if the contractor fails to:

■ Deliver products or perform services within the time specified in the contract

■ Perform other contract provisions

■ Make progress, endangering performance of the contract.

Human nature being what it is, contracting officers try very hard not to let conditions deteriorate to the point where they must terminate a contract for default. First, it shows poor contract management. Second, it brands a contractor as a "non-performer" and endangers future business. Most contracting officers much prefer to terminate a contract using termination for convenience procedures, which enables them to negotiate the remaining contract requirements with another contractor.

When a contract is terminated for default, the contracting officer provides the contractor with a written notice of termination. This written notice of termination for default must be unequivocally clear and must state:

■ The contract number and date

■ The acts or omissions constituting the default

■ That the contractor's right to proceed with further performance of the contract has been terminated

■ That the products and services under the terminated contract are subject to reprocurement against the contractor's account and that the contractor is liable for any excess costs

■ That the notice constitutes a decision of the contracting officer that the contractor is in default as specified and the contractor may appeal according to the procedures stated in the disputes clause.

If the government terminates a contract for default, the contractor becomes liable for expenditures on undelivered work and must repay any advance payments. The contracting officer may direct the contractor to transfer title and deliver all completed or partially completed (but not yet accepted) products and materials to the government. The government then pays the contractor the contract price for any completed products and negotiates a value for the remaining materials.

Termination for default is serious business. Not only does a contractor lose its contract, but it must also pay the government for any excess reprocurement costs. The contractor is therefore responsible for the costs the government pays to an alternate source that exceed the price payable under the existing contract.

Suppose a contractor defaulted on its contract to build five computer network mainframes for $250,000. The contractor completed and installed two mainframes but was behind schedule on the others. A termination for default notice was issued.

5 computer mainframes	$ 250,000
Payment for 2 completed mainframes	$ 100,000
Balance of contract	$ 150,000

Next, the government decided to purchase the remaining mainframes from an alternate source for $175,000. The defaulted contractor must pay the difference:

Alternate source price	$ 175,000
Original contract price (3 mainframes)	$ 150,000
Balance owed by default contractor	$ 25,000

Terminations for default are not abrupt. A contractor typically has the chance to improve performance or to explain why the contract should continue. If a contract was terminated for default and it is subsequently determined that the contractor's delay was excusable, the termination for default may be converted to a termination for convenience. Excusable circumstances include:

■ Defective specifications

■ Late or defective government-furnished property

■ Suspensions of work and stop-work orders received

■ Strikes

■ Floods or fires

■ Freight embargoes.

If the contractor believes that the termination for default was improper, it may file a claim under the disputes clause.

CONTRACT CLOSEOUT

Contract closeout, as you probably guessed, is the action that occurs when a contractor completes the contract. You're out of the woods, so to speak—at least for this job! The contract is considered fully completed when:

■ The contractor has completed the required deliveries and the government has inspected and accepted the items

■ The contractor has performed all services and the government has accepted these services

■ All option provisions, if any, have expired

■ The government has given the contractor a notice of complete contract termination.

Proper contract closeout helps ensure that the contractor has complied with all the contractual requirements and that the government has fulfilled its obligations.

■　■　■

Contract performance is just the tip of the iceberg when it comes to fulfilling your contractual obligations. Contractors also must comply with applicable laws, prepare required reports, seek contract modifications, prepare invoices, retain contractual records, and carry out other administrative duties. All requirements that apply to your contract are spelled out in the contract document.

■　■　■

Closing Remarks

To quote a famous tennis phrase, "The ball is now in your court." This book tells you what you need to know to break into and succeed in the federal government marketplace. If you learn the system and are patient and persistent, you can make good money, even big money, doing business with the federal government.

Acronyms

Copyright 2003 by Randy Glasbergen.
www.glasbergen.com

GLASBERGEN

"I knew it was time to simplify our organization when we started creating acronyms for our acronyms."

If you are looking to do business with the federal government, you'll have to speak its language and know a multitude of acronyms. The following list will help get you started.

ACO	Administrative Contracting Officer
ADR	Alternative Dispute Resolution
AF	Air Force
AGAR	Department of Agriculture Acquisition Regulation
AID	Agency for International Development
AIDAR	Agency for International Development FAR Supplement
AMS	Acquisition Management System
B&P	Bid and Proposal
BA	Basic Agreement
BOA	Basic Ordering Agreement
BPA	Blanket Purchase Agreement
CAGE	Commercial and Government Entity

CAO	Contract Administration Office
CAR	Department of Commerce Acquisition Regulation
CAS	Cost Accounting Standards
CASB	Cost Accounting Standards Board
CBD	*Commerce Business Daily*
CCR	Central Contractor Registration
CDRL	Contract Data Requirements List
CFR	*Code of Federal Regulations*
CICA	Competition in Contracting Act (1984)
CLIN	Contract Line Item Number
CO	Contracting Officer
COC	Certificate of Competency
COR	Contracting Officer's Representative
COTR	Contracting Officer's Technical Representative
CPAF	Cost Plus Award Fee
CPFF	Cost Plus Fixed Fee
CPIF	Cost Plus Incentive Fee
D&B	Dun & Bradstreet
DAASC	Defense Automatic Addressing System Center
DARPA	Defense Advanced Research Projects Agency
DCAA	Defense Contract Audit Agency
DCMC	Defense Contract Management Command
DEAR	Department of Energy Acquisition Regulation
DFARS	Department of Defense FAR Supplement
DFAS	Defense Finance and Accounting Service
DLA	Defense Logistics Agency
DLIS	Defense Logistics Information Service
DOC	Department of Commerce

DOD	Department of Defense
DOE	Department of Energy
DOJ	Department of Justice
DOT	Department of Transportation
DRL	Data Requirements List
DUNS	Data Universal Numbering System
EC	Electronic Commerce
EDI	Electronic Data Interchange
EFT	Electronic Fund Transfer
EPA	Environmental Protection Agency
EPS	Electronic Posting System
ESB	Emerging Small Business
FAA	Federal Aviation Administration
FAC	Federal Acquisition Circular
FAR	Federal Acquisition Regulation
FARA	Federal Acquisition Reform Act (1996)
FAS	Federal Acquisition Service
FASA	Federal Acquisition Streamlining Act (1994)
FBO	FedBizOpps
FFP	Firm-Fixed-Price
FOB	Free on Board
FOIA	Freedom of Information Act
FPDS	Federal Procurement Data System
FP/EPA	Fixed-Price with Economic Price Adjustment
FPI	Fixed-Price Incentive
FR	*Federal Register*
FSC	Federal Supply Classification
FSG	Federal Supply Group

FSS	Federal Supply Schedule
FY	Fiscal Year
G&A	General and Administrative
GAAP	Generally Accepted Accounting Principles
GAO	Government Accountability Office
GFP	Government-Furnished Property
GPO	Government Printing Office
GSA	General Services Administration
GSAR	General Services Administration Acquisition Regulation
GWAC	Government-wide Acquisition Contract
HCA	Head of Contracting Activity
HHS	Health and Human Services
HHSAR	Department of Health and Human Services Acquisition Regulation
HUBZone	Historically Underutilized Business Zone
ID/IQ	Indefinite Delivery/Indefinite Quantity
IFB	Invitation for Bid
IFSS	International Federal Supply Schedule
IR&D	Internal (Independent) Research and Development
LCC	Life-Cycle Costing
LH	Labor Hour
MAS	Multiple Award Schedule
NAICS	North American Industry Classification System
NASA	National Aeronautics and Space Administration
NAVSEA	Naval Sea Systems Command
NCMA	National Contract Management Association
NIIS	New Item Introductory Schedule
NIST	National Institute of Standards and Technology
NOA	Notice of Award

NSF	National Science Foundation
NSN	National Stock Number
NTIS	National Technical Information Service
ODC	Other Direct Cost
OFPP	Office of Federal Procurement Policy
O/H	Overhead
OMB	Office of Management and Budget
ORCA	Online Representations & Certifications Application
OSDBU	Office of Small and Disadvantaged Business Utilization
PCO	Procuring Contracting Officer
PIIN	Procurement Instrument Identification Number
PO	Purchase Order
POC	Point of Contact
PR	Purchase Request
PSA	Presolicitation Announcement
PSC	Product and Service Code
PWS	Performance Work Statement
R&D	Research and Development
RFI	Request for Information
RFP	Request for Proposal
RFQ	Request for Quotation
RFTP	Request for Technical Proposals
SADBUS	Small and Disadvantaged Business Utilization Specialist
SAP	Simplified Acquisition Procedures
SAS	Single Award Schedule
SAT	Simplified Acquisition Threshold
SBA	Small Business Administration
SBDC	Small Business Development Center

SBIR	Small Business Innovation Research
SCA	Service Contract Act
SCF	Simplified Contract Format
SCORE	Service Corps of Retired Executives
SDB	Small Disadvantaged Business
SEC	Securities and Exchange Commission
SF	Standard Form
SIC	Standard Industrial Classification
SIP	Schedule Input Program
SML	Solicitation Mailing List
SOW	Statement of Work
SSA	Source Selection Authority
STTR	Small Business Technology Transfer Research Program
T&M	Time and Materials
TAR	Department of Transportation Acquisition Regulation
TCO	Termination Contracting Officer
TINA	Truth in Negotiations Act
UCF	Uniform Contract Format
USC	*United States Code*
USCG	United States Coast Guard
USDA	United States Department of Agriculture
VA	Department of Veterans Affairs
VAFR	Veterans Administration FAR Supplement
VBOP	Veterans Business Outreach Program
WBC	Women's Business Center
WBS	Work Breakdown Structure
WOB	Woman-Owned Business
WOSB	Woman-Owned Small Business

Federal Agencies and Departments

© 1999 Randy Glasbergen. www.glasbergen.com

GLASBERGEN

"I heard on TV that everyone is getting rich on the Internet. Is this little slot where the money comes out?"

The federal government is huge. There are so many federal agencies and departments that it would take more then 50 pages of this book to list them all. The best way to locate information on these is to visit the following website:

www.lib.lsu.edu/gov/fedgov.html

This website provides a listing or directory of most government agencies and departments (including links to their websites).

Glossary

Copyright 2001 by Randy Glasbergen. www.glasbergen.com

GLASBERGEN

"Yes, I have some management experience.
When I was ten, I ran a lemonade stand.
I had 40 lemons working for me."

> The glossary terms that are enclosed in a box represent a little government contracting humor (which may or may not be more accurate than the term's formal definition).

Acceptance
The act of an authorized government representative assuming ownership of identified supplies tendered or approving specific services rendered as complete in performance of a contract.

Accumulating Costs
The collecting of cost data in an organized and consistent manner, such as through a chart of accounts.

Administrative Contracting Officer (ACO)
A contracting officer who is responsible for administrative functions after a contract is awarded.

Advance Payments
Advances of money by the government to a contractor, prior to contract performance.

Affiliates
Business concerns, organizations, or individuals related, directly or indirectly, when (1) either one controls or has the power to control the other, or (2) a third party controls or has the power to control both.

Agency
One party, known as the principal, appoints another party, known as the agent, to enter into a business or contractual relationship with a third party.

Agency Supplements
Regulations issued by individual federal agencies for the purpose of supplementing the basic Federal Acquisition Regulation (FAR).

Allocable Cost
A cost that is assignable or chargeable to one or more cost objectives in accordance with the relative benefits received.

Allowable Cost
A cost that (1) meets the tests of reasonableness and allocability and (2) complies with generally accepted accounting principles and cost accounting standards, as well as specific exclusions set forth in FAR 31.

Amendment
A change (correction, deletion, or addition) to a solicitation *before* it is due. The amendment becomes part of the resulting contract.

Appropriation
Authority to obligate public funds that will result in immediate or future outlays.

AUDITORS—People who go in after the war is lost and bayonet the wounded.

Basic Ordering Agreement (BOA)
A written instrument of understanding negotiated between a contractor and a federal buying office that contains (1) terms and clauses applying to future contracts (orders) between the parties during its term; (2) a

description of supplies or services to be provided; and (3) methods for pricing, issuing, and delivering future orders. It is not a contract.

Bid
An offer in response to an invitation for bid (IFB).

BID—A wild guess carried out to two decimal places.

Bid and Proposal (B&P) Costs
Costs incurred in preparing, submitting, or supporting any bid or proposal, which are neither sponsored by a grant nor required in the performance of a contract.

BID OPENING—A poker game in which the losing hand wins.

Bidder
A contractor who submits a bid in response to an IFB.

Bidders' List
A register maintained by a contracting activity that lists contractors that have expressed an interest in furnishing a particular supply or service.

Certificate of Competency (COC)
A certificate issued by the Small Business Administration stating that the holder is responsible (with respect to elements of responsibility, including capacity, credit, and integrity) for the purpose of receiving and performing a specific government contract.

Closeout
The process for closing out the contract file following contract completion.

Commercial Items
Products that are sold competitively to the general public.

Competitive Range
All proposals that the contracting officer determines to have a reasonable chance of being selected for award based on cost/price data and other factors stated in the solicitation.

COMPLETION DATE—The point at which liquidated damages begin.

Contingent Fee
Any commission, percentage, brokerage, or other fee that is contingent upon the success that a person or concern has in securing a government contract.

Contract
A mutually binding legal relationship obligating the seller to furnish supplies or services and the buyer to pay for them.

Contracting Officer (CO)
A government agent with the authority to enter into, administer, or terminate contracts and make related determinations and findings.

Contracting Officer's Technical Representative (COTR)
A federal employee to whom a contracting officer has delegated limited authority (in writing) to make specific contract-related decisions.

CONTRACTOR—A gambler who never gets to shuffle, cut, or deal.

Cost Accounting Standards (CAS)
Standards designed to achieve uniformity and consistency in the cost accounting principles followed by government contractors and subcontractors on selected large-dollar-value contracts (see Part 30 of the FAR).

Cost and Pricing Data
All facts, as of the date of price agreement, that prudent buyers and sellers would reasonably expect to affect price negotiations.

Cost-Reimbursement Contracts
Contracts that provide for payment of allowable incurred costs to the extent prescribed in the contract. These contracts establish an estimate of total cost for the purpose of obligating funds and establishing a ceiling that the contractor may not exceed, except at its own risk.

CRITICAL PATH METHOD—A management technique for losing your shirt under perfect control.

Debriefing
Informing unsuccessful offerors of the basis for the selection decision and contract award. This information includes the government's evaluation of the significant weak or deficient factors in the offeror's proposal.

DELAYED PAYMENT—A tourniquet applied at the pockets.

Delivery Order
A written order for supplies under an indefinite-delivery contract.

Direct Costs
Any cost that is specifically identified to a contract.

Emerging Small Businesses
Firms that are no larger than 50% of the applicable small business size standard.

ENGINEER'S ESTIMATE—The cost of construction in heaven.

Evaluation Factors
Factors in selecting an offer for award.

FedBizOpps
The single government point of entry on the Internet for federal procurement opportunities over $25,000.

Federal Acquisition Regulation (FAR)
The body of regulations that is the primary source of authority over the government procurement process.

Federal Register
A daily publication that informs the public of proposed rules and other legal notices issued by federal agencies.

Federal Specifications (Specs)
Specifications and standards that have been implemented for use by all federal agencies.

Federal Supply Schedules
Indefinite-delivery contracts established by the General Services Administration with commercial contractors. These schedules provide federal agencies with a simplified process for obtaining commonly used supplies and services at prices associated with volume buying.

Fee (or Profit)
Money paid to a contractor over and above total reimbursements for allowable costs.

Fixed-Price Contract
A contract type that establishes a firm price regardless of the actual cost of contract performance.

Government Accountability Office (GAO)
The audit agency of the U.S. Congress. GAO has broad authority to conduct investigations on behalf of Congress and to review certain contract decisions, including contract award protests.

Government-Furnished Property
Property in the possession of, or directly acquired by, the government and subsequently made available to the contractor.

Indefinite-Delivery Contract
A type of contract used when the exact times and/or quantities of future deliveries are unknown at the time of contract award. There are three variations of indefinite-delivery contracts: definite-quantity, requirements, and indefinite-quantity.

Independent Research and Development (IR&D) Cost
The cost effort that is neither sponsored by a grant nor required in performing a contract that falls within any of four areas: (1) basic research, (2) applied research, (3) development, and (4) systems and other concept formulation studies.

Invitation for Bid (IFB)
The solicitation document used in sealed bidding.

> **LAWYERS**—People who go in after the auditors and strip the bodies.

Letter Contract
A written preliminary contractual instrument that authorizes the contractor to begin manufacturing products or performing services immediately.

> **LIQUIDATED DAMAGES**—A penalty for failing to achieve the impossible.

> **LOW BIDDERS**—Contractors that are wondering what they left out of their bids.

Micropurchases
Purchases that are $3,000 or less.

Modifications
Written changes to an *existing* contract, such as changes to the specifications, delivery schedule, contract period, price, quantity, or other contract provisions.

Option
The unilateral right in a contract by which, for a specified time, the government may elect to purchase additional supplies or services called for by the contract and/or extend the term.

Order of Precedence
A provision that establishes priority among various parts of a solicitation.

Pre-award Survey
An evaluation by the government of a prospective contractor's capability to perform a proposed contract.

Pre-bid/Preproposal Conference
A meeting held with prospective offerors before bid opening or before the closing date for proposal submission. The purpose of this conference is to brief the offerors and explain complicated specifications and requirements.

Progress Payments
Payments made under a fixed-price contract on the basis of costs incurred by the contractor as work progresses under the contract.

> PROJECT MANAGER—The conductor of an orchestra in which every musician is in a different union.

Protest
A written objection by an interested party to a solicitation, proposed award, or contract award.

Request for Proposal (RFP)
The solicitation document used in negotiated procurement procedures.

Request for Quotation (RFQ)
A document used in soliciting quotations. RFQs are used when the government does not intend to award a contract on the basis of the solicitation but wishes to obtain price, delivery, or other market information for planning purposes.

Sealed Bidding
Method of procurement (prescribed in Part 14 of the FAR) in which the government publicly opens bids and awards the contract to the lowest responsive, responsible bidder.

Set-Aside
An acquisition reserved exclusively for offerors that fit into a specified category. Set-asides are commonly established for small businesses and businesses in labor surplus areas.

Simplified Acquisition Procedures (SAP)
Procurement procedures used for obtaining supplies and services that are under $100,000.

Simplified Acquisition Threshold (SAT)
The $100,000 ceiling (or limit) on purchases of supplies and services using simplified acquisition procedures.

Size Standards
Measures established by the Small Business Administration to determine whether a business qualifies as a small business for purposes of implementing the socioeconomic programs enumerated in Part 19 of the FAR.

Small Business Concern
A concern (including its affiliates) that is independently owned and operated, is not dominant in the field it bids on government contracts, and qualifies as a small business under the size standards in 13 CFR Part 121.

Small Disadvantaged Business
A small business that is at least 51% owned and operated by one or more persons who are both socially and economically disadvantaged.

Sole Source Acquisition
A contract for products and services that is entered into with only one source.

Source Selection
The process of soliciting and evaluating offers for award.

Specification
A document prepared by the government that describes the technical requirements of the products and services being acquired, including the criteria for determining whether these requirements are met.

Standard
A document that establishes engineering and technical requirements of materials, processes, designs, and practices. It includes any related criteria deemed essential to achieve the highest practical degree of uniformity in materials or products, or interchangeability of parts used in those products.

Statute
A law enacted by the legislative branch of the government and signed by the President.

Task Order
A written order for services under an indefinite-delivery contract.

Time and Materials (T&M) Contract
A type of contract that provides for acquiring services and materials on the basis of (1) direct labor hours at specified fixed hourly rates that include wages, overhead, general and administrative expenses, and profits and (2) material handling costs as part of material costs.

Unallowable Costs
Any cost that, under the provisions of any pertinent federal law, regulation, or contract, may not be included in prices, cost reimbursements, or other settlements under a government contract.

Uniform Contract Format (UCF)
The solicitation/contract format used in most Invitations for Bids and Requests for Proposals.

Unsolicited Proposal
A written proposal that is submitted to an agency on the offeror's initiative for the purpose of obtaining a government contract. It is not submitted in response to a formal or informal request.

Index